Gerald O'Hara

FDR's
SPLENDID
DECEPTION

Also by Hugh Gregory Gallagher:

Advise and Obstruct: The Role of the United States Senate in Foreign Policy Decisions

Etok: A Story of Eskimo Power

By Trust Betrayed: Patients, Physicians and the License to Kill in the Third Reich

FDR's SPLENDID DECEPTION

*The moving story of Roosevelt's massive disability—
and the intense efforts to conceal it from the public*

HUGH GREGORY GALLAGHER

IF THE PARALYSIS COULDN'T KILL HIM,
THE PRESIDENCY WON'T.
—*Eleanor Roosevelt*

REVISED EDITION

VANDAMERE PRESS
a division of AB Associates

P.O. BOX 5243
ARLINGTON, VIRGINIA
22205

Published by
Vandamere Press
A Division of AB Associates
P.O. Box 5243
Arlington, VA 22205
USA

Copyright 1994
Hugh Gregory Gallagher

ISBN 0-918339-33-2

First Edition published by Dodd, Mead, & Co., Inc., 1985,
ISBN 0-396-08521-0

All rights reserved, which includes the right to reproduce this book or any portion thereof in any form whatsoever, except as provided by U.S. Copyright Law. For information contact Vandamere Press.

This book is dedicated to

Lauro S. Halstead and Lorenzo W. Milam,

without whom it would not have been written;

Paul Fredrick Waggaman,

without whom it could not have been written;

Lisbeth Mark,

without whom it would not have been published.

Contents

CONTENTS

Preface to the Second Edition

1995 marks the 50th anniversary of the death of FDR. The Franklin Delano Roosevelt Memorial is now under construction in Washington, D.C., with dedication scheduled for 1996.

Although *FDR's Splendid Deception* has been out of print for five years, the demand for the book continues. In college courses, teachers xerox copies for class use. Polio support groups pass tattered, well-worn copies of the book from member to member. Historians make continual reference to it and it has changed forever the way Roosevelt is perceived by scholars.

For these reasons and more, I am pleased that Vandamere Press is issuing a revised, second edition of *FDR's Splendid Deception*. This allows me to add new material and new photographs which have been uncovered, further illustrating the extent of the President's disability and the efforts made to disguise it.

FDR was a great American, a disabled American: this is his book. I am glad it is back in print.

HUGH GREGORY GALLAGHER
Cabin John, Maryland

Preface

This book is written as the result of a lifelong interest in Franklin D. Roosevelt as a handicapped person. My interest is natural enough:

Like FDR, I had polio. I contracted the disease at the age of nineteen in 1952. For six weeks I was encased in an iron lung and for many months completely paralyzed. Like FDR, I have had to use a wheelchair ever since.

Over these years, I have met hundreds of polios* with varying degrees of paralysis. I have never met any person for whom the paralysis was not a vital—if not the most vital—shaping event of his life. These polios are as scarred by their experience as concentration camp survivors are scarred by theirs.

This is what has puzzled me so about the biographies of Franklin D. Roosevelt: the man was a paraplegic, yet this important fact is given very little attention. FDR's disease and seven years of convalescence are treated as an episode in an early chapter in these books and never mentioned again. This is absurd and unreal. A visible paralytic handicap affects every relationship, alters the attitudes of others, and challenges one's self-esteem. It requires meticulous minute-by-minute monitoring and control to an extent quite unperceived and unimaginable by the able-bodied. This condition of being handicapped generates a range of emotions, whether expressed or not, that

---

*The term "polio" is used throughout the text to denote a person who has a residual paralysis caused by the disease poliomyelitis. This is used in preference to such terms as polio victim, polio survivor, etc.

must be dealt with, not just at onset, but continuing throughout the rest of the patient's life.

The central key to understanding FDR's personality and motivation—the impact of his handicap—has been all but ignored
by historians. I have written this book in an effort to rectify this
anomaly.

I have been preparing for this book for thirty years. At Warm
Springs, where I went for rehabilitation in the 1950s, I talked
with many persons who had vivid memories of FDR. I think,
particularly, of the late Fred Botts, cofounder with FDR of the
rehabilitation center. My physical therapists told me stories of
the President and his treatment, some of which have reached
print, many of which have not. Over the years I have talked
about Roosevelt's handicap with his associates whenever I had
the chance—particularly with Grace Tully, Rex Tugwell, and
Louis Brownlow. And perhaps most important, I have discussed
my assessment of FDR with fellow polios, testing my own
interpretation and conclusions with theirs—in particular, with
writer Lorenzo W. Milam and physician Lauro Halstead.

The basic facts of the life of FDR are well known and are set
out without change in my book. All quotations used are au-
thentic and sources have been indicated. What cannot be documented is my interpretation of these quotations and facts. This
interpretation is based upon my observation and understanding
of the way the disability of polio works upon the individual and
upon the individual's relationship with others in the community.

What follows may not be Roosevelt exactly—he was a reserved and immensely subtle man—but it is far closer to the
mark than previous studies have been.

Introduction

I greatly admired the courage with which
he fought his way back to active life and
with which he overcame his handicap. . . .[1]
—HERBERT HOOVER

Franklin Delano Roosevelt was the only person in the recorded
history of mankind who was chosen as a leader by his people
even though he could not walk or stand without help.

Roosevelt was paralyzed from the waist down. As the result
of an attack of polio in 1921, he was forced to live the rest of his
life using a wheelchair. He was able to stand for only short periods
of time and only with the aid of braces and the support of
crutches. Roosevelt stood only for ceremonial occasions.

Nevertheless, Roosevelt was elected President by a landslide
in 1932 in the depths of the Great Depression. He was reelected
by similarly large majorities in 1936, 1940, and again in 1944.

Although there are over thirty-five thousand still photographs of FDR at the Presidential Library, there are only two of
the man seated in his wheelchair. No newsreels show him being
lifted, carried, or pushed in his chair. Among the thousands of
political cartoons and caricatures of FDR, not one shows the man
as physically impaired. In fact, many of them have him as a man
of action—running, jumping, doing things. Roosevelt domi-

nated his times from a wheelchair; yet he was simply not perceived as being in any major sense disabled.

This was not by accident. It was the result of a careful strategy of the President. The strategy served to minimize the extent of his handicap, to make it unnoticed when possible and palatable when it was noticed. The strategy was eminently successful, but it required substantial physical effort, ingenuity, and bravado.

This was FDR's splendid deception.

FDR's
SPLENDID
DECEPTION

I

Onset

I know that he had real fear when he was first taken ill.[1]
—ELEANOR ROOSEVELT

ON the afternoon of August 9, 1921, thirty-nine-year-old Franklin Delano Roosevelt fell overboard. He was sailing the Bay of Fundy aboard the yacht *Sabalo*. The waters were cold, and he was chilled clear through. "I'd never felt anything so cold as that water. I hardly went under, hardly wet my head because I still had hold of the tender, but the water was so cold it seemed paralyzing." He complained of the "icy shock in comparison to the heat of the August sun and the tender engine."[2]

This sudden chill, "so cold it seemed paralyzing,"[3] was most likely an early symptom of the onset of poliomyelitis, or "infantile paralysis." Very likely, Roosevelt's central nervous system was already under attack from the polio virus and this would have produced heightened sensitivity to changes of light, temperature, and pressure upon his skin. The chill was a warning, but it was a warning he did not heed.

The ability of the human body to resist the attack of the polio virus is dependent upon both the body's physical and psychological condition. A healthy person, free of great stress, presents the greatest resistance to disease. FDR was neither rested nor stress-free. By his own admission, he was extremely tired that August day, at the Roosevelts' summer home at Campobello, New Brunswick. Had he had the prescience to rest and place no strain upon his muscles, the severity of the attack and the extent of the resultant permanent paralysis would have been lessened. But this was not FDR's style.

Franklin was a vigorous man. To everything—work or play—he brought great energy and enthusiasm. This summer of 1921 he had planned his first lengthy vacation with his five children since America's entry into World War I. Life at Campobello with the Roosevelts was extremely strenuous. Days were filled with fishing, sailing, swimming, hiking, and rock climbing. For hours on end, Roosevelt would lead his children, their governesses, and the various members of the little summer colony through games of paper chase and hares and hounds along the rocky shore and cliffs. His children adored him. They loved these games, although his wife did not. Eleanor, in her matter-of-fact way, wrote, "Quite a number of persons really did not enjoy Franklin's games at all."[4]

The following day, August 10, FDR took his older children (Anna, Elliott, and James) for a sail on board the twenty-four-foot keel sloop, the *Vireo*. They noticed a forest fire on an island and went to put it out. After hours of flailing the flames with evergreen branches, "Late in the afternoon we brought it under control. . . . Our eyes were bleary with smoke; we were begrimed, smarting with spark burns, exhausted." Thinking that a swim would make them feel better, FDR and the children jogged two miles across Campobello Island, swam a freshwater lagoon, and plunged into the icy bay. This did not help. "I didn't get the usual revitalization, the glow I'd expected. When I reached the house the mail was in, with several newspapers I hadn't seen. I sat reading for a while, too tired even to dress. I'd never felt quite that way before."[5]

Remarking that he seemed to have a slight case of lumbago, he put down the papers, climbed the stairs unassisted, and went to bed. He would never walk again.

Roosevelt was a determined man who wanted to be President. He had this desire clearly in mind at least as early as 1907 when, as a law clerk in a Wall Street law firm, he told a fellow clerk he intended to become President of the United States. He would first, he said, get into the New York State Legislature. This would be followed by an appointment as Assistant Secretary of the Navy, like his cousin Theodore. He would then run for governor of New York in a Democratic year. "Once you're elected Governor of New York, if you do well enough in that job, you have a good show to be President, don't you?" he asked.[6]

In 1921, FDR's career was right on schedule. He had served four years in the New York State Senate, a Democrat elected by a normally Republican district. Woodrow Wilson had appointed him Assistant Secretary of the Navy in 1914, and he had served with some distinction and considerable popular attention throughout World War I. FDR continued in the footsteps of his Republican cousin when, in 1920, he was nominated as his party's vice-presidential candidate. The Democratic leaders of that year had compromised on James M. Cox of Ohio as their presidential nominee, and Roosevelt seemed to them a natural for second place: he was from New York; he was a Wilsonian; he had a well-known, popular name. He was a skilled speaker; he had a charming personality; and he made a most attractive, although not too serious, candidate. Wilson-hater Henry Cabot Lodge was perhaps not far wrong when he said of the FDR of the time: "He is a well-meaning, nice young fellow, but light. . . ."[7]

Unlike his cousin, however, FDR lost, as the Cox–Roosevelt ticket went down to defeat. It may be that no Democrat could have won in 1920, but the race did Roosevelt no harm. He made political contacts from coast to coast; he became a nationally known figure; and in the summer of 1921, he was quite clearly a man with a bright political future.

Few men are so fortunate as to have a childhood as blessed as Franklin D. Roosevelt's. His had been a life of stability, security, and serenity. He was born on January 30, 1882, at Hyde Park, New York, the family seat of the Hudson Valley Roosevelts. His wife, Eleanor, and her uncle Theodore Roosevelt were of the Oyster Bay branch, but they were all direct descendants of one of the earliest and proudest of New York families.

Franklin's father led the life of a country squire. Although already in his fifties he devoted much time and attention to his son, teaching him the values and behavior of a Victorian gentleman. His mother, a Delano fully as aristocratic as her husband, adored her only child and surrounded him with love and affection. Franklin grew up in a world now gone—of wealth and privilege, of nannies and governesses, ponies and sailboats, voyages to Europe, and summers in Campobello.

Although the young FDR was loved, he was not unduly protected. Initiative, enthusiasm, and adventure were encouraged and applauded. Franklin was supported as he developed his interests over a wide array of subjects: ornithology, stamp-collecting, ships, history, reading, sailing, hunting, riding, fishing, skating. He brought great good humor, vast self-confidence, and the personal reserve of a correct young gentleman to all the projects in which he involved himself.

These qualities are displayed and repeated in the childhood letters and anecdotes that were so carefully and lovingly preserved by his mother. In an early letter to her he said: "My dear Mama, We coasted yesterday, nothing dangerous yet, look out for tomorrow!! Your boy." He was no less enthusiastic in the themes he wrote for his tutors, as in this one on ancient Egypt: "The working people had nothing. . . . The kings made them work so hard and gave them so little that by jingo! they nearly starved and by jinks! they had hardly any clothes so they died in quadrillions."[8]

Franklin's almost sublime self-confidence is revealed in his mother's account of his coming into the house to fetch a pellet gun. He told her he had seen a winter wren sitting on a tree branch, and he wanted the wren for his collection. "Do you think," she asked, "that wren is going to oblige you by staying there while you come in and get your gun?" "Oh yes," said Franklin, "he'll wait." And a few minutes later Franklin returned with his wren.[9]

One summer, at Campobello, he was accidentally struck in the mouth with a stick. He lost one tooth; another was broken in half and the raw nerve was exposed to the air. Roosevelt did not complain of the pain. Indeed, he showed neither discomfort nor emotion during the two hours it took to cross to the mainland and find a dentist. This was, his mother believed, thoroughly appropriate behavior, and she was pleased that Franklin went through the entire incident "without fuss."[10]

Pampered by his parents and servants, young Franklin lived isolated from other children. He was educated at home and taken to play with the children on other estates only under carefully monitored conditions. His closest friend, young Archibald Rogers, died of diphtheria when Franklin was seven. He took the loss without recorded emotion or fuss and transferred his friendship to Archibald's brother Edmond.

There seemed to be a distinct distance between Franklin and other children, though he was not aloof nor was he shunned. He was, in fact, popular, and a hearty participant in the games. But he did not share his emotions and he was more often the director of the playground activities. His mother noted in her diary that he always seemed to be the child who issued the orders—which were "for reasons I have never been able to fathom" usually obeyed. When she pointed this out he replied, "But Mommie, if I didn't give the orders nothing would happen."[11]

The disease poliomyelitis has been with man throughout civilization. Egyptian mummies have been found with polio withered limbs. Pieter Brueghel, in the sixteenth century, painted a crippled beggar almost certainly a polio victim. Epidemics of polio, however, were not recorded until the nineteenth century. The spread of epidemic polio in North America and Europe coincided with the development and widespread utilization of basic modern public health procedures, and there is a reason for this. In a real sense, polio is a disease associated with cleanliness. In societies where hygiene is poor, children are early and often exposed to polio. And as a result, most children are infected by the virus in infancy while they are still carrying maternal antibodies. This attack is usually mild, with seldom any permanent paralysis, and it confers a degree of lifelong immunity to the child. For example, it has been found in Cairo that close to 100 percent of the children are immune to one or more

5

polio strains by the age of four. This is an immunity denied to the protected child of the upper classes such as Franklin D. Roosevelt.[12]

Franklin, as a child, was kept clear of the sick and the dirty. Unlike most children, he was not exposed at an early age to the various contagious diseases that plague society. He had great vitality, he was vigorous, but he was vulnerable. His body lacked resistance and he was often ill. In childhood he had typhoid fever and contracted it again in 1912. At Groton, his prep school, living for the first time with boys his own age, Roosevelt came down with such usual childhood diseases as measles and scarlet fever. He repeatedly suffered from various stomach complaints. He was operated on for appendicitis. He suffered from severe throat infections, related no doubt to his lifelong difficulty with acute sinusitis. He had many colds, a grim case of influenza in 1918, and double pneumonia in 1919. He had recurrent bouts with lumbago (a painful rheumatism of the lumbar region of the back). It was his experience with back pain that led FDR to ignore the first stage of active polio, dismissing it as nothing more than "a touch of lumbago."

Roosevelt had been sickly during the closing months of the Wilson Administration. Like other people, however, Roosevelt was healthiest when he was doing what he liked to do best. He loved campaigning and, as a result, he had been particularly healthy during the summer and fall of 1920. As a vice-presidential candidate, he had campaigned more widely and actively than any national candidate ever had before. After the election, he had returned to private life for the first time in six years. With great zest he worked on Wall Street in the mornings, practiced law in the afternoons, and worked on his burgeoning political career at all times with speeches, articles, and a vast correspondence.

The politically ambitious Roosevelt was always anxious to avoid the slightest criticism and was easily upset by unfavorable publicity. In the early part of the twentieth century, the personal standard expected of political figures was considerably more rigid than that of today. It was this rigid standard that had dictated the outcome of the confrontation between Franklin and Eleanor in 1918 over his love affair with Lucy Mercer. Not much is certain about this episode. Eleanor is reported to have pressed for divorce. Divorce, however, would have ruined FDR's political career. To avoid divorce, and to preserve the outward formalities of his marriage, Franklin agreed to forgo Lucy forever and, according to son Elliott, to give up all claim to his conjugal rights. Whether or not Elliott's report is correct, it is clear that Roosevelt was willing to sacrifice a great deal to protect his public life from scandal.[13]

And scandal certainly threatened during the summer of 1921, which placed Roosevelt under substantial emotional stress—both political and sexual.

During World War I, the Newport Training Station, constructed to house two thousand men, had been jammed with upward of twenty thousand recruits. There were, throughout the period, continuing reports of extensive drinking, drug use, and homosexual activities on the base. In the spring of 1919, FDR set up a vice squad to clean up conditions at Newport. This squad was, for administrative purposes, attached to his office as "Section A—Office of Assistant Secretary." In carrying out its mission, the squad employed entrapment procedures—using enlisted men as decoys. These decoys did, in fact, on several occasions engage in sodomy.

FDR first learned in September 1919 of what he called these "highly improper and revolting methods," and, as he later stated, "Immediate orders went out from me . . . that day to stop it." These orders were too late, and the matter was to become a public scandal. In 1921, the Republican Senate, as part of its politically oriented investigation of the Wilson Administration's war effort, looked into the Newport sex scandal. A special subcommittee of the Senate Committee on Naval Affairs, made up of two Republicans and a single Democrat, conducted the investigation. The subcommittee chairman promised Roosevelt (according to Roosevelt) that he would be given an opportunity to appear before the subcommittee to present his case in full. FDR was therefore caught by surprise, on a Thursday afternoon

7

in July, by a wire from his associate, Louis Howe, informing him that the subcommittee had completed its work and filed its report, which would soon be made public. Roosevelt rushed to Washington, a city sweltering under a tropical heat wave. He demanded the opportunity to be heard by the subcommittee. A hearing was scheduled and then canceled. He requested an opportunity to review the evidence and the final report before its release. He was given only one night to do so. He found the report to be extremely damaging—fully as bad as he had feared.

The report charged that a secret Roosevelt order had authorized the entrapment practices, stating: "That Assistant Secretary Roosevelt should have allowed enlisted men to be placed in a position where such acts were even liable to occur is, in the opinion of the committee, a most deplorable, disgraceful and unnatural proceeding." Roosevelt's actions displayed, said the subcommittee's report, "an utter lack of moral perspective."

In 1921, such charges, perhaps even more than today, were dynamite. Whether they were true or not, their disclosure could turn Roosevelt into a political untouchable. His career could be over. Roosevelt was extremely upset.

Roosevelt spent that night reviewing the fifteen volumes, six thousand pages of testimony, and preparing a statement for the press. The subcommittee at last agreed to hear from him the following evening at 8:00 P.M. With his assistant from Navy days, Steve Early, and with his new secretary, Missy LeHand, Roosevelt worked on his rebuttal all night and on into the fearfully hot day. At 4:00 P.M. that afternoon he was infuriated to learn from newspapermen that the report was already in the hands of the press for release the following day.

Roosevelt completed his statement, presented it to the subcommittee at its 8:00 P.M. meeting, and released it to the press. He denied all responsibility. The vice squad "was at no time supervised by me personally." As soon as he learned it was using "highly improper and revolting methods" he issued "orders to stop it." The denial was detailed and persuasive, and it contained a vigorous attack on the subcommittee: "As an American, irrespective of party, one hates to see the United States Navy . . . used as a vehicle for cheap ward politics."

8

Fortunately for Roosevelt, the newspapers incorporated his statement into their accounts of the subcommittee's report. The report was so shrill, its political purposes so blatant, that it soon died away, doing no lasting harm to FDR's reputation.[14]

The fracas, however, left Roosevelt physically exhausted and emotionally drained. "It must be dreadfully disagreeable for you," Eleanor wrote from Campobello, ". . . I know it worries you."[15] A few days later he sailed aboard the *Sabato* to join her and the children. "I thought he looked tired when he left," Missy LeHand later reported to Mrs. Roosevelt.[16]

It is not unusual for a man under great emotional strain to become ill. In Roosevelt's case, his records indicate a pattern linking stress and illness. Biographer Kenneth Davis makes note of this during the climax of the Lucy Mercer affair:

> There is evidence of unprecedented tensions in Roosevelt in the growing and increasingly open irritability. . . the increased incidence of his bouts with ill health (colds, throat infections, sinus headaches), beginning with his return from Haiti in early 1917.[17]

In the summer of 1921, at Campobello, FDR was exhausted and under emotional strain—vulnerable to the polio virus.

II
Crisis

By the end of the third day practically all muscles
from the chest down were involved.[1]
—FRANKLIN D. ROOSEVELT

WHAT he had thought was lumbago was clearly something
else, much worse. "The next morning when I swung out
of bed my left leg lagged. . . . I tried to persuade myself that
the trouble with my leg was muscular, that it would disappear
as I used it. But presently it refused to work and then the other."[2]
This account in Roosevelt's own words is taken from a campaign biography published in 1932. The author, Earle Looker,
based his book on interviews with Roosevelt at the Governor's
Mansion in Albany, ten years after his polio attack. In 1924, three
years after the attack, Roosevelt had written a lengthy case history of his illness for a South Carolina doctor who sought information on the care and treatment of a patient with polio. FDR
wrote:

> First symptoms of the illness appeared in August, 1921, when
> I was thoroughly tired from overwork. I first had a chill in
> the evening which lasted practically all night. The follow-
> ing morning the muscles of the right knee appeared weak
> and by afternoon I was unable to support my weight on my
> right leg. That evening the left knee began to weaken also
> and by the following morning I was unable to stand up. This
> was accompanied by a continuing temperature of about 102

and I felt thoroughly achy all over. By the end of the third day practically all muscles from the chest down were involved.[3]

Looker's interview with FDR and this letter are the only existing accounts in Roosevelt's own words of the onset of his polio. Curiously, they are not consistent. In the first account it is his left, in the second his right leg that is first affected. The onset of permanent paralysis is such a significant event in a man's life that it seems unlikely Roosevelt could have confused the sequence—yet he did so.

Whether the paralysis started in the left or the right leg, it was obvious that morning that something was seriously wrong. Eleanor called the family doctor, who, after examining Roosevelt, decided he was suffering from nothing more than a heavy cold—a most unsatisfactory diagnosis considering his temperature was 102, the paralysis was progressing, and the patient was in great pain throughout his body. That was on Thursday. On Friday Roosevelt was worse. By Saturday he was completely paralyzed from the chest down, his arms and shoulders were weak, and even his hands were involved. His skin and muscles had developed a sensitivity to touch so painful that he could not stand the pressure of the bedclothes, and even the movement of the breezes across his skin caused acute distress.

By Saturday morning the doctor and Mrs. Roosevelt decided to seek more expert advice, and an eminent specialist, Dr. Keen, was located at Bar Harbor. After careful examination, Keen announced that the trouble was "a clot of blood from a sudden congestion . . . settled in the lower spinal cord, temporarily removing the power to move though not to feel."[4] For treatment of this extraordinary problem, the doctor had an extraordinary prescription—heavy massage. A few days later, in a chatty, thoughtless letter to Eleanor, Dr. Keen changed his diagnosis from "a blood clot" to a "lesion of the spinal cord," and whereas he had been quite hopeful of early recovery he was now less sanguine: It would be "a longer business." He also enclosed a staggering bill for six hundred dollars.[5] The Roosevelts never forgave him for the extent of his misdiagnosis or for the size of his bill.

Ten days after the massage treatments had begun, arrangements were made for a specialist in infantile paralysis, Dr. Robert W. Lovett, to come to the island from Boston. He was called because the family was dissatisfied with the diagnosis by Dr. Keen and frightened by FDR's paralysis and his extreme suffering. Dr. Lovett immediately made a positive diagnosis of polio. He ordered an immediate halt to the massage; he suggested hot baths, and he prescribed bromides as needed for sleepless nights. The doctor explained that medicine could do no more for the polio patient than relieve some of the discomfort and he expected that the patient would find this a frustrating situation. Further, he warned, "There is likely to be mental depression and sometimes irritability in adults in the case of polio."[6]

Roosevelt lay completely paralyzed from the waist down. His upper trunk was very weak, his arms were weak, and even his thumbs were unable to function. He could not sit up, nor could he turn himself from side to side. He was in great pain. His legs were placed on pillows to lessen the pressure (and thus the distress) caused by direct contact with the bed. The bedclothes were propped up in a tentlike manner so that they would not touch his legs and cause them further distress. Roosevelt was nursed night and day by Eleanor, who slept on a camp bed in his room. She was relieved only by FDR's close and trusted political advisor, Louis Howe. Roosevelt's legs caused him extreme discomfort no matter how they were arranged. He was in danger of developing bedsores at the base of his spine from the pressure of lying in an unmoving position. Such sores, before the advent of modern rehabilitation techniques, were both serious and dangerous. Throughout the long nights Eleanor rubbed his back and buttocks to stimulate circulation and to ease the pressure; she moved his legs, and moved them again and moved them again. She hauled his heavy, inert body back and forth across the bed, turning him first on one side and then on the other. FDR's bowels were affected and so she had to administer enemas. His urinary tract was also affected and so he had to be catheterized. This meant she had to insert a rubber tube up through the urethra of his penis into the bladder, thus allowing the urine to flow out through the tube. This process is not easy; it is painful, and it invites local infection.

In addition to all this, Eleanor had been instructed by Dr. Keen to give her patient deep massage. This she had done. There could be no more perverse or harmful instruction. The pain caused FDR by massage was as great as any conceivable torture. Furthermore, it actually served to prolong and to heighten the hyperesthesia and tenderness. Most tragically, it actually hastened and worsened the extent of the paralysis. Through no fault of her own, Eleanor had been not only torturing her husband, she had been worsening his affliction. At last a stop was put to this by Dr. Lovett.

The summer vacation had become a nightmare. Eleanor later called it "a trial by fire."[7] Both she and Franklin were terrified of polio. Large-scale epidemics of the disease in the United States were a rather new event, and the Roosevelts worried that their five children were in peril. There had been an extensive epidemic in 1916, and FDR had Eleanor keep the children at Campobello until well into the fall and then actually sent a U.S. Navy destroyer to the island to bring his children to Hyde Park, landing them on the Roosevelt private dock to keep them from contact with others. And now he had the disease.

In panic, Eleanor kept the children from him, allowing them to come to the door of the sickroom only once a day or so. She instructed the children to be quiet, and she did not tell them what was wrong with their father. They knew he was very sick, and young Elliott thought perhaps he had had a heart attack. They were extremely frightened and nervous. Soon they succumbed to cold-like illnesses. This could have been a light form of polio but, more probably, was of sympathetic psychosomatic origin.

Franklin and Eleanor responded to the crisis in a manner typical of their class and background. They concealed their true feelings from others, from each other, and perhaps even from themselves. This took tremendous self-discipline.

Franklin had lost the use of his muscles. He lay helpless, dependent for the most basic bodily needs upon his wife, with whom he had not been physically intimate for years. His feelings, her feelings, cannot be known. Many years later she told her friend and biographer Joseph P. Lash that "in nursing his body, the sight of his legs had reminded her of Michelangelo's *Pietà*, a statue whose beauty and sadness had reduced her to tears when she had seen it as a girl."[8] This, of course, was the proper emotional reaction of a well-brought-up young woman of Eleanor Roosevelt's class. There are other, stronger emotions usually associated with a great trauma. If Eleanor experienced these feelings, she told no one and kept them to herself.

The unique bond between these two extraordinary persons was surely forged in this "trial by fire." They were never affectionate, nor were they in the least demonstrative. Over the years, as public figures, their lives became increasingly separate, their relationship distant, almost formal. Nevertheless, after the "trial by fire" there was always FDR's absolute confidence in Eleanor and Eleanor's complete dedication to him. Their marriage was indeed real, but it was different.

It is likely that FDR knew terror and despair during his illness. How or when they manifested themselves is not known. Louis Howe reported that during the height of the disease Roosevelt would repeatedly moan, "I don't know what is the matter with me, Louis, I just don't know."[9] Eleanor said, after his death, "I know that he had real fear when he was first taken ill."[10] In the 1930s, as First Lady, Eleanor wrote her autobiography for publication. In the draft manuscript, speaking of the illness, she wrote: "One night he was out of his head"—and the President blue-penciled it out of the manuscript.[11] If indeed Roosevelt was "out of his head" it was surely due to hysteria and not some form of delirium. His doctors found no form of polio-encephalitis, which is extremely rare except in the bulbar form of the disease, and his temperature was not high. Hysteria is caused by some overwhelming combination of fear and anxiety. A letter written at the time by Eleanor to Franklin's half brother, James Roosevelt, seems to confirm some sort of "out of his head" episode. She said, ". . . and I think he's getting back his grip and a better mental attitude though he has, of course, times of great discouragement."[12] As the doctor had warned, it was in no way unusual for a patient to be irritable, upset, or depressed by the drastic, tragic events occurring within his body. What is so very unusual about FDR's case is that the "out of his head" reference is virtually the only trace of a genuine or honest reaction to his loss, either then or later.

Roosevelt was not yet aware that he faced a years-long struggle to regain partial use of his paralyzed body. His doctor was certainly aware. He knew the crucial, critical nature of the adjustment to be made by his patient. Writing at the time about Roosevelt to another doctor, he warned:

> He has such courage, such ambition, and yet at the same time, such an extraordinarily sensitive emotional mechanism that it will take all the skill which we can muster to lead him successfully to a recognition of what he really faces without crushing him.[13]

FDR had been a withdrawn child, fairly shy with strangers, personable and charming but always somehow distant. He had no great friends in whom he confided, no bosom buddies, no intimates. He kept his own counsel and shared his confidences with no one. Now, in this "trial by fire," he was nursed by the two persons closest to him: his wife and Louis Howe. Howe, an ugly, sickly little man, was a political genius who had already decided FDR could achieve the presidency and who was now to dedicate his life effort toward getting it for him. Howe moved into the Roosevelt household when FDR got polio, and he never moved out. In the White House years he and Eleanor—and they alone—called the President by his first name, Franklin. If Roosevelt ever talked to anyone about his illness and the resulting paralysis it would have been to one of them. According to Eleanor he did not do so. There is no record of his ever having discussed it with *anyone*.

According to his mother he never spoke of it to her. She was in Europe when he became sick. Upon her return on September 1, FDR arranged what has been called "a major act of cheer, nonchalance for her benefit."[14] As she described it in a letter to her brother:

> I got here yesterday at 1:30 and at once . . . came up to a brave, smiling, and beautiful son, who said: "Well, I'm glad you are back, Mummy, and I got up this party for you!" He had shaved himself and seems very bright and keen. Below his waist he cannot move at all. His legs (that I have always been proud of) have to be moved often as they ache when long in one position. He and Eleanor decided at once to be cheerful and the atmosphere of the house is all happiness, so I have fallen in and follow their glorious example.[15]

This illustrates how total and resolute were FDR's defenses. The lessons of youth—one must endure a painful broken tooth "without fuss"—had been well learned. They were under severe test but they were holding.

Determined cheer was the rule, and all abided by it. Of her mother-in-law, Eleanor later wrote, "I am sure that, out of sight, she wept many hours but with all of us she was very cheerful."[16] So too the children, frightened and bewildered, were cheerful in the presence of their father. He helped them immensely by his own enforced cheer. His son James recalled: ". . . even before the paralysis had receded fully from the upper regions of his body, Father was unbelievably concerned about how we would take it. He grinned at us, and he did his best to call out, or gasp out, some cheery response to our tremulous, just-this-side-of-tears greeting."[17]

The pattern for dealing with his affliction was developed by FDR during these first weeks of the disease and was followed throughout the rest of his public and private life. It was based on the values he learned in his childhood, which were simple, straightforward, and unconflicted.

First of all, FDR had absolute confidence in his recovery. He would walk again. He would regain full use of his muscles. No matter how long, how painful, or how arduous, he would get better and eventually fully well. This confidence, like his childhood confidence that the bird in the tree would wait for him, was absolute and basic.

Next, FDR refused to acknowledge unpleasant facts. They were simply avoided, dismissed, or denied. They were certainly not discussed either in public or private. Years after her husband's death, Eleanor recalled: "There were certain things he never talked about—he would just shut up."[18] These things included death and his disability. He loved golf and was very good at it, but once he had lost the use of his legs he never mentioned the game again, said Eleanor. Years later, musing on FDR's attitude toward his handicap, she said, "You know that he has never said he could not walk."[19]

Third, FDR insisted upon good cheer at all times, no matter how difficult. There would be no complaints, no matter how great the pain. During his convalescent period, the paralyzed muscles in his legs began to tighten, bending his legs backward and pulling his heels toward his hips. To halt this grotesque deformity, it was necessary to place his legs in plaster casts and to force his legs straight by hammering ever wider wedges into the casts behind the knees. This was extremely painful—a torture drawn out over many days. Roosevelt took it all without complaint. Negative feelings were simply not acknowledged or expressed. This pattern would apply throughout the years, whether the negative feelings were over the loss of his legs or the death of his mother or Missy. They were not allowed.

And last, from his sickbed as later from the Oval Office, FDR directed the whole show. From a child explaining to his mother why he directed the other children, he became the man who was unquestionably in charge. During the rehabilitation years after his illness, Eleanor and Howe had to stand in for FDR, working to keep his name alive in elective politics, but they did so quite clearly at his direction, under his supervision.

After four weeks, Roosevelt was judged well enough to be moved from the island to a hospital in New York. FDR was most anxious that the press should not know how severely paralyzed he had become. From the onset of the illness, Louis Howe had consciously misled the reporters. To inquiries from the press concerning FDR's health, Howe at first reported a heavy cold, later influenza from which he was "now improving."[20] Now it was necessary for Howe to work out a scheme to transfer FDR without the reporters becoming aware just how ill he was.

In fact, Roosevelt's body was stiff and unbending due to muscular contractions. He was still suffering acute pain. He could not sit up. He could be transferred only on a pallet and only with great pain. The move was extremely difficult. Howe had to engineer the transfer process from the second-story bedroom down the steep hill to the wharf. This required that FDR be strapped to a canvas-type stretcher and lowered down the cliff, passed down by strong hands. Roosevelt's stretcher was loaded onto a small boat, which took him across a two-mile sea to a sardine dock. There he was loaded onto an iron-wheeled baggage cart and hauled over cobbles to a siding where a private railroad car was waiting. A window was removed from the car so that the stretcher could be passed through to a waiting berth. All this was done while the press was diverted by Howe to the other end of the port.

By the time the reporters caught up with Roosevelt, he was arranged in his berth, resting on pillows, his famous cigarette holder cocked at a jaunty angle in his mouth. As the *New York World* reported the next day, "Mr. Roosevelt was enjoying his cigarette and said he had a good appetite. Although unable to sit up, he says he is feeling more comfortable."[21]

This was the first public test of FDR's resolve. He had just experienced several hours of excruciating pain throughout his entire body. Eleanor speculated that during the move he had felt extremely helpless and frightened at the thought of being dropped, particularly as he was being transferred into and out of the bobbing boat.[22] But neither the fear nor the pain was expressed. He simply would not let it show.

III
Convalescence

I must get down the driveway today—all
the way down the driveway.[1]
—FRANKLIN D. ROOSEVELT.

AFTER Roosevelt was placed in the hospital, an announcement about his illness was made to the press. He was still
virtually helpless, his arms were still weak, the muscles of his
legs and buttocks were continuing to atrophy, his body below
the waist was paralyzed. The account to the press was inten-
tionally misleading. Reported *The New York Times:*

F.D. ROOSEVELT ILL OF POLIOMYELITIS

Brought on special car from Campobello, Bay of Fundy, to
hospital here.

Recovering, doctors say.

Patient stricken by infantile paralysis a month ago, and use
of legs affected.

Although the *Times* reported there had been some temporary
paralysis of Roosevelt's legs below the knees, the paper assured
its readers "he will definitely not be crippled."

The next day FDR dictated a cheery little note to *Times* publisher Adolph S. Ochs:

> . . . while the doctors were . . . telling me . . . that I was
> not going to suffer any permanent effects . . . I had, of

course, the usual dark suspicion that they were just saying nice things . . . but now that I have seen the same statement officially made in *The New York Times*. I feel immensely relieved because I know it must be so.[2]

Thus was the private policy of good cheer and denial of the unpleasant truth turned to public and political purpose.

FDR was in the hospital for six weeks, and in November he went home. He was still sick, still in pain. Gradually, the muscles in his arms and trunk were gaining strength. He had learned to turn himself by using a trapeze suspended over his bed. He could sit up in a wheelchair, wearing a corset for back support. Soon he learned how to transfer from his bed to the chair. Slowly, over the months, the pain receded, his health returned, and his energy and endurance grew. The long, tedious process of recovery and rehabilitation had begun.

Roosevelt grew in strength, but the muscles in his lower back and legs did not improve. From the very first, FDR was absolutely determined that he would recover the use of his legs and that he would walk again. For seven years, from 1921 through 1928, walking again was to be Roosevelt's principal interest, major goal, and full-time occupation. Over this period, it is beyond question that he devoted far more time and thought to his rehabilitation than he did to his political career, which, although certainly under his direction, he left in the hands of Louis Howe and Eleanor. Roosevelt devoted himself to his recovery with a monomaniacal passion.

Much has been written about the struggle between Franklin's mother and his wife over the path his life should take. Eleanor, backed by Louis, believed he must continue his political career. His mother believed that polio must put a close to his public life and that he should now retire to Hyde Park to lead, as his father had before him, the life of a semi-invalid country squire. It was, in the words of biographer John Gunther, "a battle to the finish between these two remarkable women for Franklin's soul."[3]

Of course, in the overall sense, Eleanor and Louis triumphed. Roosevelt would take up his political career with great lifelong success. Nevertheless, what is not often realized is that in another sense his mother also won. Roosevelt *did* in fact retire from public life for seven years. He spent months of each year at Hyde Park; he was away each winter seeking treatment, first at the Massachusetts shore, then in Florida, and then finally in Warm Springs, Georgia. Less than 25 percent of his time during those years did he live in the Roosevelt Manhattan townhouse where he was able to attend to business and politics in person. When he was away from Manhattan he attended to other things: gentlemanly pursuits such as fishing, stamps, ornithology, model boats, and, of course, his physical therapy. His guests, and the people with whom he spent his time, were Harvard classmates, Hyde Park neighbors, and the heirs of the old New York families who made up his mother's circle of friends. His mother found great pleasure having him back home, surrounded by people of suitable social background.

The Roosevelt townhouse on East Sixty-fifth Street was four stories tall, and it was jammed from top to bottom that first winter of 1921–22. Tensions ran high as FDR, his wife, mother, and family attempted to adjust themselves to the new fact of Roosevelt's paralysis. There were unpleasant scenes and bitter words. Roosevelt was in pain psychologically as well as physically, but he endured, in his mother's words, "without fuss" and he always insisted upon good cheer around him. He dealt with the struggle between his wife and mother by ignoring it in a particular Roosevelt manner: he simply refused to acknowledge its existence. He would not choose between them, and he continued to placate both concurrently.

By the spring of 1922, the various roles had been sorted out. Eleanor and Louis remained in the city working on politics, while Roosevelt went to spend the summer with his mother at Hyde Park. Increasingly their lives as husband and wife were to be become more separate and independent, yet as always Eleanor's activities were dedicated to him, and he retained his absolute confidence in her.

During these years Eleanor became a nationally acknowledged leader in the Democratic Party. She was active in both state and national campaigns. She took positions of her own on the issues of the day, and it is indicative of her own rising importance that the papers gave front-page coverage on February 1, 1924, to the news that both Mr. *and Mrs.* F. D. Roosevelt were endorsing the candidacy of Al Smith for President.[4]

At first, it seems, Roosevelt had periods of isolation and retreat. There were times when he seemed to take little interest in anything beyond his illness and therapy. Howe and Eleanor were afraid of this apathy. "Mr. Howe felt that the one way to get my husband's interest aroused was to keep him as much as possible in contact with politics." And this they did.[5] Nevertheless, there is some evidence that he remained in a state of repressed emotional depression. For three winters he lived in semi-retreat aboard a houseboat in Florida waters. He had gone there once, saying to Eleanor, "I don't want to be a burden to my family."[6] This was, according to her, the only time he decried his condition, although she once reported another such occasion to a biographer: ". . . he said it would be easier for him to go by boat than train. That was the only time I ever heard him acknowledge that he was not just as he had been before."[7]

On the houseboat, there were good times, of course, as his sons or the friends of his childhood would come down to join him for days of clowning and fishing. There were also bad times, periods of genuine depression. His secretary, Missy LeHand, who was by his side during these years, once confided to Secretary of Labor Frances Perkins (as quoted by Roosevelt's biographer Frank Freidel), "There were days . . . when it was noon before he could pull himself out of depression and greet his guests wearing his lighthearted facade."[8]

Roosevelt's family and friends have insisted that he never became depressed and that he was never troubled by his handicap. In the words of his White House doctor, "From the testimony of his friends and my own observation I can say truthfully that no one ever saw him indulge in so much as a moment of self-pity." This, if true, would be superhuman, but it is not true.

The doctor goes on to say, "Periods of depression, if any, were hidden and never at any time shadowed the smile with which he faced the future."[9] This is more accurate. As Missy indicates, Roosevelt *did* indeed have periods of depression but he kept them hidden.

During the winter of 1921–22, Roosevelt began the long struggle to rehabilitate himself. It was a struggle he both won and lost. He won it by any general definition of rehabilitation: that is, the extent to which the handicapped person is able to make optimum use of the faculties and abilities available to him. He lost, however, by the measure of his own ambition: he was determined, absolutely determined, to walk again without the use of braces and crutches. And this he never did.

Over the first winter of his illness there had been marked improvement in his condition. The functions of his body controlled by the autonomic nervous system, including his bowels and bladder, had returned to normal as, gradually, had sensory perception over the whole body. His arms now had normal strength, as did the muscles of his upper trunk. The muscles of his stomach and lower back, although weak, were strengthening. His legs, however, had not improved. In the new year, the doctors ordered crutches and braces with a pelvic band attached to provide support and stability. By the spring, making use of this equipment, FDR could stand erect.

FDR's arm and trunk muscles seemed well on the way toward full recovery. The prospects for recovery of his hip and leg muscles were not as hopeful; those muscles were still painful, tight, and quite paralyzed. Although he was not able to move his legs, the leg muscles had clear signs of life: each of the major muscle groups had at least a flicker, a ripple of movement. It was his hope of coaxing the flicker into movement, and the movement into normal function, that drove Roosevelt onward.

In his search for an effective therapy, Roosevelt consulted expert medical opinion across America. He developed an extensive correspondence with polio victims and the doctors treating them, which he carried on throughout the rest of his life. At first he was seeking advice and exchanging ideas. In due course

23

he was providing advice, as he became expert and an innovator in the new field of rehabilitation medicine.

He tried everything: massage, saltwater baths, ultraviolet light, electric currents, walking on braces with parallel bars at waist height, walking while hanging from parallel bars mounted above his head. He tried horseback riding, and an electric tricycle his mother brought from Europe. He tried exercises in warm water and exercises in cold water. He tried various theories of muscle training: working with gravity, against gravity, with resistance and without. He tried osteopathy. Even the eminent Dr. Émile Coué ("Every day in every way I'm getting better and better") was consulted on his behalf.

Roosevelt developed a daily routine: exercises in the morning, walking practice in the afternoon. These sessions were arduous and invariable and continued for seven years.

Daily he worked out on the floor. He would sweat and strain, pulling himself across the carpet on his stomach. Sitting up he would inch himself backward, dragging along his useless legs. The Roosevelt townhouse in Manhattan had four floors: FDR's bedroom was on the top floor. He taught himself a way of getting up and down stairs in case of fire. Sitting on the bottom step with his hands on the step above, he would lean backward, straighten his arms, and hitch himself up to the next step. And in this way he would slowly bump himself upstairs.

Every day he worked out on the parallel bars. Wearing his corset and braces, leaning into his arms, he would drag his legs along—first the one and then the other—to the end of the bars and back again.

FDR was no different from other handicapped patients in the diligence and concentration with which he worked. What was unusual about FDR's sessions was that he liked, indeed insisted upon, the presence of family members and visitors. As he struggled along the parallel bars, his muscles straining, his brow furrowed and sweating from the intense effort, FDR would carry on a conversation with his visitors, laughing, joshing, telling anecdotes, entertaining everyone present. He made the sessions entertaining for the people who were watching him. This was, of course, his political personality hard at work. It was good practice. FDR was learning how to be entertaining and diverting even as he was devoting virtually his entire effort and attention to another quite different and more difficult task. This is a skill that most successful politicians seem to have. They know how to appear pleased with their guests, interested in their issues, and confident of the future, even as they struggle with the task before them.

FDR did not like to be alone. He did not like introspection or deep thoughts. He liked to have people about him and he gained support and confidence from their presence. Essentially a shy man, he did not confide his feelings to others; instead he entertained them. In a sense, his patter, his song and dance, was the price he paid for companionship.

At first, his teenage children were frightened by their father's affliction and were uncomfortable in his presence. FDR changed this by involving them in his rehabilitation efforts. He would call them to his bedside, throw back the covers, and explain to them the names and functions of the major muscle groups. He would demonstrate the difference between a muscle with good motor power and one with only fair power. He would explain the exercises he was using to reeducate the muscles in his legs, and he would point out improvement as it occurred. Soon enough the children were at ease with their father's condition. In fact, upon occasion the children became so enthusiastic about his progress they would break into cheers when he reported a strengthened gluteus maximus. The four Roosevelt boys grew to be strong, strapping six-footers. As FDR gained strength in his arms and shoulders, he challenged his boys to arm wrestling matches and he would roughhouse with them on the floor.

Roosevelt had been a glamorous and dashing father to his children, but distant. Politics did not leave him much time to be with them. They had adored him, but from afar. Now, because of his illness, he was home, perhaps for good. Furthermore, now he needed them, needed their help, their strength. This the children gave then and later. They loved their father, and the help they gave him, at some sacrifice to their own lives, from the Democratic Convention of 1924 to Yalta in 1945, made life easier for the handicapped Roosevelt.

When he was at Hyde Park during the rehabilitation years, in the afternoon he would have his braces put on, take up his crutches, and set out to "walk" to the road at the end of the driveway two hundred yards away. He would "walk" a few paces and then lean into his crutches and rest. It was very hard work. He had to concentrate all his attention upon the effort. Often he fell. If there was no one about to pick him up he would lie helpless until someone came along.

His daughter, Anna, recalled what it was like:

> I think it's a bit traumatic, when you're 15 years of age and you look up and see your father, whom you have regarded as a wonderful playmate, who took long walks with you, sailed with you, could out-jump you, and do a lot of things, suddenly, you look up and you see him walking on crutches—trying, struggling in heavy steel braces. And you see the sweat pouring down his face, and hear him saying, "I must get down the driveway today — all the way down the driveway."[10]

Roosevelt worked like this for many hours each day, virtually every day for seven years. He never made it to the end of the driveway. Experiences such as this were quite new to Roosevelt. All that he had done hitherto had been successful and easy. This was hard, terribly hard, and, in spite of all his efforts, a failure.

Of course he never admitted that it was a failure. His letters of the time are as full of optimism and good cheer as always. According to his accounts, each new therapy that he tried offered promise of remarkable recovery; the failure of his last therapy was quite forgotten. His good cheer and confidence were quite contagious. Everyone wanted to believe along with him that progress was possible. His mother wrote him in 1925, four years after the attack,

> I feel so hopeful and confident! Once able to move about without crutches and without braces, strength will come,

and now for the first time in more than a year I feel that
work is to be done for *you*, my dearest. . . .[11]

Unfortunately, his paralysis was reality and his therapy a
failure. Eleanor said later she thought the experience had taught
him patience. She thought it had given him an understanding
of the suffering of others. She called it "perhaps a blessing in
disguise."[12] Probably she was right, but "blessing" is a strange
word for it.

After the first two years, Roosevelt's leg muscles had not improved significantly. Since he had come to know everything there
was to know about polio and physical therapy, Roosevelt certainly knew the chances of total recovery (or even further significant recovery) had become very slight. Nevertheless, he did
not slacken his desperate efforts for further recovery. Actually
such superhuman effort was not necessary: what muscles were
coming back would continue to do so, given moderate exercise
and favorable conditions. The extent of the recovery would be
determined by the degree of permanent damage caused by the
polio virus to the anterior horn cells of the central nervous system. Recovery was not increased or improved by extraordinary
amounts of exercise. Too much exercise, in fact, constituted a
hazard. Weak muscles could be strained by overwork, and the
rate of returning strength could be slowed or even reversed.

There was great and unflagging determination in Roosevelt's
efforts; there was also desperation. He was trapped. His entire
effort was dedicated to what was now clearly an impossible task:
the recovery of his muscles. After the first two years, his sin-
gle-minded concentration had begun to take on the characteristics of an unhealthy obsession. Instead of putting his life in
order and proceeding with such business activities as he could
handle, Roosevelt shook his fist at the fates and seemed psychologically unable to acknowledge the permanence of his
paralytic condition.

IV
Attitudes

But it's a bitter blow.[1]

—LILY NORTON

THE situation faced by FDR and his family is nicely caught and expressed by a visitor in a letter to a friend dated November 14, 1921:

> I am staying up here with a dear friend: Mrs. James Roosevelt. . . . It's a lovely region, but tragedy rather overshadows this once so happy and prosperous family, for Mrs. R's only son: Franklin Roosevelt was struck down in August with a terribly serious case of infantile paralysis. He is only 39—both too old and too young for such a fell germ to disable him. He's had a brilliant career as Assistant (Secretary) of the Navy under Wilson, and then a few brief weeks of crowded glory and excitement when nominated by the Democrats for the Vice Presidency. Now he is a cripple—will he ever be anything else? His mother is wonderfully courageous and plucky, but it's a bitter blow. . . .[2]

Medical treatment for the handicapped in the 1920s was inadequate, ineffectual, and grim.

Most paralytic patients died at the onset of their illness, either from the illness itself, from accompanying infection, or from the usual "complications." Paraplegics died routinely of kidney infections. Pneumonia carried off the bedridden. Therapies were ineffective; drugs to counteract complications were often nonexistent. Mortality rates were high, and only a small percentage of patients with serious illness survived long enough to enter the rehabilitation phase of treatment.

Patients who did survive disappeared into the general population. Upon their discharge from hospital, most did not seek, nor did they receive, any continuing form of rehabilitative therapy.

In the 1920s, to be handicapped in some visible way carried with it social opprobrium. The handicapped were kept at home, out of sight, in back bedrooms, by families who felt a mixture of embarrassment and shame about their presence. The well-to-do were able to afford custodial nursing care for their handicapped family members, and the loving family was able to care at home for its crippled loved ones. Many of the handicapped, however, were simply ignored by their families and society. A New York State study of handicapped children found them to be "neglected at home, rejected by the public schools, incapacitated by physical disability and unable to care for themselves."[3] There was very little help for such persons.

Even if the patient and his family should decide to seek continuing rehabilitative therapy—and even if they had the money to pay for it—such treatment was not easy to find.

In 1890, there were but five rehabilitative orthopedic hospitals for children in the United States. By 1920, there were seven times as many: thirty-five to forty. They could handle, at the most, only a few thousand patients at a time, when there were quite literally millions of persons who could benefit from therapy.

These hospitals were often grim, depressing places—dark, gray piles indistinguishable from prisons and asylums. They had names such as House of St. Giles the Cripple, Children's House of the Home for Incurables, and the New York Society for the Relief of the Ruptured and Crippled. Treatment was spartan and severe—and purposely so: fresh air in all seasons; windows open at all times; no central heating; basic institutional cooking, without luxury or frill; strict rules and firm discipline. In a very real although subconsciously motivated sense, the handicapped were viewed as flawed in moral character as well as in body. The physical handicap was, as it were, an outward sign of some inner weakness. It was widely held that treatment, to be effective, must have a punitive quality to it. Those who administered this painful treatment did so in fulfillment of their Christian duty, in answer to their calling to a life of Christian service. It was unpleasant but necessary work, like visitation to the prisons, or operation of Salvation Army kitchens. The superintendent of the Society for the Ruptured and Crippled exemplified this attitude as he explained the mission of his society: to provide "Science to prune and brace and train the poor little shrunken forms into a development of symmetry and grace; earnest and loving hearts and hands to minister to their material comfort; devoted teachers to stimulate and train the neglected minds and stagnant brains into an activity that will transform from ignorance and vice into moral purity and beauty . . ."[4]

R. C. Elmslie, a leading medical authority in the early part of the century, in a textbook widely circulated, issued a clear warning of the evil nature of the handicapped: "A failure in the moral training of a cripple means the evolution of an individual detestable in character, a menace and burden to the community, who is only too apt to graduate into the mendicant and criminal classes."[5]

Such treatment often was not rehabilitative; it was in fact the contrary—debilitating in the extreme. Helpless and fearful patients were subjected to severe and often painful exercise therapy in prison-like surroundings, for their own good and moral uplift. Strict, long-term hospitals are like prisons; they teach their inmates to be highly dependent. Social contacts and needs are subordinated to discipline. The childish and humiliating routine of institutional life rewards regressive, infantile behavior. It robs the patient of whatever ability he has to function on his own. As Dr. Elmslie warned from his experience, it is small wonder that "In a hospital devoted to the care of chronic deformities in childhood the wards, after a time, become almost hopelessly encumbered with convalescent patients."[6]

Admittedly, the health professionals administering these places were severely frustrated by inadequate facilities and ineffective therapies. There was little they could do in any real sense to benefit their patients, and this must have caused them severe frustration. Almost in desperation they took to surgery; where they could not heal, they butchered. Dr. Elmslie, in a discussion on the treatment of paralysis arising from poliomyelitis, stated: "When a leg is completely useless—i.e., when it cannot be swung forward and backward—it is better to amputate it through the thigh."[7] This is, of course, a disastrous policy; the loss of a limb simply adds the hindrance of an artificial leg to the problems of paralysis and creates vast new psychological trauma. A properly braced leg performs better in virtually every case than a false one. This, however, did not stop the doctor. Even in a case where the leg can be "swung backward and forward," the doctor believed that "persistent chilblains (from cold temperatures and poor nursing) on a badly paralyzed leg form a good reason for advising amputation." This same doctor found that braces and crutches *can* be helpful for bringing a paralyzed leg to use but he advised against supplying such equipment to the poor, who cannot be trusted "to look after them well." In the treatment of poor patients, he prefers amputation, but upon occasion he found it possible "to provide cheap but efficient forms [of braces] which will serve the purpose, although because they are a little unsightly or inconvenient they would not satisfy the parents of well-to-do children."[8]

Of course, in the 1920s, few available orthopedic devices satisfied anybody. Wheelchairs were large, bulky, wooden wicker contrivances, which could not be folded for travel, could not be carried up steps, could only with great difficulty be propelled up curbs, and could rarely pass through narrow bathroom doors. It was virtually impossible to live an independent life confined to such a chair. Braces were heavy iron and leather—difficult enough for a limb with normal muscle power to handle, and painful, tiring, and awkward for an impaired limb. Various pieces of iron, cage-like equipment and frames—painful and ugly—were used to prevent increased deformity caused by growth and muscle imbalance.

It is not inaccurate to state that these hospitals, in the course of their treatments, practiced maiming and torture.

Handicapped children were not allowed into the mainstream of public education. The vast majority received no formal education at all. Efforts were made in a few places to provide segregated teaching and vocational training. For example, in 1910, Boston was providing such training, but only for forty handicapped students. Typically, this training was in the form of stitchery and needlework for women, chair caning and basketwork for men. Although well intentioned, efforts like these simply served to reinforce the sense of helplessness and isolation felt by the crippled. A quite perceptive 1914 report of the Sage Foundation pointed out that the handicapped were being trained to make unwanted things: "It is hard to secure steady employment or reasonably good wages by making such articles outside the institution and away from the possibility of a 'charity' demand for the things made."[9] The handicapped were being trained to so limit their skills and their expectations as to be permanently unemployable anywhere but in a charity supported sheltered workshop.

Of course, behind these jumbled practices of ignorance, apathy, and oftentimes cruelty, there lay the lingering primordial fear, unspoken but nearly universal, of the crippled. Throughout history—with specific, glorious exceptions—the crippled have been cursed, tormented, abandoned, imprisoned, and killed. The Spartans hurled their disabled citizens off a cliff to their death. Martin Luther believed deformed children were fathered by the devil and killing them was no sin. The Jews banished their cripples, forcing them to beg along the roadside. American Indians took their deformed newborn and buried them alive. In the eighteenth century, the handicapped were confined to asylums—to be cared for, perhaps, but also to remove their deformed appearance, offensive to sensitive persons, from the streets. Not until the nineteenth century were institutions for the care and treatment of handicapped persons established. These were primitive and inadequate, but they were a legitimate effort to minister to the crippled.

In America, in the 1920s, such age-old fears and taboos associated with the crippled were largely denied by right-thinking, well-meaning people who tried to be modern and forward-looking. Nevertheless, these fears were not far beneath the surface.

Clearly, the person who survived a severe case of paralytic polio in the 1920s faced a depressing and uncertain future. Standard medical treatment offered very little in the way of encouragement or support. There was no program pushing for the reentry of the handicapped into the mainstream of society. There were no role models to follow, no organized group of experienced peers, no society of concerned citizens to provide help and advice.

It is difficult in our own time to appreciate how very depressing was FDR's situation, and how great were the obstacles to his overcoming them and returning to his career in public life. His legs were paralyzed and would always be so. No one severely paralyzed had ever been active in public life; current social attitudes discouraged anyone from attempting it. Yet Roosevelt was still young, vigorous, and healthy, and he was manifestly ambitious. What was he to do?

V

Warm Springs

This is really a discovery of a place . . .[1]
—FRANKLIN D. ROOSEVELT

FRANKLIN Roosevelt went to Warm Springs, Georgia, for the first time on October 3, 1924.[2] As was usual after his illness, he was accompanied not only by his wife but also by his secretary, Missy LeHand, and his chauffeur-valet. He arrived on board the milk train from Columbus, thirty-five miles away. As a Roosevelt and a former vice-presidential candidate, he was already something of a celebrity. The townsfolk knew he was coming, and some fifty of them gathered at the station. He was to stay at a cottage on the grounds of an old resort hotel, the Meriwether Inn. Even though the season was over, the hotel's owner had spruced up the gardens and hung Japanese lanterns from the trees in his honor.

The crowd watched in silence at the train station as FDR was lifted from the train and slowly moved with braces and crutches to a waiting car. He was greeted by the mayor and other local dignitaries.

Warm Springs was then—as it is now—a town of fewer than 550 people. Located eighty miles southwest of Atlanta, it was ten miles from the nearest paved road. In 1924, the town was a sleepy, desperately impoverished farm community. Farming in the Deep South had been in depression since the end of World War I. The Meriwether Inn was a ramshackle, rambling, wooden Victorian structure, long ago painted in gaudy yellow and green.

34

It had been a popular place for Atlanta society some fifty years before, but was now in as depressed a state as the community.

What had made the hotel so popular—what was indeed the most important feature of the town itself—were the remarkable warm springs. Rising from deep within Pine Mountain, pure, highly mineralized water flowed at the rate of 1,800 gallons per minute. The temperature of the water was a constant eighty-eight degrees. It was said that the minerals and the temperature provided a remarkably buoyant, refreshing bath, without the normally enervating effects of a lengthy swim.

Roosevelt learned of Warm Springs in a letter from his friend, the wealthy Wall Street banker George Foster Peabody. In the course of the letter, he told of a young man, confined to a wheelchair since childhood by a severe case of polio, who had received substantial benefits from swimming in the waters of Warm Springs, where Peabody was coowner of the hotel. Perhaps, he suggested, Roosevelt, too, could benefit from hydrotherapy at Warm Springs. Roosevelt, who had tried everything else, was willing to try.

Roosevelt came to Warm Springs and met the young man, Louis Joseph, who indeed was now able to walk with the help of two canes. According to his story, he had begged his aunts to allow him to go into the Springs' pool with them. He kept afloat with a pair of water wings. The buoyancy of the water served to counter the heavy pull of gravity, and thus relieved, his polio-weakened muscles were able to do in water what they could not do on dry land. Relieved of gravity, subjected to gentle exercise in the water, his muscles gradually regained strength and, in time, the boy was able to walk again, using only canes for support.

On FDR's first morning, Louis told his story and demonstrated the exercises and procedures that had helped him. Roosevelt was much impressed. Together the two devised exercises that they felt would benefit Roosevelt's wasted legs. FDR was delighted to discover that he could work in Warm Springs' waters for as long as two hours at a time without excessive fatigue or dehydration. After these exercises, Roosevelt stretched out un-

35

der the rays of the hot Georgia sun. After a leisurely Southern lunch, he took the first of many drives over the countryside. That very first day, Roosevelt established a routine he was to follow throughout the rest of his life whenever he visited Warm Springs.

Eleanor saw FDR safely lodged and, after a few days, hastened back to New York City and her political activities. Roosevelt wrote her of his new life at Warm Springs:

> The life is just the same day after day and there is no variety to give landmarks. The mornings are as you know wholly taken up with the pool and for the afternoons we have sat out on the lawn . . . and I have worked at stamps or checks or accounts or have played rummy with Missy. The other three afternoons we have gone motoring. . . . The legs are really improving a great deal. The walking and general exercising in the water is fine and I have worked out some special exercises also. This is really a discovery of a place and there is no doubt that I've got to do it some more.[3]

The hotel season was over and the hotel itself was closed. Roosevelt and Missy were staying in one of the cottages on the grounds. The cottages were little more than simple wooden structures resting upon four brick columns. The cottages were so poorly constructed, recalled Eleanor, "I could look through the cracks and see daylight." They were without running water or electricity and the kitchens were primitive. Indeed, life at Warm Springs was simple. Eleanor had driven out to buy chickens one day when she discovered "to her perfect horror" that she must buy them live. "They ran around in our yard, until the cook wrung their necks amid much squawking and put them in the pot. . . . Somehow I didn't enjoy eating them," she said later.[4] There was not much about Warm Springs she *did* enjoy. The acute poverty saddened her, and she was angered by the active prejudice against the blacks. She was never able to be comfortable at Warm Springs and came as seldom as possible.

Tom Loyless, coowner of the hotel with George Peabody, lived in a cottage across the way. In the evenings, FDR would roll out on the porch of his cottage and bellow across to Tom: "Come on over." The two would sit and talk late into the night. Loyless had hopes of revitalizing Meriwether Inn. He thought it had a future as something of a European spa with people coming to Warm Springs to take a "cure." Loyless and Peabody had hoped that Roosevelt would be interested in the project, and he most certainly was. Roosevelt's concept of Warm Springs as a convalescent rehabilitation center for the victims of infantile paralysis had its inception in these leisurely late-night conversations with Loyless.

Like Eleanor, FDR was bothered by the poverty and the prejudice, but he was able to see the worth of these friendly people in their depressed community and the townspeople were most pleased to have such a famous man in their midst. It was hoped his presence would put Warm Springs on the map the way a visit of President Taft to Macon had once brought publicity to that town. Everyone wanted to meet Roosevelt and, over the course of the next several weeks, virtually everyone did. One by one, Georgia's politicians and public men stopped by to pay their respects. Roosevelt delighted in the attention. He was comfortable with the people; he found them warm and quite different from New Yorkers.

In his afternoon drives he began to explore the country—a terrain, climate, and culture that seemed quite alien and remote from upstate New York. Different as it was, he soon came to love the countryside, the red clay roads, the rolling hills, the tall and stately pines. Roosevelt saw the beauty of the place and responded to the hospitality of the people. He felt at home.

The *Atlanta Journal* learned of Roosevelt's visit to Warm Springs and sent reporter Cleburne Gregory to do a feature story. FDR suggested the man stay a while, long enough to get a thorough understanding of Roosevelt's activities. In a letter written some twenty years later, Gregory recalls: "I went swimming in Warm Springs with Mr. Roosevelt two or three times a day for five days. We ate hot dogs at a small, unsanitary stand adjacent to the pool and washed them down with an occasional bottle of beer.

37

"Mr. Roosevelt laughed at the claims of the Cherokee Indians that the springs had medicinal value, but he said the water's temperature of 89 degrees soothed muscles drawn by infantile paralysis and encouraged mild exercise. I wrote a story about his visit for the *Journal*'s Sunday magazine with the title 'Franklin D. Roosevelt Will Swim to Health.' The article appeared on October 26, 1924."

Sixteen years later, when FDR was considering running for a third term, he called Georgia political leaders to meet with him at Warm Springs. One of the leaders called was Gregory. The President stared at Gregory repeatedly during the meeting and later asked: "Haven't you and I been on a junket somewhere together?" Gregory reminded the President that he had visited him during his first days at Warm Springs. The President was delighted. "Didn't we have a good time in the Springs and weren't those hot dogs good?"[5]

Gregory's article received much attention and it sparked the beginning of Warm Springs as a treatment center for polio patients. The article said, in part:

> Franklin D. Roosevelt, New York lawyer and banker, Assistant Secretary of the Navy during the World War, and Democratic nominee for vice-president in 1920, is literally swimming himself back to health and strength at Warm Springs.

The article described Roosevelt's life at Warm Springs: the morning exercise in the pool; the leisurely lunches; the afternoon naps; the pleasant drives through the countryside. The story was full of cheerful optimism and good humor. While the article did not claim that Roosevelt had found a cure for polio at Warm Springs, it came close. It quoted FDR as saying: "The best infantile paralysis specialists in New York told me that the only way to overcome the effects of the disease was to swim as much as possible, and bask in the sunlight. Conditions here are ideal for both prescriptions."[6] This was a typical upbeat feature story. The theme—celebrity struggles to overcome the effects of a dread disease—guaranteed its wide appeal. The article was syndicated, and widely printed across the country. Inevitably it was read by many polio patients.

The daily existence of many of these polios was in stark contrast with the pleasant and cheerful life described by Gregory. According to the article, Warm Springs had extended a "hearty welcome" to polio patient Roosevelt, and presumably would similarly welcome others. Treatment at the Springs had undeniably helped Roosevelt and would presumably help others. Not surprisingly, there was a quick response from polios who had seen the article. Letters came pouring in addressed to Roosevelt at Warm Springs. Some desperate polios simply packed their bags and set off for the Springs without so much as invitation, permission, or warning. They had come drawn by Roosevelt's example, and he took an immediate and genuine interest in their plight.

This response took Roosevelt and hotel coowner Tom Loyless by surprise. They were simply not equipped to take care of handicapped boarders. The old Meriwether Inn was still trying to attract able-bodied vacationers. The old building had many steps, and the bathrooms in the hotel were inaccessible to wheelchairs. The cottages had no bathrooms at all. The hotel had no therapeutic equipment, and Roosevelt and Loyless had no therapeutic experience. Quite clearly, by any standard of good judgment—to say nothing of legal responsibility—they were in no position to accept polio patients.

It is a serious responsibility, and today a complicated matter, to offer a program of treatment for the handicapped. Studies must be made. Medical clearance must be obtained. State and national standards must be met for the equipment to be used, the procedures to be followed, even for the dimensions of the living and treatment quarters. The medical and professional credentials of the persons giving the treatment must be certified. The costs for such things are extraordinary, and outside sources of funds must be obtained. Today it takes years of effort and much paper work to create a new hospital.

It didn't work that way at Warm Springs. Roosevelt and Loyless simply took specific steps to meet immediate requirements. As Roosevelt explained years later, "One day Mr. Loyless and some of the neighbors—the Harts, Miss Wilkins, Joseph, and some of us—were sitting around when a messenger came up the hill to Mr. Loyless and said, 'Two people have been carried off the train down at the station. What shall we do with them? Neither of them can walk.' Well, we held a consultation. It was long before anything was done here in the way of a hotel or cottages. We decided that we could take care of them in the village overnight, and then in a couple of days, we could fix up what is now 'the wreck' and put them in it. Well, before we could put that cottage in order, eight others had arrived. They came like Topsy and got here before we knew it."[7]

Warm Springs had begun its life as a treatment center. As the article had implied, the polios were indeed welcomed by the people of Warm Springs. From the very beginning, even before cottages had been opened for them, the townspeople took the polios in with an easy, neighborly acceptance, which was, for its time, surprisingly free of fear or unease.

From the very beginning, the polios had a spirit of self-help and make-do. Life at first was rough, funds were low, treatment was sketchy at best, but there was always great fun about the place. For many of the newly arrived patients, Warm Springs was like a life rediscovered. The oppressive hostility of the Victorian hospital routine, the pain of body bracing and muscle stretching, had been replaced overnight by a world of sunlight and warm water, laughter, encouragement, and hope.

That was in the fall of 1924. By the summer of 1925, there were more than twenty-five patients at Warm Springs. By then, Loyless, who was dying of cancer, was too ill to continue his work at the hotel. He and FDR had talked about turning Warm Springs into a therapeutic center. Now the work had begun, but Loyless, who was to die the following year, would be unable to see it carried forward. That second summer, Roosevelt took over direction of the operations. He built ramps into the Meriwether Inn, had additional cottages repaired and opened for patients, and designed a treatment table for use in the pool. The table, twelve inches below the surface of the water, is now standard equipment for all water therapy. The regular guests at the Meriwether Inn complained about the presence of polio patients at the resort. They found it distasteful to dine in the same dining room, to swim in the same pool with crippled people. Whatever Roosevelt thought of these complaints, he resolved them—at least temporarily—by establishing a dining room in the basement for the polios with a level entrance from the outside, and by having a small treatment pool dug next to the large outdoor pool, separate and away from the nonhandicapped paying guests. The treatment pool was covered for use in rainy weather and in the winter.

Working with the other patients, Roosevelt evolved exercises and treatment procedures. He drew up a crude but serviceable muscle chart, which listed the major muscle groups of the body, left side and right side. With this chart, Roosevelt undertook to give his "patients" muscle tests on a regular basis so as to record gain or loss of strength over the weeks and months of treatment.

They called him—as he called himself—"Doctor Roosevelt" and they adored him. He was their leader and he was one of them. There was much laughter, and the excitement of doing new things and doing them together. Roosevelt recalled that summer:

> I remember there were two quite large ladies; and when I was trying to teach them an exercise, which I had really invented, which was the elevating exercise in the medium of water, one of these ladies found great difficulty in getting both feet down to the bottom of the pool. Well, I would take one large knee and I'd force this large knee and leg down until the foot rested firmly on the bottom. And then I would say, 'Have you got it?' And she would say 'Yes,' and I would say, 'Hold it, hold it.' Then I would reach up and get hold of the other knee very quickly and start to put it down and then number-one knee would pop up. This used to go on for half an hour at a time; but before I left in the spring, I could get both those knees down at the same time.[8]

Fred Botts arrived that summer. Severely handicapped and confined to a wheelchair, he had spent nine years trapped in the back bedroom of his parents' house. Botts was an affable man with a splended singing voice who had planned a career in opera before he was struck by polio. The railroad refused him and his wheelchair passage in a Pullman car, and so he was forced to ride to Warm Springs in a mail car confined to a wooden boxlike structure that had been constructed for the trip. Botts came because he had read the "swimming his way to health" article. He came without an invitation and he stayed for over thirty years.

Said FDR, "That is when Fred Botts was carried off the train—yes, he was a man in those days! And we thought he is going to look like a skeleton, or die of tuberculosis before night. We did not have any doctor down here and I acted as doctor. I did not know what to do and so I fed him cream. It put flesh on him. We got him in the pool and he was scared to death, and in about a week he began to walk in the pool and that is one of the things we discovered—that people can walk in water when they cannot walk alone on land."[9] Botts became a lifelong friend of the President. FDR made him registrar of the Georgia Warm Springs Foundation, in charge of admissions. Botts, in an unpublished memoir, remembered that "first summer" of 1925: "In those pioneer days was born the new era we are now living in and enjoying; and, in those pioneer days we did well.

"Those who came into our midst that first summer of '25 came from distant places, and have come back each year since then and remained longer each time. They did only one thing and that was improve in every respect. One came with crutches and a brace, and left with a cane only. Others came in wheelchairs and *nearly* put them aside that summer. The writer of this article came in a wheelchair accompanied by his brother, and before the summer had passed was walking with crutches and was loath to use his chair." Botts lists the polios at Warm Springs that summer, ending with "The Honorable Franklin D. Roosevelt from New York City, dearest of friends and noblest of mentors, and now owner of the famous Georgia Warm Springs."[10]

Certainly the patients were having a wonderful time, but so

42

too was "Doctor" Roosevelt. His ebullience and enthusiasm were running full throttle. He positively bubbled in a letter to a friend, "In addition to all this I am consulting architect and landscape engineer for the Warm Springs company—and giving free advice on the moving of buildings, the building of roads, setting out of trees, and remodeling the hotel. We, i.e., the company plus FDR, are working out a new water system, new sewage plan, a fishing pond, and tomorrow we hold an organization meeting to start the Pine Mountain Club which will run the dance hall, the tea room, picnic grounds, golf course, and other forms of indoor and outdoor sports."[11] He was not exaggerating.

It is unclear when Roosevelt decided to buy Warm Springs. His family and friends were opposed to the idea. His law partner, Basil O'Connor, tried to stop him. O'Connor saw Warm Springs as no more than an overpriced, broken-down resort: "To me the place was just a big old hole. But it was one of those things where Roosevelt sort of had a seventh sense. And I didn't." When O'Connor heard that FDR intended to proceed with the purchase, he wired, "Don't do anything, am taking train." He was unable to stop the deal, however.

Roosevelt bought Warm Springs in the spring of 1926. He committed $200,000—over two-thirds of his fortune—to the purchase. The terms worked out between George Foster Peabody and Roosevelt were complicated. O'Connor handled the arrangements, remarking, "Something tells me Peabody's doing all right."[12] Peabody was: he had doubled his money in three years.

Eleanor had written to FDR: "I know you love creative work, my only feeling is that Georgia is somewhat distant for you to keep in touch with what is really a big undertaking . . . don't be discouraged by me; I have great confidence in your extraordinary interest and enthusiasm. It is just that I couldn't do it."[13] To Eleanor's concern that the money would be needed to educate the children, Roosevelt replied: "Ma will always see the children through."[14] To allay his mother's concerns, FDR wrote: "It looks as if I have bought Warm Springs. If so I want you to take a great interest in it, for I feel you can help me with many

43

suggestions, and the place, properly run, will not only do a great deal of good but will prove financially successful."[15] Certainly Warm Springs did do a lot of good, but it was never successful in financial terms.

VI
Rehabilitation

The work . . . has never been done
in this country before.[1]
—FRANKLIN D. ROOSEVELT

THE decision to buy Warm Springs was extraordinary. During the 1920s, Roosevelt had invested in many rather foolish projects: a helium-filled dirigible passenger service between New York and Chicago; automatic vending machines; private forests; and lobster farms. In none of these projects, however, did he invest much money. Warm Springs was the only major risk he ever took with his money.

Roosevelt's reasons for taking this risk were based more on his feelings than on a keen business sense. With Loyless dying, Roosevelt had decided to continue on his own. He personally had benefited from the treatments in the Springs' water. He was comfortable and happy with the people and the countryside. He obviously found great satisfaction working with the other polios, and they valued immensely his confidence, skill, and enthusiasm. The work and the place gave him much pleasure.

It is possible—perhaps more than possible—that FDR was actually giving consideration to making the Warm Springs treatment center the focus of his career. Certainly his wife thought so. Eleanor said once that had he not accepted the nomination as Democratic candidate for governor of New York in 1928, he would have remained as manager of "that place," as she called Warm Springs.[2] In later years he made joking reference to his continuing desire to return to Warm Springs. For example, in his Thanksgiving Day remarks at Warm Springs to his fellow polio patients in 1934, he told the story of his work with the fat ladies in the pool. "I called that my medical practice, the first and last time that I have ever practiced medicine and physiotherapy. After I get through at the White House, I hope the medical fraternity will allow me to come back and practice here. . . ."[3]

Roosevelt wanted the endorsement of the American Orthopedic Association (AOA) for his center at Warm Springs. He felt it would lend dignity to the operation. He learned the association was holding its annual convention at Atlanta, and he wrote asking permission to address the body. In his letter he explained the work under way at Warm Springs, the exercises given, and the beneficial results experienced by the polios. He asked the association for "technical guidance and help." He was surprised when he received a flat turndown from the doctors. This was an unusual experience for FDR, who was seldom turned down for anything by anyone, and he did not like it one bit. It made him angry. Roosevelt called an official of the association for an explanation. He was told that he was a man without standing. He was not an orthopedist. He was not even a doctor. He could not appear before the convention. It is reported that this conversation infuriated FDR. He called for his car and went to the convention uninvited. In his wheelchair, he prowled the corridors of the convention hotel explaining the project to every delegate he could locate. He lobbied the convention with all the political skill he possessed. As a result, a resolution was submitted on the floor and approved by the delegates to set up a committee of three orthopedic surgeons to receive and to pass upon a report of the work at Warm Springs to be submitted by a physician in residence. Roosevelt was satisfied.

He called upon Dr. LeRoy W. Hubbard, an orthopedist with the New York State Department of Health. At Roosevelt's insistence, Dr. Hubbard, who had had nine years' experience in the treatment of polio, came to Warm Springs to be in charge of the medical program. He brought with him physical therapist Helena Mahoney, who had worked with polio since the New York epidemic of 1916. She was an immensely strong-willed, tough, and innovative person whom not even Roosevelt dared call by her first name. The treatment center that they created at Warm Springs was fully as much a product of her vision as it was of FDR's. Hubbard observed and monitored the progress of twenty-three patients who were receiving exercise and treatment at Warm Springs for periods of from five to seventeen weeks from June to December 1926. He found marked improvement in each of the twenty-three cases and was able to so certify to the AOA. And so, after due consideration, the American Orthopedic Association, in January 1927, endorsed "the establishment of a permanent hydrotherapeutic center at Warm Springs."[4]

It is important to point out that no miracles were claimed by Warm Springs; there had been no "cures." Dr. Hubbard's report said that "all twenty-three seemed to make some improvement." This is generally what would be expected of a post-polio receiving a careful and continuing series of therapeutic treatments. The experiment proved that no harm was done by the Warm Springs procedures. It established that as much progress was made by the treatment as by any other. Nevertheless, the AOA recommendation was extremely helpful to Roosevelt. Within a month of receiving it he and his law partner, Basil O'Connor, established the Georgia Warm Springs Foundation as a nonprofit, permanent institution under the laws of New York and thus under the purview of the New York State Board of Charities. This meant the Foundation was eligible to receive tax-free gifts and grants. A board of trustees was named, made up of various eminent bankers and financiers, in addition to Dr. Hubbard, Louis Howe, Basil O'Connor, and, of course, Roosevelt. Roosevelt became president of the new foundation just as he had been president of the preceding corporation. The Foundation bought the hotel grounds and springs from FDR in exchange for a dollar demand note.

Roosevelt was now deeply committed to Warm Springs. In 1926 and 1927, he purchased farmland on Pine Mountain, adjacent to the Foundation. Eventually his holdings exceeded 1,750 acres. As private citizen and later as President, he kept close watch over the operation of his farm. He hoped that the right crop and modern farming methods would demonstrate that it was possible to make a profit operating a farm in rural Georgia. He was determined to find a crop that would pay its way. He refused to plant cotton, which he believed was the cause of the rural depression. Over the years, he tried various vegetables, grapes, goats, poultry, and timber. He settled on cattle. He tried to demonstrate that, by careful breeding practices, it was possible to improve the quality of the local stock of scrub cattle. Roosevelt's resident farm manager recalled that FDR was a real cattleman who "remembered the names and registration numbers of herds at Hyde Park years ago."[5] Letters concerning the farm always went directly across the President's desk, such as the one from a D. M. Boggs, February 19, 1940, which complained that Roosevelt's livestock had got into Boggs's bean patch and destroyed five hundred pounds of beans. Boggs asked for compensation because he needed "money to buy feed for the cow." At FDR's direction, Boggs got his money.[6]

Roosevelt's demonstration farming in Georgia was helpful and instructive to local farmers. It was, however, a financial failure and FDR never made a penny from his farm. It did, however, provide him with much interest and recreation. During the war years, when food supplies were scarce and rationed, the Roosevelt farm supplied the patients at the Warm Springs Foundation with fresh vegetables and meats. This, too, was a satisfaction to Roosevelt. Upon his death, the farms were willed to the Foundation.

Not only had FDR bought farmlands, he had also commissioned the construction of a small cottage on the grounds of the Foundation. This was completed in the early spring of 1927. He wrote to his mother in high spirits and cloying hyperbole: "The new cottage is *too* sweet, really very good in every way, the woodwork covering all walls and ceilings a great success, and the new furniture fits perfectly and it's just the right color."[7]

Roosevelt's enthusiasm was running at a high level during this creative period. In a letter to Eleanor's Aunt Bye Cowles, he bubbled:

> I am sending you some of our folders about Warm Springs. The work of starting a combined resort and therapeutic center has been most fascinating for it is something which, so far as I know, has never been done in this country before.
>
> We have already thirty patients there this summer and our total capacity for this coming year will be only fifty, a figure I think we shall reach in a few weeks.
>
> Most of the patients are suffering from infantile paralysis. . . . It has to be a success as the doctors are most enthusiastic and, at the same time, the climate is a delightful one all the year round. . . .
>
> . . . The whole property I have put under the Georgia Warm Springs Foundation and am now busily engaged in trying to raise two or three hundred thousand dollars to carry out the improvements and pay the mortgage on the property.
>
> . . . You would love the informality and truly languid Southern atmosphere of the place! My one fear is that this gentle charm will appeal to some of our rich friends who are suffering from nervous prosperity and that they will come down there and ruin our atmosphere. . . .[8]

This fear was not justified. The rich were never to flock to Warm Springs and money would always be a problem for the Foundation. Though the rich stayed away, the polio patients certainly did not. Applications came from across the country. Roosevelt was right about the uniqueness of what he was doing; it had never been done before, anywhere. In his intuitive way— making use of that seventh sense of which O'Connor spoke— he was developing a rehabilitation center in which the psychological and social aspects of being handicapped were acknowledged to be fully as important as the medical treatment.

Under Roosevelt's direction, the Georgia Warm Springs Foundation began a rapid development. FDR called architect Henry Toombs down from New York. Together they drew up a master plan for construction over the next twenty years. The plan called for a small cluster of buildings similar to a college campus. The ramshackle Meriwether Inn would be torn down and replaced by a central recreation hall and dining room connected by covered walkways with various dormitory, hospital, and treatment outbuildings. These would be placed about the perimeter of a large, grassy quadrangle. The Foundation grounds consisted of 1,200 acres of virgin pine forest. This would be left in its natural state, dotted here and there on the hillside by small white cottages, to be owned by resident polio patients or as seasonal homes by polios who lived elsewhere. All central buildings were to be level, easily accessible, and without obstacles to persons in wheelchairs. Roosevelt chose for these buildings a simple architectural style derived from the local antebellum architecture, and it suited the countryside well. These plans were for buildings that would take several million dollars to construct, yet the plans were drawn at a time when the total of charitable gifts received by the Foundation was less than $12,000. Roosevelt seemed confident that the money could be found.

Patients were to be treated at cost. Rates were set at forty-two dollars a week—not cheap, but still one-third the cost of hospital care at the time. This amount was not really adequate to cover patient expenses. Additional endowment would be needed to make up the shortfall.

In addition, Roosevelt had undertaken all sorts of necessary improvements. Running water with bath and toilet had been installed in each cottage. Ramps and level walkways had been constructed between the cottages, the inn, and the treatment pools. An old van had been purchased that circled through the woods each morning picking up patients from the cottages and taking them to the large treatment pool. A concrete walking court had been poured with various parallel bars, railings, and practice steps.

In the summer of 1927, FDR sent away the last of the paying guests from the old Meriwether resort. The guests had continued to complain about the presence of the polios. The income from the regulars would be missed, but clearly the two groups were incompatible. Roosevelt expressed no qualms about sending the regular guests packing.

Roosevelt's expenses were mounting. He needed to raise funds to finance the present activity and the planned growth at Warm Springs. He commissioned his friends and retained a commercial fund raiser to launch a nationwide fund drive to raise $1.25 million. In the course of the preparations for this drive, materials and pamphlets were prepared under Roosevelt's supervision. The first of these demonstrates that even early on FDR knew what he was trying to achieve.

"The hydrotherapeutic center at Warm Springs," said the pamphlet, is "to be developed and administered on a nonprofitmaking basis for the treatment of patients . . . at actual cost.

"It is not the desire or intention to make the hydrotherapeutic center at Warm Springs a hospital or sanitarium, but a place where . . . patients can live as far as possible normal lives."

The pamphlet lists three aspects of the treatment to be offered:

First, "heliotherapy or exposure of the body in graded periods to the sun's rays."

Second, "directed and general exercises in the water of the pools" along with examination and tests of muscle groups as the exercises proceeded.

Third, "expert training and supervision in walking" and other functional training.

The pamphlet emphasizes that "to the special methods of treatment must be added the psychological effect of the group treatment, the stimulus caused by a number of people pursuing the same end, and each spurring the other on to more and better effort."

The pamphlet concludes: "Add to this . . . much sunshine, a simple normal life with good food, pure water . . . plenty of sleep and recreation and we have a nearly ideal plan of treatment. . . ."[9]

The publicists also prepared press releases and materials, which were reprinted in many of the nation's newspapers. A story printed in *The New York Times* on January 5, 1930, is typical.

This story repeats the point made in the brochure: "Warm Springs is not a sanitarium or a hospital. It is a year-round health resort for persons suffering from the loss of muscle control that follows infantile paralysis." The article describes the forms of treatment, mentions the endorsement of the American Orthopedic Association, and illustrates the value of peer-group support, which had been emphasized in the pamphlet: "A young man who found relief and established partial recovery from infantile paralysis at Warm Springs said that in his opinion one of the most beneficial features of the resort is being able to talk to other people who had the same problems, to meet and together overcome them." The article explains that "Authorities at the Warm Springs resort believe that talk helps to relieve the minds of persons brooding over ailments. Doctors and nurses mingle freely with the patients. They do not wear uniforms." The article concludes by summarizing the average daily activities of the patients: a round of treatments and exercises, capped by pleasant social activities—dinners, gossip, games, and excursions.[10]

A similar article of the period makes a most important point, emphasized by Roosevelt over and over again: " 'Nobody at Warm Springs has infantile paralysis now,' says Arthur Carpenter, business manager. 'They have already had it.' " Carpenter wanted people to know that the disease, which had caused the paralysis of the clients at Warm Springs, had come *and* gone. " 'Except for being crippled they are as healthy as anybody else.' "[11]

VII
Principles

Oh Toi, wasn't it fun![1]

—ANNE IRWIN BRAY

B Y the late 1920s, the policies and procedures followed by the Georgia Warm Springs Foundation had been firmly established. Over the next thirty years, new buildings would be constructed, the rehabilitation equipment would become more sophisticated, and treatment policy would evolve. Nevertheless, the basics remained unchanged.

What Roosevelt conceived at Warm Springs seems, on reflection, to be both sensible and obvious, but it was, in fact, revolutionary. So far as rehabilitation practice is concerned, Roosevelt grasped certain principles intuitively; his actions and decisions were based upon these principles even though they had not yet been formulated into words or placed within the context of an organized, philosophical structure. At Warm Springs, Roosevelt and his associates were busy *doing* rehabilitation. As a result, they discovered various principles, and these were later incorporated into a coherent theory of rehabilitation.

This intuitive understanding of a problem and its solution, this development of the principle of the solution in concert with the practical application of the solution, was the method Roosevelt would use later in the New Deal.

From the first, Roosevelt seemed to understand that rehabilitation of the polio patient was a social problem with medical

53

aspects. It was not a medical problem with social aspects, as previous American treatment efforts had assumed. Most modern hospitals and rehabilitation centers give lip service to this concept, but even now remarkably few seem willing to act upon it.

Patients came to Warm Springs after the acute stage of their illness, sometimes years after. They were often in a state of mind bordering on shell shock. They were hurt and grieving still from the loss of use of their paralyzed limbs. They felt helpless and angry as a result of the hospital treatment they had received. The impact of a severe hospital regime upon the paralyzed often causes a regression into infantile behavior. Responsibility for eating, urinating, and bowel movements, for getting up and going to bed, are removed from the patient and exercised by medical authority, assuming the role of a strict parent. The good patient, like a good child, does what he is told. Such a patient is rewarded for his dependent behavior; the rebel is punished. Obviously, this procedure is not rehabilitative; it is, in fact, debilitative.

Such treatment was universal when Roosevelt began Warm Springs. It produced anger and confusion, and it was particularly difficult for teenagers. Adolescents are in the process of separating from their families and parents. They have not yet established themselves as full-functioning, self-reliant adults. Typical hospital routines complicated or blocked these efforts. Teenagers were particularly vulnerable in another way. During the adolescent years there is generally great concern about body development as the frame develops and sexual characteristics mature. The adolescent child is particularly sensitive to, and self-conscious about, body changes. Severe paralysis of the adolescent child can have a catastrophic psychological impact, destroying concepts of self-worth, raising vast self-doubt.

The Warm Springs experience had an immediate impact upon such shell-shocked patients. For the long-term patient who had come from the grim Victorian hospitals, the effect was sometimes quite stunning. The Warm Springs setting was physically of great beauty: flowers everywhere, manicured lawns, tall green pines, and blue skies. Rooms were bright and sunny; the food was excellent; help was readily available; and the importance of fun was both appreciated and cultivated.

The patient realized from the first that Warm Springs was quite different. This difference produced a change of attitude in him or her—a very positive change.

Under Roosevelt's direction the medical treatment at Warm Springs was divided into segments: the polio patient would receive the physical therapy treatments necessary to maximize muscle recovery and would learn the techniques necessary to allow functioning in society to the maximum extent possible.

The physical therapy provided at Warm Springs was always of excellent quality. The staff was highly competent. As the Foundation's reputation grew, therapists from across the country sought admission to its training programs. The brace shop at Warm Springs acquired a nationwide reputation for excellence and innovation. Warm Springs innovated water treatment techniques and developed numerous creative and useful prosthetic devices. Many professional articles by staff members on various aspects of this treatment were published in medical journals.

From the first, Warm Springs placed unusual emphasis on functional training. This was quite new. Patients at Warm Springs took part in classes in which they learned how to make use of whatever muscles were available to them so as to get in and out of bathtubs, on and off toilets, in and out of cars, and how to perform the routine tasks of day-to-day living. The class concept was important. Patients with similar degrees and kinds of paralysis worked together. They gave each other suggestions and ideas and, equally important, they gave each other encouragement and support. These classes were occasions of much laughter. Severe paralysis often causes absurd predicaments, which can be very funny. It was a warm and cheerful experience to work with others to overcome these problems.

For a generation, Warm Springs was a community of the handicapped. A permanent population of polios came to live at the Foundation or nearby. Many of these people worked at the

Foundation as officials, staff people, and teachers. In 1930, there were eight polios on the rehabilitation staff. Other resident polios were well-to-do people who found life comfortable and protective at Warm Springs and simply decided to stay. Still others came down for the winter season from their homes in the North. The presence of these people helped both the functional training and the social aspects of the Warm Springs treatment.

Leaders of the functional training classes would invite the older resident polios to demonstrate their techniques—the tricks and methods they had devised to perform the daily tasks of life with partially paralyzed muscles. This was of benefit to the new patients in practical terms, but also in psychological terms more difficult to describe and define. New polios saw the old polios as persons with a paralysis pattern similar to their own, living a normal life, functioning as productive human beings. The value of such an example was enormous.

At Warm Springs, social life served a purpose greater than simple morale building. It provided a way for polio patients to relearn their social skills. Warm Springs provided an opportunity to meet people, undertake joint activities, make friends, date, fall in love. The whole range of normal social activities went on at Warm Springs much the way it does elsewhere in the world. New patients were welcomed into the group. Their handicap did not isolate them from the norm; it *was* the norm. The parties, dinners, and activities at Warm Springs gave new patients the opportunity to exercise the skills, traits, and habits they developed and utilized in interpersonal contact before their illness. And, of course, in most cases, the patients found that people responded in much the way they had before the illness. He or she was as attractive, as witty, and had the same positive and negative traits as before. This realization was helpful in the reconstruction of self-image.

At Warm Springs, parties were as important to rehabilitation as the treatment table or the walking court. The Foundation was a microcosmos, a protected halfway house. The social practice available in this protected environment gave patients a confidence that would allow them to move more easily in the world of the able-bodied upon their return to their home environment.

Life at Warm Springs was never puritanical. The gray pall of institutional life never threatened the Foundation. Meals were important and festive. The tables were set with good china and linen napkins and tablecloths. The food was fresh, well cooked, and served by well-trained waiters in dinner jackets. Places at table were reserved, the makeup of the table at dinner carefully planned. There were bridge tournaments and poker games, classes, movies, excursions, amateur theatricals, and visiting professional artists. There were private dinners, cocktail parties in the cottages and, as always with the Roosevelts, picnics. Many of these activities were spontaneous; none was forced. As at Greenbrier, White Sulphur Springs, or Saratoga in season, Warm Springs was a cheerful, active, lovely resort in the country. And, of course, during the twelve years when FDR was in the White House, it was a place of great glamour and excitement.

In the United States, polio struck most heavily at teenagers. The youthful patient population at Warm Springs added to its vitality. Roosevelt is said to have felt strongly that these young people needed to be encouraged not only in their social life but also in their sexual life. He hired local high school boys—he called them "push boys"—and they were available at all hours to push the patients in wheelchairs where they might wish to go. Push boys were not in short supply—one was almost always within earshot. They were to be used not simply to go to and from treatment, but to the coffee shop, post office, the movie theater—wherever the patient might wish to go. From a local girls' college, Roosevelt obtained the services of eight girls majoring in physical science. These were employed as assistant physical therapists. In a very tangible sense, the presence of these young women and men interacting with the patients helped keep Warm Springs a lively place. There was flirting, falling in love, sexual hanky-panky—and much gossip about it all.

In 1980, at a meeting in Washington called to consider the disposition of the Warm Springs property, Anne Irwin Bray, whose father had been medical director, was reunited with Toi

Bachelder, herself a Warm Springs polio, who had served as a secretary to President Roosevelt. As they began to exchange stories of the FDR days, their memories flooded in upon them. "Oh Toi," said Anne, *"wasn't it fun!"*

VIII
Triumph

On the stage is Franklin Roosevelt . . .
a figure tall and proud even in suffering.[1]
—WILL DURANT

THERE was no such thing as "mainstreaming" for the severely and visibly handicapped in the 1920s. Often they were not allowed to use public transportation or to attend theaters or movies. Their clumsy gait and movement were still the object of fun and ridicule: vaudeville entertainers could always raise a laugh with a limp, palsy, or a speech impediment. In fact, for the handicapped to appear in public was considered by many to be in dubious taste. They, along with pregnant women, were expected to keep out of sight. The idea that the severely disabled could participate in elective politics was quite simply unheard of.

And so it took a good deal of scheming by Eleanor and Louis Howe to get Governor Al Smith to ask Franklin Roosevelt to give the speech placing Smith's name before the Democratic Convention of 1924. In so doing, Smith displayed a fair amount of courage and a lot of smart politics. FDR was a patrician Democrat from rural upstate New York, far removed from machine politics. He appealed to the sections of the party where Smith was weakest. Smith, a big-city Tammany man, needed Roosevelt's support. For Roosevelt, it would mark his first major appearance in public since his polio attack three summers before.

At this point, of course, Roosevelt was still obsessed with his search for total recovery. His therapy thus far had been almost entirely dedicated to muscle care and reeducation. He had not yet devised the means and devices that would allow him to function in public with a minimum of apparent effort. He could take some steps with corset, braces, and crutches, but it was very hard work, and it showed.

FDR asked his son James to serve as his aide during the convention. He concentrated his greatest attention on rehearsing the physical aspects of his appearance, leaving the preparation of the speech largely to Smith's staff. Roosevelt accepted the proposed text virtually without objection. He did, however, dislike the ending—a quotation from Wordsworth about the happy warrior. Roosevelt thought it was too poetical, but he was overruled and the phrase stayed in.

James surveyed the convention hall (the old Madison Square Garden), staking out the exits, the speakers' platform, and the location of the New York delegation. From the very first, Roosevelt was determined not to be seen in a wheelchair unless absolutely necessary, and not to be lifted up stairs in view of the public. James mapped the way this could be achieved.

FDR attended every session of the convention. He and James arrived early each day in order to get to their seats before the arrival of the other delegates. James would take his father by wheelchair to the hall entrance closest to the seats of the New York delegation. At the door, Roosevelt's braces would be locked, and he would be pulled to a standing position. With James on one arm and a crutch under the other, he would slowly make his way down the aisle. At times he gripped James's arm so tightly that James had to concentrate to keep from crying out in pain. The effort was exhausting, the summer heat intense. A large, solid oak armchair was placed in the aisle by the New York delegation. The chair arms provided Roosevelt with essential stability and security. Here he sat, greeting friends and well-wishers throughout the long and dreary hours of the session. He did not leave the hall until the session had ended and the hall had cleared. Even so, although the floor of the hall was empty, the galleries were often still filled, and Roosevelt of course would be recognized and applauded as he struggled down the aisle.

On the day of his nominating speech, FDR, leaning on James, slowly made his way down the aisle to the back of the speakers' platform, where he stood waiting, leaning on James's arm and a crutch. As FDR was being introduced, James passed him the other crutch, doing it carefully so as not to upset his father's balance. Eleanor, accompanied by the other children, was in a box in the gallery. Quite nervous, she knitted intensely throughout the speech. Roosevelt gave no sign of being nervous; he was, rather, determined. "Let's go," he said to his son.

FDR was determined to get to the podium by himself. The walk to the podium was not far—not more than fifteen feet or so—but it took a long time. He would place the left crutch forward, shifting his weight over onto his left leg, freeing his right leg and hitching it forward; and then move his right crutch up, shifting his weight back on his right leg and hitching his left leg forward. His entire attention was taken with the effort and with doing it right. His eyes were riveted to the floor, watching and measuring his steps. His face was serious and concentrated. He broke into a heavy sweat, with perspiration running down his forehead. Behind him a pace or two, James followed, watching his father's every move. James had seen him fall many times, and he was prepared to catch him should he lose his balance. He knew how disastrous a fall would be to his father's ambition. James was as tense as FDR.

The delegates and galleries were hushed, watching. FDR had been a popular figure at the convention four years before. Many of the delegates knew Roosevelt personally, having met him during his years with the Wilson Administration or as the result of his campaigning in 1920. His polio attack had been widely reported and there was much interest in his appearance. His name was applauded as he was introduced, but then the applause fell away as he made his slow progress. Step by slow step, he struggled forward. It was an arduous business. At last he reached the lectern. He had made it. He looked up at the hall.

He threw back his head in that exaggerated gesture that was to become his hallmark, and across his face there flashed a vast, world-encompassing smile, and the audience went wild. Applause and then cheers filled the Garden. It was an electric moment, remembered for many years by all who were present.

Clearly he had their sympathy. He needed more than that, or his political career would be over. He must have their respect. He must make them think of him as a leader and not as a cripple. Roosevelt took hold of the lectern, handed his crutches to James, and began his speech. From the first he had the complete attention of every person in the hall. He spoke in his fine, clear tenor, and he spoke with powerful effect. The speech surely ranks as one of the great political addresses of the century.

The audience, already moved by his courage, was soon swept up by the power of his delivery. As he concluded with the peroration upon Al Smith as the "happy warrior" there was a silence, and then the hall exploded with an ovation louder and longer than any in the history of the Garden. It lasted an hour and fifteen minutes. Although the speech did not win Smith the nomination, it was the high point of the convention.

Roosevelt was absolutely exhausted. It had been a tremendous effort, not just of muscle but of will. He asked James to bring his wheelchair and, in view of all, allowed himself to be helped to take his seat and be wheeled from the hall. "We made it, James," he said, "We made it."[2] Thirty-five years later James wrote: "At that moment I was so damned proud of him that it was with difficulty that I kept myself from bursting into tears."[3]

As a politician, Roosevelt had seized an opportunity to assert his place as a leader of his party. For three years, Louis and Eleanor had kept his name alive by appearing in his stead at meetings and rallies. He had maintained a vast correspondence with party leaders across the country and worked to retain an active voice in the press. In this he had been remarkably successful. Over the three years of his convalescence, and the four more years that were to follow, his name appeared on the front page of The New York Times more than two hundred times. This was, however, not enough. To be a leader he had to lead. He had to be seen and be seen to lead. Political reality demanded that he appear, ready or not, before the Democratic Convention of 1924. He did so, and dragged his body along as an act of will.

This act of will overcame the reluctance of the newly handicapped to allow their limitations and vulnerability to be seen by others. The stares of strangers are unpleasant. The fear of falling, of lying helpless in a public place, is strong. Roosevelt, in pursuit of his political career, pushed right through this barrier of fear and did so without talking about his feelings to anyone. It was an astonishing performance. As a child he had been taught to bear adversity "without fuss." As a child he had confidence the wild bird would wait for him. Now, in Madison Square Garden, he simply assumed the crowd would wait for him, would accept him, and he made his way to the platform "without fuss."

It was an extraordinary event, completely without precedent. Roosevelt showed his party that he was, legs or no, an able contender. By so doing he helped to change the way American society viewed the handicapped, and he helped to alter the way the handicapped see themselves.

Four years later, at the Houston Convention of 1928, he was absolutely determined to appear before the delegates as a man who had not merely struggled, but had triumphed over his crippling disease. In order to do this Roosevelt believed it critical that he appear to be able to walk to the podium without crutches. "I'm telling everyone," Eleanor wrote him at Warm Springs, "you are going to Houston without crutches, so mind you stick to it."[4]

Once, at Warm Springs, his physical therapist, Helena Mahoney, had asked him what he was working for, what he hoped to achieve from therapy. "I'll walk without crutches," he said. "I'll walk into a room without scaring everybody half to death. I'll stand easily enough in front of people so that they'll forget I'm a cripple."[5] This quotation, if reported accurately, indicates that in a conscious and specific way Roosevelt had accepted the fact that if he were to reenter public life he must do so as a crippled man. This Roosevelt quotation, it should be pointed out, is quite out of character. It states an implicit acceptance of his paralysis as a permanent condition. It implies further that the purpose of his efforts was no longer the recovery of the full use of his legs but rather the development, to the extent possible, of such means and strategies as will allow him to do the things he wishes in spite of his by now permanent crippled condition. This is the true and basic (yet often misunderstood) purpose of rehabilitation. Unfortunately, when, how, and to what extent Roosevelt reached such a conclusion cannot be known. It probably came to him gradually over the years between the 1924 and 1928 conventions. Certainly he still continued to talk of total recovery. He told friends and family that with a year or two more of progress he would be able to discard his braces and walk unassisted. "It seemed constantly to be 'another two years,'"[6] reported his son Elliott laconically. Most probably this is also what he told himself for, as always, he preferred not to confront the unpleasant if it could possibly be avoided or postponed. Whatever he may have told himself and others, his exercises in therapy shifted in focus and now were directed toward solving functional problems: how to get in and out of cars with braces on; how to propel himself from a chair to a standing position with a minimum of floundering and fuss; and how to appear to "walk into a room without scaring everybody to death."

In 1953, Turnley Walker, a professional writer, himself a polio and a former Warm Springs patient, wrote a book that was heavily inspirational—Roosevelt would have called it sob sister stuff—entitled *Roosevelt and the Warm Springs Story*.[7] The book is without footnotes or bibliography. Quite obviously some of its dialogue is reconstructed, if not actually made up out of whole cloth. Walker, however, interviewed many of the original Warm Springs residents, and his account is based upon their memories. It is accurate in its essentials.

According to Walker, Roosevelt himself, in 1928, thought up the idea that made it possible for him to appear to be walking. He had been working with Mahoney, hours a day, every day, for months trying to improve his walking ability, with his braces, canes, and crutches. And, says Walker: "On one of these eve-

nings a great idea came to him. 'With my hand on a man's arm,
and one cane, I'm sure. . . . Let's try it.' "

Roosevelt practiced first with Mahoney and then he sent for
one of his sons, eighteen-year-old Elliott. The boy, often in
trouble, and starved for attention, was "delighted at the chance
to be with his father." Together, father and son worked for over
a month perfecting the new technique.

Elliott would stand, holding his right arm flexed at a ninety-
degree angle, his forearm rigid as a parallel bar. Roosevelt would
stand beside Elliott, tightly gripping his son's arm. In his right
hand Roosevelt held a cane. His right arm was straight and held
rigid with his index finger pressed firmly straight down along
the line of the cane. In this posture he could "walk," although
in a curious toddling manner, hitching up first one leg with the
aid of the muscles along the side of his trunk, then placing his
weight upon that leg, then using the muscles along his other
side, and hitching the other leg forward—first one side and then
the other, and so on and so on. He was able to do this because
his arms served him in precisely the same manner as crutches.
His right arm transmitted the weight of his body through the
index finger along the full length of the cane to the floor. His
left arm, leaning on his son's arm, similarly took the weight off
his body.

Because his quadriceps and the other leg muscles were so
weak, he was unable to move each leg forward as is done in
normal walking. Instead he had to "hitch" the leg off the ground
and at the same time swing the leg out and forward in a semicircular arc. It was this that gave his gait its toddling nature.

It was very dangerous. A single slippery patch on the floor
could cause his cane to scoot out from him and down he would
fall. A fall in the full view of the convention delegates would
do incalculable harm to his political career. He wanted to con-
vince the delegates by his appearance that his long struggle had
concluded with victory, that he had triumphed over adversity.
He simply could not allow himself to be seen to be helpless.
Roosevelt wished to be thought "a cured cripple." In a rare reference to his own condition, he once said in a campaign speech

in the 1928 race for governor, "I myself furnish a perfectly good example of what can be done by the right kind of care. . . . Seven years ago . . . I came down with infantile paralysis. . . . By personal good fortune I was able to get the best kind of care, and the result of having the best kind of care is that today I am on my feet."[8]

To be "cured," to be "on my feet," he devised the walking technique with Elliott. Mahoney warned Elliott, "Don't forget, if he loses his balance, he'll crash down like a tree." "Don't scare us," said FDR.

It was not only necessary to appear to be walking; it was necessary to appear to be relaxed, smiling, and at ease. FDR told Elliott, "As soon as you feel confident, Son, look up and around at people, the way you would do if I weren't crippled." As Walker tells the story they worked hour after hour through the weeks.

This technique for walking was devised for the sake of appearance. It was not in any sense a practical means of locomotion. It was treacherous, slow, and awkward. It would have been much more sensible to use crutches. With crutches he could have moved about in a reasonably practical and safe manner. Crutches, however, are a universal symbol of the cripple. They arouse fear, revulsion, and pity—emotions quite opposite to those a leader would wish to stir. Roosevelt, throughout his political career, projected a supreme confidence and a cheerful command. He could not have done so using crutches.

FDR worked on the speech he would give again placing the name of Governor Al Smith in nomination as the Democratic candidate in 1928. As in 1924, it had been ghostwritten by a member of Smith's staff. Roosevelt was allowed to make only minor alterations, principally of style, bringing the text into line with his own natural speech rhythms. This was to be his first radio address, and he tailored the speech to meet the requirements of this new medium. Nevertheless, Roosevelt devoted far more time and much more effort to the physical aspects of his appearance than he did to the content of his speech. These efforts paid off in a spectacular manner. His performance was flawless.

Roosevelt moved slowly across the platform on the arm of his son, laughing, joshing with Elliott, greeting people, throwing back his head with that great grin to receive the wild and warm cheers of the spectators. At the podium, with his legs spread wide for stability, he gripped the lectern with one arm and waved to the delegates. He appeared the very essence of vitality and restored health. He stood triumphant before that convention on his own two feet.

The speech, as in 1924, was hugely successful. He was again nominating Al Smith. He ended his speech superbly, projecting his fine, clear tenor voice across the hall and by radio across the nation, offering the delegates "one who has the will to win— who not only deserves success but commands it. Victory is his habit—the happy warrior, Alfred E. Smith!"

The cheers were fully as much for Roosevelt as for Smith. To many of the delegates it was Roosevelt who deserved success, for whom victory was a habit, who was most certainly "the happy warrior." Roosevelt's political career was now fully restored, and by consensus he had made himself a major, and possibly the most attractive, figure in the Democratic Party.

Historian and popularizer Will Durant was covering the convention for *The New York World*. In purple prose, he wrote:

> On the stage is Franklin Roosevelt, beyond comparison the finest man that has appeared at either convention. . . . A figure tall and proud even in suffering; a face of classic profile; pale with years of struggle against paralysis; a frame nervous and yet self-controlled with that tense, taut unity of spirit which lifts the complex soul above those whose calmness is only a stolidity; most obviously a gentleman and a scholar. A man softened and cleansed and illumined with pain. . . . This is a civilized man.[9]

Such adulation was almost universally expressed. *The New York Times* praised it as a "high-bred speech . . . a model of its kind,"[10] and even rock-ribbed Republican Colonel McCormick, publisher of the *Chicago Tribune*, later to be one of the great Roosevelt haters of all time, gave FDR the highest tribute: Roosevelt, said the Colonel, was "the only Republican in the Democratic Party!"[11]

IX
Governor

. . . like a sack of potatoes.[1]
—JAMES ROOSEVELT

Tʜɪs time—in 1928—Governor Al Smith of New York was nominated by the Democratic Party as its candidate for President. Smith was a good man but his limitations did not make him a particularly attractive national candidate. A product of New York City and Tammany Hall politics, he knew little of farming and nothing of the West. For example, he was surprised to learn, during the course of the campaign, that Wisconsin lies to the west of Lake Michigan. It was the dawning age of radio, and Smith was not successful with the new medium. He had a Bronx accent and an annoying voice—raspy and whiny. Most difficult of all, he was a Roman Catholic. Smith was running in what was widely considered a Republican year. His opponent was a greatly admired hero of World War I, Herbert Hoover.

Clearly, if Smith was to have any chance at all of a national victory, he had to carry his own state. And so, apparently with the counsel of Eleanor Roosevelt, he soon came to the conclusion that he needed FDR on the ticket with him. The strongest New York ticket possible would feature Smith for president and Roosevelt for governor.

Roosevelt said he was not a candidate. He was at Warm Springs when Smith offered him the nomination. FDR turned it down, and Smith turned up the pressure. Roosevelt received many telegrams and letters from Smith supporters urging him to run. Smith himself called repeatedly. Louis Howe, Roosevelt's political advisor, felt, with some justification, that the timing was wrong, and he urged Roosevelt to resist a draft, suggesting that he use his handicap as an excuse, telling Smith he was not yet strong enough to campaign. In a wire, Howe said, "There is no answer to the health plea, but any other reason would be overruled by the Governor [Smith]"[2] On the eve of the state convention that was to nominate the gubernatorial candidate, Roosevelt sent a lengthy telegram to Smith that seemed to be final. He would not run, he said. He would not serve as governor at the sacrifice of his health. His legs had been making rapid improvement, and he must "give the present constant improvement a chance to continue. It probably means getting rid of leg braces during the next two winters, and that would be impossible if I had to remain in Albany."[3] Once again, FDR was saying two more years; two more years, and I will be well. Intellectually, he knew this was untrue. Emotionally, however, he found it hard to admit; politically—in this case—it served him to believe it to be true.

Smith was desperate. The day before the nominating session, he tried again to reach Roosevelt by phone. Roosevelt made himself unavailable all day. In the morning he was in the pool doing his exercises. In the afternoon he was at a picnic on Dowdell's Knob. In the evening he was at neighboring Manchester giving a speech, ironically, in support of Al Smith's candidacy. If FDR would not speak to him, Smith was sure Roosevelt would accept a call from Eleanor. He begged her to place the call, and she did. On her third try FDR sent word that he would accept her call if she would wait on the line for him. His speech had been given in an auditorium on the third floor of a high school. The school had no phone. Roosevelt had to be carried down the flights of stairs and driven to the town drugstore to take Eleanor's call. FDR was lowered onto the seat in the phone booth with his leg braces still locked. His legs stuck straight out of the booth into the night air. During that call and one received later that evening, FDR allowed Smith to talk him into reentering politics—seven long years after his polio attack.

FDR was hesitant, but Smith brushed aside every objection. The campaign would be easy, said Smith. Roosevelt could limit himself to major addresses and give several radio talks. That would be sufficient. The able Herbert Lehman had agreed to serve as lieutenant governor. After the election, said Smith, Lehman would act as the day-to-day administrator of the state, leaving Roosevelt free to spend as much time as he wished at Warm Springs. Roosevelt would have to return to the state only for such formal occasions and critical moments as might make his presence necessary. It is implicit from the argument that Smith still thought of Roosevelt as an invalid—charming, even essential, but not really up to the hurly-burly of an active political life.

Roosevelt pleaded that he was committed, both morally and financially, to making Warm Springs successful. Even here, Smith had an answer. He put the chairman of the Du Pont Company, Democrat John J. Raskob, on the line. Raskob pledged a personal contribution to Warm Springs of $100,000 and agreed to assist in fund raising. To all this persuasion, Roosevelt was silent. Smith grabbed the phone back with "just one more question": If FDR was nominated the next day by the delegates by acclamation, would he refuse the nomination? Roosevelt paused before he answered. He could not approve his name being placed before the convention, FDR replied; but if it was, and if he were nominated, he did not know just what he would do. Smith took that as a yes, and hung up.

The next day FDR was nominated, and he did accept. Louis Howe was terribly upset. He believed that 1928 was a Republican year. The odds were that the popular Hoover would be elected. The Great Administrator, as he was called, was expected to do well as President and most probably would be reelected in 1932. If, on the other hand, Smith should surprise the experts and win unexpectedly, he, too, most likely would be reelected in 1932. As a newly elected governor of New York, attractive and dynamic, FDR would clearly be a contender for the

White House, but only if the White House stood a chance of being empty. Howe believed the next real opportunity for the presidency would come up in 1936. By this timetable, Roosevelt should not run for governor of New York until 1932. Now, FDR had allowed himself to enter the race four years early, and Howe was disgusted. "Mess is no name for it. For once, I have no advice to give," he wired FDR.[4]

FDR made his political decisions—as he made all others—by intuition. His intuition to run in 1928 was not wrong. The political situation was such that he was honestly drafted by his party to run for office. Such an opportunity is rare, even for a Roosevelt. It might not come again. He could not continue to use the excuse of health. His legs would get no stronger. In politics, as everywhere else, time is all: one must fish or cut bait. His reluctance, the draft, and his final acquiescence, gave fine drama and momentum to his campaign—a momentum his career never lost.

At once, and in an underhanded manner, Roosevelt's physical condition became an issue of the campaign. Throughout the rest of his political life the state of his physical and mental health was to be the subject of persistent rumor and conjecture. The issue surfaced in an outrageous editorial in the Republican *New York Post*: "There is something both pathetic and pitiless in the 'drafting' of Franklin D. Roosevelt by Alfred E. Smith. . . . Stung by the presidential bee, driven by the necessity of getting New York's electoral vote, the governor made this most loyal of friends agree to serve his ambition at a price that is beyond all reason." The editorial spoke movingly of Roosevelt's paralysis and his continuing efforts to overcome it. It spoke of his refusal to accept the nomination and the means used to make him change his mind. "Even his own friends," concluded the editorial, "out of love for him will hesitate to vote for him now."[5]

FDR reacted immediately and forcefully. He hit the issue hard and head on. By press release he responded:

> I am amazed to hear that efforts are being made to appear that I have been "sacrificed" by Governor Smith to further

his own election, and that my friends should vote against me to prevent such "sacrifice."

I do not believe that appeals to personal friendship should form any part of a plea to the electorate. But if I did, my own appeal would be: "Not only do I want my friends to vote for me, but if they are my real friends I ask them to get as many other people to vote for me as possible."

I trust this statement will eliminate this particular bit of nonsense from the campaign from the very beginning.[6]

Of course, Roosevelt's press release did not end the "nonsense." Throughout the entire campaign, the state of his health was a very real issue. The newspapers had said at the time of his nomination that he was not expected to campaign actively, giving perhaps no more than four or five speeches. His wife, according to the papers, would do his campaigning for him. There were rumors that he was running only because his win would add strength to the Smith ticket. It was said that immediately after the election he would resign the office he had just won, turning the office over to Lieutenant Governor-elect Lehman. Roosevelt determined that the best way to counter these rumors would be to demonstrate to the electorate just how extremely healthy and fit he was. This he intended to do by waging an unexpectedly active campaign.

And he did. For the entire month of the campaign, Roosevelt barnstormed the state. He gave more campaign speeches in more places than had any candidate before him. He exhausted the members of his staff and the reporters assigned to travel with him. The unique novelty of a handicapped candidate waging an active campaign in spite of rumor and previous reports created a sensation—from which Roosevelt took every advantage.

It was during this campaign that FDR developed many of the techniques and practices he was to use successfully in later years. He led his cavalcade of party members and reporters from town to town, riding in the back seat of an open touring car. He had ordered a steel bar to be mounted above the back of the front seat. Driving through a new town to the site of the rally, FDR would wave to the townspeople. At the rally, with his car parked in front of the gathered crowd, Roosevelt would use the bar to pull himself to a standing position, snapping his braces locked. According to the *Herald Tribune* reporter present, each speech was very like the last. "A few words of fulsome praise for Alfred E. Smith, a reference to his last call in the town . . . an allusion to himself as an 'upstate farmer, too,' a description of the campaign as one of reactionaryism vs. progressivism, and an invitation for the crowd to take a look and judge for itself the state of his health." The last he would do with a grand sarcasm. For example, at one point he listed the speeches he had given over the last several days in his hectic schedule: "Herkimer, Fonda, Gloversville, Amsterdam . . . and then, for good measure, we just dropped into Schenectady and spoke there early in the evening, and now here we are in Troy." Here FDR paused. "Too bad about this unfortunate sick man, isn't it?"[7] The crowds would roar with laughter.

In fact, the campaign was extremely difficult for Roosevelt. This was his first time out, and the party organizers did not appreciate the extent of FDR's physical limitations. Time and again meetings were scheduled in inconvenient places. Roosevelt, of course, never complained about such occasions, but they were ingrained in the memory of his children and his friends. Daughter Anna remembered one time when the only way to get up to an auditorium without being seen by the public was a narrow fire escape in the back of the building. However, the iron staircase was too narrow to allow Roosevelt to be carried up in someone's arms. The only way he could reach the rally was to haul himself up the stairway using only his arms, dragging his body up, step by agonizing step. By the time he reached the top he was sweating profusely, his neck muscles straining prodigiously. "It's all in knowing how," he joked.[8] At the top he rested briefly, adjusted his clothing, turned, and walked into the hall as though nothing had happened.

Friend and associate Frances Perkins remembered another such occasion. She was awaiting the arrival of the candidate in a small hall in the New York City district of Yorkville. "The only entrance was up the broad stairway from the street, then down narrow aisles to the small stage." The hall was very crowded. "The only possible way for any candidate to enter the stage without being crushed by the throng was by the fire escape" at the rear of the hall.

"I stood in the wings backstage, being among the fifty-odd people who were to sit upon the platform that night. I realized with sudden horror that the only way he could get over that fire escape was in the arms of strong men. That was how he arrived.

"Those of us who saw this incident, with our hands on our throats to hold down our emotion, realized that this man had accepted the ultimate humility which comes from being helped physically. He had accepted it smiling. He came up over that perilous, uncomfortable, and humiliating 'entrance' and his manner was pleasant, courteous, enthusiastic."[9]

Perkins had known Roosevelt when he was a young man serving in the State Senate, and she had not been impressed. She was mightily impressed by the Roosevelt she saw that night.

Perkins noticed during the campaign that FDR's polio had altered his relations with other politicians and the voters. Roosevelt had first achieved state prominence by bucking Tammany Hall. As a state senator he had annoyed many of New York's Democratic Party officials. Now, because Governor Smith wanted him, he was campaigning for state office. "He was politically inexperienced," remarked Perkins, "from the point of view of the old-time state politicians, but his heart was in the right place and his purposes were politically sound from the politicians' point of view. Their affection, based partly on a protective sense, began to develop. There was no question that his handicap made it possible for many of the old politicians to forgive old scores." And, she noted, as so many were to note after her, "It made it possible for the common people to trust him to understand what it is to be handicapped by poverty and ignorance, as well as by physical misfortunes."[10]

FDR's son Jimmy was there the night he was carried up the fire escape. Jimmy wrote many years later that he found such episodes extremely upsetting. Jimmy spoke of "the humiliating and physically uncomfortable experience of being lifted up and over obstacles like a sack of potatoes. Whenever I saw this and remembered that the big, smiling, physically helpless man was the same father with whom I once ran and roughhoused at Hyde Park and Campobello, the emotion was almost more than I could endure."[11]

On Election Day predictions turned out to be correct. Nationwide, the Republicans swept the election. Al Smith went down to defeat, losing even his home state of New York. Roosevelt, however, won. His barnstorming campaign across upstate New York had been highly effective. He had found and developed issues of interest to the voters; he had aroused substantial editorial support from the papers; and at the polls he was able to buck the Republican tide. He won by but half of 1 percent of the vote, but that was enough. His victory received nationwide attention. He was a Democrat winning in a Republican tide; he was a man triumphing over a crippling disease; and most of all, he was a Roosevelt, governor again of New York. Roosevelt was still a magic name. As governor and President, Theodore Roosevelt had been extremely popular. He was remembered and revered by many. Throughout FDR's career he was to benefit greatly from the name association with his famous cousin.

When the Roosevelts moved into the governor's mansion at Albany, Al Smith stood ready to play the role of power behind the throne. He had assured Roosevelt over the phone at Warm Springs that FDR need not be a full-time governor. Now he was prepared to help out by suggesting appointments, staff members, even by drafting the governor's message and legislative program. FDR, of course, had no intention of being a part-time governor. He intended to be governor in every sense of the word. His position and his record would be part of his campaign for the presidency. Furthermore, as he explained to Frances Perkins, "I didn't feel able to make this campaign for governor, but I made it. I didn't feel that I was sufficiently recovered to undertake the duties of Governor of New York, but here I am. After Al said that to me I thought about myself and I realized that

I've *got* to be Governor of the State of New York and I have got to be it MYSELF."[12] And so he was.

The mansion was altered for Roosevelt's use. An elevator was installed. A swimming pool was built in the backyard, and ramps were placed over unavoidable steps. As governor, of course, Roosevelt had the use of state cars, chauffeurs, and bodyguards. No longer would he be blocked by architectural barriers. He retained the services of Gus Gennerich, a New York City policeman who had been detailed to protect Roosevelt during the campaign. Gennerich went on leave from the force, served on the governor's staff, and later went with Roosevelt to the White House. State Trooper Earl Miller also served as bodyguard to FDR.

Earl and Gus became skilled at working with Roosevelt. They were big men with very strong, solid arms. They learned how to provide solid support for FDR as he "walked" with a cane. They knew how to lift him in and out of cars. They even developed a technique for carrying him up flights of steps. FDR would walk to the base of the steps with Gus on one side and Earl on the other. The two men would each take an elbow and lift the governor up the stairs in a standing position. To all but the closest observers it looked as though Roosevelt himself were climbing the stairs.

Roosevelt's doctor said publicly that he felt FDR should have no problems handling the governorship. He suggested a schedule involving working in bed each morning until about 9:30 and an hour of rest and massage therapy in the afternoon. Roosevelt discovered it was practical for him to work in bed. He would awake each morning at about 8:00 and read the New York papers. As he was having breakfast in bed, he would take phone calls, confer with staff members, and dictate to Missy, who was lodged in an adjoining bedroom.

Roosevelt was in his office in the Capitol by midmorning. He would most often have lunch at his desk. When the legislature was in session, he would work very long hours, indeed, but usually by midafternoon he would return to the mansion for his exercises and massage, and lie down. With the Roosevelts, family life often merged with official life, and the house was full of politicians and reporters. The Roosevelts seldom dined alone.

The Roosevelts' four sons were in and out of the house. The two youngest went to school at Groton during the week but were home for weekends. Daughter Anna was now married. In due course, her young children, Buzz and Sisty Dall, were about the house and underfoot. FDR's mother was a constant visitor, when she was not away on her many trips to Europe. Missy, Earl, and Gus ate with the family. Louis Howe had a bedroom in the house, and he, too, was usually present. Always there were Roosevelt cousins, nephews, and nieces mixing with visiting reporters and politicians. FDR was surrounded by flow and movement. Everyone was always coming or going somewhere. Conversation was lively, and life was informal.

This extraordinary hubbub of confusion and activity reflected the Roosevelt family way of life. They took it with them when they moved from the Governor's Mansion to the White House. Franklin's mother, Sara, was neither pleased nor comfortable with the stream of strange and varied guests brought to her table at Hyde Park by the younger Roosevelts. In fact, members of the family—Eleanor and Franklin's cousins—were puzzled to find FDR's secretary and Eleanor's state trooper bodyguard dining with the family. Nevertheless, it suited FDR. Since his ability to move about was severely limited, he could not get out or roam the countryside or city at will. He could not move out in the world; and so, in effect, the world came to him. Not only was his mobility limited, so were his activities. No longer could he play golf, go sailing, hiking, or play ball with the boys. Going to the theater was difficult; shopping was close to impossible. It was easier to bring movies to him than for him to go out to a movie. In a very real sense, the presence of his staff, his family, reporters, politicians, crackpots and visionaries, people with missions, people with stories, people with problems—all this served to entertain FDR and to keep him as busy and occupied as he wished. Boredom is a major curse of the severely handicapped. Roosevelt used the presence of people to escape boredom.

As governor, Roosevelt continued to visit Warm Springs at least twice a year, in the spring and in the fall. His visits brought much attention to the Foundation and its work. Roosevelt continued to help with the fund-raising activities, giving speeches, hosting lunches, and such. He had a genuine, constructive interest in the affairs of the handicapped—considerably advanced for its time—even though he continued to see himself as a "cured" cripple, or as one soon to be completely cured.

For example, in his first Annual Message to the Legislature in 1929, Roosevelt declared it the responsibility of the State to rehabilitate the handicapped and to pay for their care and treatment. He said, "I conceive it to be the duty of the State to give the same care to removing the physical handicaps of its citizens as it now gives to their mental development. Universal education of the mind is, after all, a modern conception. We have reached the time now when we must recognize the same obligation of the State to restore to useful activity those children and adults who have the misfortune to be crippled." Pointing out the continuing costs of providing constant care to the disabled, FDR argued, "As a matter of good business, it would pay the State to help in restoring these cripples to useful citizenship."[13]

Roosevelt's call for universal care and rehabilitation of the physically disabled was a radical proposal for 1929. More than sixty years later, it is still a radical proposal. The restoration of such persons to useful citizenship is still only imperfectly attempted, and nowhere in the United States is it yet perceived to be the duty of the State.

Roosevelt's proposal met with little interest from the legislature, and it disappeared in the onslaught of the Great Depression.

At first the Roosevelts were not entirely comfortable about appearing in public. They were testing different ways of coping with FDR's disability. His appearance of being completely at ease, later familiar to the world, had not as yet been worked out; nor had the understanding about such things yet been struck with the press. In the early days, the Roosevelts had no good reason to be confident about FDR's ability to cope with his infirmity and, at the same time, continue his political career. An appearance in public was a strenuous production, which demanded FDR's full concentration and called upon Eleanor's extraordinary social skills. Philip Hamburger, writing some thirty years later in *The New Yorker*'s "Talk of the Town," recalled:

> But what we remember most about that far-off afternoon . . . was the departure of the Governor and his wife from the hall. The only way out was down a narrow aisle running the narrow length of the hall, past the camp chairs on which the audience had been sitting. The distance from desk to street could not have been more than a hundred feet, but it took the Governor an agonizingly long time to traverse it. His legs were in heavy braces, and he walked with the aid of two canes—first one foot and one cane forward, then the other. The audience, as though hypnotized, did not leave. It stood and watched the Roosevelts depart. Mrs. Roosevelt, walking alongside her husband, adapted her pace to his. The Governor was intent upon the task before him: to reach the street and the sanctuary of his limousine without help. Occasionally, she leaned over to whisper something in his ear, and he smiled and put the other foot forward. The slow procession became extremely impressive. Mrs. Roosevelt seemed to sense that we knew we should not stay but that we could not leave. Moving slowly along, she thanked many of us for coming, and expressed the hope that we had enjoyed the Governor's remarks. She greeted many of us with a wave of her hand. She turned again to say something to her husband, who smiled again, and moved forward. She never took his arm, and yet we knew that he was leaning as heavily upon her as upon his canes. Finally, the Roosevelts reached the street. The audience, still hypnotized, followed them outside. Mrs. Roosevelt and a chauffeur helped the Governor into his car. He put his head back against the cushions with the expression of a man who has accomplished his mission. Mrs. Roosevelt opened a window of the car and waved again. An audience of strangers had become

a group of friends. "Goodbye!" she called out. "Good-bye!"[14]

Eleanor's role, always important, was now central and vital. She could do it; she *did* do it, but at a cost to her nerves. She was often quite anxious about her husband's safety and his acceptance by the public. At FDR's appearance before the 1924 Democratic Convention he had been aided by his son James. Though Eleanor was present throughout the ordeal, sitting in the Roosevelt family box, knitting ferociously, she could not bring herself to attend the 1928 convention.

Eleanor's concern for her husband was noticed in 1931 by Louis Brownlow, director of the Public Administration Clearing House. He had invited Governor Roosevelt to a conference on regional planning to be held at Charlottesville, Virginia. Roosevelt accepted the invitation and agreed to appear at a round table. According to Brownlow, Roosevelt "adjusted his braces, stood up, and began to speak." On the platform with him was his friend and aide, Henry Morgenthau, Jr. In the audience was Mrs. Roosevelt. The governor spoke for about half an hour and then called for questions. Said Brownlow, "Mrs. Roosevelt became much agitated. Her husband was standing too long. She sent a note up to Morgenthau, who handed it to me and asked would I please pull the governor's coattail and ask him to sit down. I couldn't do that, but told Morgenthau to do it. Morgenthau didn't dare." Roosevelt continued on his feet for well over an hour and, according to Brownlow, "that was the longest time he had ever stood up with his braces."[15]

Beneath their genuinely gracious manner and behind the bonhomie, both FDR and Eleanor were extremely sensitive to slights, real or intended. Roosevelt ran four times for the presidency. He was personally fond of two of the men he ran against—Willkie and Landon—but he did not like Dewey. His aversion to Hoover, however, was both mysterious and complex. They had served side by side in Woodrow Wilson's wartime Cabinet and, according to Hoover, "We met socially during this period and were good friends." In fact, there are indications that the two men actually discussed running together on the Democratic ticket in 1920 as heirs to Wilson, supporters of the League. The two men corresponded in a desultory way throughout the 1920s. Roosevelt even served—at Hoover's request—as chairman of the American Construction Council, a trade association of the period launched under the aegis of Hoover's Commerce Department.

Both men were sensitive, intelligent persons, ambitious for the same office. Each had lost a father at an early age, and both had seen President Wilson as a strong father figure in their lives. Both were competing heirs for the Wilson tradition. Each had reason enough to distrust and fear the other. It is, however, perhaps not surprising that the event that served to trigger Roosevelt's animus toward Hoover concerned FDR's handicap.

An unspoken issue—yet one that was on every mind—was whether FDR, with his handicap, was strong enough to campaign and to serve as President. As in the gubernatorial campaign, Roosevelt was intent upon demonstrating his strength by displaying his stamina at every opportunity. In fact, of course, both his stamina and his strength had real and narrow limits. The governors' conference in 1932 was held in Richmond. President Hoover invited the governors and their wives to the White House for a reception. Governor and Mrs. Roosevelt attended. [See photo.] And they were, of course, the center of much attention from the press and from the other governors—particularly the Democratic ones. The Roosevelts arrived early, knowing that it would take FDR a long time to navigate—with braces, cane, and the arm of his bodyguard—from the front door of the White House to the East Room, the site of the reception. The governors gathered but, unfortunately, President Hoover was delayed. The governors were kept waiting, and FDR was forced to stand on his braces, gripping Eleanor's arm tightly as his only support. He chatted manfully with the other reception guests, but it was a painful business and the sweat ran from his forehead. Twice, White House ushers offered FDR a seat; both times he refused, unwilling to appear handicapped and weak, seated while all others were standing.

Certainly, President Hoover knew nothing of what was occurring in the East Room. According to intimate friends, he would not have allowed such sadistic torture to take place had he been aware.[16] As a matter of fact, Hoover had much respect for the way FDR mastered his handicap. "I greatly admired the courage with which he fought his way back to active life and with which he overcame the handicap which had come to him," wrote Hoover in an unpublished memoir in 1962, adding that, "I considered that it was a great mistake that his friends insisted upon trying to hide his infirmity, as manifestly it had not affected his physical or mental abilities."[17] This respect of Hoover's was genuine, but Eleanor and Franklin always believed that Hoover had purposely delayed his entrance at the reception in order to take political advantage of FDR's handicap. Such was not the case, but they went to their graves believing it so. And they never forgave Hoover for the imagined slight.

Roosevelt was already a national figure before he was governor. His election to that position catapulted him into the top ranks of presidential contenders, simply because his win in New York was just about the only bright spot in the Democratic debacle of 1928.

In those years the New York governor's term was but two years long. In 1930, Roosevelt ran for a second time. During the campaign, Roosevelt repeated the technique and tactics he had used in 1928. Again, he campaigned in a touring car. By 1930, the stock market had crashed. Unemployment was increasing, and people were frightened as the Great Depression took hold. As FDR went from town to town, he spoke to the people from the back of his car, but also he listened to them. He took questions from the audience and, often as not, the rallies became town meetings of concern. In 1928, FDR had carried the state by 25,000 votes. In 1930, he carried it by 725,000 votes, the largest majority ever won by a Democrat in the State of New York. Clearly, the voters of New York were not bothered by FDR's physical limitations.

It was not an accident that, during the compaign, Roosevelt took out a much publicized $560,000 life insurance policy with the Georgia Warm Springs Foundation as beneficiary. In order to qualify for the policy, which was underwritten by twenty-two different companies, Roosevelt had to submit to a physical examination. The doctors performing this examination reported they had found him to be in excellent health. Their report on his condition, and the fact that twenty-two life insurance companies found him insurable, received widespread publicity and attention. This, too, served to counteract the health rumors.

FDR's record in the office was not distinguished. He was steady and innovative, but by no means radical. He was a *popular* governor, seen by many people as he moved often across the state, and he was widely featured in the press. He logged a respectable record as he struggled with a Republican legislature; and, after the onset of the Depression, he received much favorable attention for his efforts on unemployment compensation. He was remarkably deft in his handling of the politically explosive Mayor Walker scandal involving New York City finances. All in all, Roosevelt's governorship did not, in itself, provide justification for his campaign for the presidency. His record did not alarm or arouse antagonism, so in this sense it was not harmful to the campaign. And as it provided a platform from which to be seen, a pulpit from which to be heard, it was certainly helpful. It was, in fact, a part of the logical progression to the presidency, for as Roosevelt had said long ago, anyone who finds himself governor of New York has a pretty good shot at the presidency.

The strategy by which Franklin Roosevelt obtained the Democratic nomination for president was masterful. He gathered about him men and women of great political acumen—even, in some cases, genius. At the center of it all was Louis Howe, joined by James Farley and, of course, Eleanor. Roosevelt's handicap was never central to their strategy. It was, however, an important issue: FDR believed a whispering campaign suggesting that he was unable to handle the duties of the presidency because of health could wreck his chances for the nomination.

It was thought the best response to such rumors would be his record as governor. He had worked hard; he had served effectively as a full-time governor in every sense of the term. His actions and his speeches had been reported fully in the press. The Roosevelts never made any effort to hide their private life from public gaze. As a result, they received a great amount of press attention, and their every activity was heavily reported. The bright light of all this publicity made the charges that the governor was a helpless cripple, or that the paralysis had deranged his mind, seem difficult to believe.

However, James Farley found, in his trips across the nation drumming up support for FDR's presidential bid, that the politicians of other states had substantial doubts about Roosevelt's ability to withstand the pressures of the Oval Office. Roosevelt's physical condition had again became the subject of a good deal of discussion. A story in *Time* magazine quoted an observer, "This candidate, while mentally qualified for the presidency, is utterly unfit physically."[18] Roosevelt and his advisors were concerned about such talk. James Farley reported he was asked at every point in a swing across the West about the state of Roosevelt's health. As a move to counter such talk, Roosevelt's advisors accepted what was reported to be a challenge by a writer with Republican credentials, Earle Looker, to investigate frankly and honestly the governor's physical condition and to report the results of his investigation in popular *Liberty Magazine*. It appears the challenge was a cooked-up affair. Looker was an old friend of Roosevelt's cousin, Teddy, and he had even ghostwritten articles from time to time for FDR. Nevertheless, he had a good reputation as an independent journalist. As part of the Looker investigation, the New York Academy of Medicine was asked to choose three doctors to give the governor a complete physical. Looker, in the course of his research, followed Roosevelt about as he worked his way through the schedule of a busy day. Looker's report was published in the July 25, 1931, issue of the magazine. Not surprisingly, it was a paean of praise. "Insofar as I have observed him, I have come to the conclusion that he seemed able to take more punishment than many men ten years younger. Merely his legs were not much good to him."[19]

Roosevelt's advisors reprinted thousands of copies of the article. They were sent to each Democratic Party county chairman in the country, to prominent Democrats everywhere, and as answer to the many correspondents who had written to the governor asking about his health.

The article, of course, did not end the whispering campaign. Nothing did. Even up to the last year of FDR's life, after twelve years in the presidency, there were continuing rumors of physical decrepitude and mental incompetence caused by the supposed progressive nature of his paralysis. Those who wanted to believe that Roosevelt was incompetent continued to do so. But what the *Liberty* article and the doctors' report accomplished was to provide a responsible and dignified rebuttal. The widely distributed article presented the medical facts in the best possible light. Democrats who wanted Roosevelt as their candidate did not want to believe that his handicap would stand in the way of his ability to campaign for, or to exercise the duties of, the presidency. The article simply served to reinforce them in their belief.

Such strategies as the article and the publicized life insurance policy served to minimize the handicap issue during the campaign for the Democratic nomination as well as the actual campaign itself. The presidential election campaign of 1932 was waged in a nation deeply divided and emotionally depressed by the Great Depression. The nation's economy was caught in the grip of a progressive paralysis, which had produced a crisis in the national life as grave as the Civil War. Roosevelt's handicap played little direct role in his candidacy or the campaign he waged.

Indeed, the style of his campaign was distinctly reminiscent of the way he had met the challenge of polio. He tried at every turn to offer a message of confidence and affirmation. While Hoover was painted as the prisoner of the old policies, which had failed—thus causing economic disaster and great and continuing hardship—Roosevelt pledged new ways, better ways.

His willingness to break with tradition, and an example of the excitement and novelty of the Roosevelt style, were shown when FDR flew with his family to the convention to accept his party's nomination in person. This had never been done before. Hitherto, the candidate had awaited a formal notification from a committee appointed by the convention. The drama of the flight, when scheduled air service was still in its infancy, and the excitement of the unexpected speech to the convention, carried nationwide by the radio networks, served to generate an immense amount of publicity. The impact was sensational.

The flight itself, in a cramped Ford Trimotor plane, was uncomfortable in the extreme. The plane skirted thunderstorms a good part of the way. The Roosevelt children were sick. The sons had difficulty manipulating their upright six-foot-three-inch father, with his braces and cane, down the narrow, low-ceilinged aisle and out the door in front of the waiting press of the world. FDR, however, appeared to love every moment of it.

FDR was advised that it would not be necessary to campaign extensively. Men before him—McKinley and Harding, for example—had won the presidency handily by staying home, addressing visiting delegations from their front porch. Such a campaign was thought to be safer politically. The candidate was less apt to get into trouble with an unfortunate remark or the failure to touch base with all the political factions in the communities visited during a lengthy campaign. Furthermore, a front porch campaign would make it possible to keep his handicap hidden. A whistle-stop campaign, with the risk of a fall in public, and unfortunate newsreel footage, was considered too dangerous to risk. The fact was, of course, that Roosevelt quite simply loved to campaign. Once he was nominated, it was doubtful that anything could have kept him from a great campaign swing across the country.

So, when a Western advisor advanced the opposite argument—that a trip across the country was necessary so that the voters could see in person that the rumors about FDR's feeble condition were false—Roosevelt seized upon it as his own. He campaigned across the length and breadth of the country.

One of his advisors, Raymond Moley, seemed to understand the joy these campaign trips brought Roosevelt. "It was broad rivers, green forests, waving corn, and undulating wheat; it was crowds of friends, from the half dozen who, seated on a baggage truck, waved to the cheery face at the speeding window, to perspiring thousands at a racetrack or fairgrounds; it was hands extended in welcome, voices warm with greeting, faces reflecting his smile along the interminable wayside."[20] Roosevelt loved the sights. He loved the sounds. He loved the excitement, and he reveled in the attention.

On Election Day, FDR swamped his opponent Herbert Hoover 472 electoral votes to 59, carrying 42 of the 48 states. Eleanor, although dreading the public rigors of life as First Lady, fully appreciated the personal significance of FDR's victory. "I was happy for my husband, of course, because I knew that in many ways it would make up for the blow that fate had dealt him when he was stricken with infantile paralysis."[21]

Late on Election Night, after the cheers, the speeches, the motorcades, the sirens, and the newly arrived Secret Service, son James helped his father to bed—taking the braces off one by one, standing them in the corner, helping him shift his paralyzed body from chair to bed, undressing him.

As James kissed his father goodnight, FDR said to him, ". . . All my life I have been afraid of only one thing—fire. Tonight, I think I am afraid of something else." James asked what, and his father replied, ". . . I'm afraid I may not have the strength to do this job." It was a perfectly rational and totally genuine fear. "Pray for me, Jimmy," FDR said, and Jimmy did.[22]

X
President

Roosevelt was simply himself—easy, confident,
poised, to all appearances unmoved.[1]
—RAYMOND MOLEY

H E loved being President. Jefferson had called it a "splendid misery" but it was no misery for FDR. He was at
home in the White House the first day he moved in. No man
ever had a grander time doing what he did best. And he did it
superbly well, handling the problems of the country with style
and skill.

FDR's personal courage, his response to crisis, was demonstrated even before the inaugural. Roosevelt was in Miami,
Florida, on the evening of February 15, 1934. He was returning
from a cruise aboard a friend's yacht. From the dock he rode in
an open car to Bayfront Park. There, sitting on the back of his
open car, the President-elect made a few impromptu remarks to
the thousands of people who had turned out to greet him. When
he had finished speaking, he hitched himself down to his place
in the back seat of the car, where he was chatting with Mayor
Antoine Cermak of Chicago, who stood beside the vehicle. At
that point an assassin, standing no more than thirty-five feet
away, opened fire with a pistol. He fired five bullets. The man
was shooting directly at Roosevelt, but his aim was not true.
Several bystanders were wounded, and Mayor Cermak fell to the
ground, fatally injured.

Through the fusillade, Roosevelt remained absolutely motionless, staring intently at the gunman. In the ensuing melee the Secret Service ordered FDR's chauffeur to speed away. FDR at once countermanded the order. The Secret Service shouted again to get Roosevelt out of the crowd, and the chauffeur moved the car forward. Again, FDR ordered that the car be stopped and backed up. He ordered that the dying Mayor Cermak be placed in the back seat with him. Only then did FDR allow the car to move, ordering it to the hospital. Roosevelt cradled Cermak throughout the trip, monitoring the dying man's pulse, talking to him the whole way, saying, "Tony, keep quiet—don't move. It won't hurt you if you keep quiet. . . ." Roosevelt remained at the hospital for some time, talking with Cermak and the other wounded victims. He then returned to the yacht and, before retiring, had a drink with his friends. He had seen closeup the bloody death caused by a bullet meant for him. His advisor, Raymond Moley, reports, "The time for the letdown among his intimates was at hand. . . . All of us were prepared, sympathetically, understandingly, for any reaction that might come from him."

Moley tells what happened. "There was nothing—not so much as the twitching of a muscle, the mopping of a brow, or even the hint of a false gaiety—to indicate that it was any other evening in any other place. Roosevelt was simply himself—easy, confident, poised, to all appearances unmoved."[2]

In the course of but a few minutes Roosevelt had shown courage in the face of the assassin's bullets; judgment by taking Cermak into his car; concern for the dying man; and had remained clearly in command throughout the episode. Courage, judgment, concern, and command—these are the attributes of a leader, and Roosevelt had them.

Roosevelt also had some less attractive traits. He was a manipulative man, devious and, upon occasion, even sadistic. While he was often thoughtful of others, he could also be quite ruthless. He used people, Eleanor once told her friend and biographer Joseph P. Lash, and then he discarded them.[3] His administrative practices—to put the best face on it—were not orderly. He would give two different persons the same job, and not tell the one about the other. He would work directly with lower level officials within the departments, without informing the department secretary he was doing so. He encouraged a vast array of persons, in government and out, to confide in him, to tell him their secrets. In conversation, he seemed, almost always, to be acquiescent and agreeable, when, in fact, he would commit himself to nothing and to no one. This characteristic misled many people and angered them, when they found supposed presidential commitments evaporating into nothing.

(A possibly apocryphal story has it that after FDR's attempt to purge the Southern Democratic Party of its conservatives, Senator George of Georgia was talking with Senator Cotton Ed Smith of South Carolina. "Roosevelt is his own worst enemy," observed George. "Not so long as I am alive," growled Smith.)

These lifelong personality traits and habits became more developed as a response to the President's paralysis. Rather than retire from the field of competition, he chose to continue. The blind are said to develop their tactile sense to an extraordinary degree as compensation for their blindness. So, too, paralytics, if they intend to function whole in the world of the "normal," make the best use of every faculty available to them.

As President, it was Roosevelt's duty to lead the people; but, more difficult, he had to persuade them to follow. To do these things successfully, he needed knowledge and control—to know what must be done and how, in fact, to get it done. FDR's vast network of gossip, intrigue, and tattletale made him arguably the best-informed man in Washington, even though he was bound to his desk by his wheelchair. His bewildering, apparently haphazard, and often overlapping method of delegating duties and assigning tasks was often an effective way of getting the job done. It made full use of FDR's understanding of the motives and ambitions of the participants obtained in part by observation, but also from the gossip he heard.

As a child, he had always been able to wheedle whatever he wished from his adoring mother. As a polio, dependent upon the help of others to get about, he had developed a contagious, cheerful bonhomie, which made it a pleasure to serve him. Now, as President, those personality tricks and skills did not change; they simply became more effective and intense.

Roosevelt was not a philosopher. He was an activist and a mover. He liked to get things done. He always knew instinctively what to do next, and he had a supreme confidence in the rightness of his judgment. People respond—with alacrity and relief—to such a man; they will follow such a leader.

The White House was an ideal place for Franklin Roosevelt to live in. His handicap was far less of a burden there than it would have been were he a private citizen. As President of the United States, the resources of the American government were available to ensure that he was able to move about as he wished. The White House was accessible to the wheelchair: the family entrance on the south side was absolutely level; there was an elevator for the use of the President; corridors were wide, and bathrooms were large; the executive offices were attached to the mansion; and there was both an indoor and an outdoor level route from the Oval Office to the family living quarters. The President took the outside path whenever weather permitted.

In the first years, Roosevelt insisted upon wheeling his own chair about the White House. Soon, however, on the longer trips to and from his office, he allowed himself to be pushed by a Secret Service agent or a military aide. He liked to move quickly. Speechwriter Judge Sam Rosenman tells how, in good weather, in the mornings the staff would keep their eyes on the windows, waiting for the President to be wheeled past at breakneck speed—a pile of papers on his lap, his cigarette holder cocked at its usual jaunty angle. FDR would wave and call a happy hello to all as he went by. "We used to marvel that he did not fall out going around the curve," said Rosenman.[4]

The chair he rode in was a simple device. The standard wheelchair of the day was a cumbersome thing made of wood and wicker. In fact, it was the old-fashioned Bath chair used for pushing invalids about in Jane Austen's time. Such a chair was impractical for work or travel. So, rather than struggle with such

a contraption, Roosevelt had a chair built to his own specifications and design. To the seat and back of a common, straight-
back kitchen chair he had a sturdy base attached, with two large
wheels in front, two small ones in back. The large wheels were
but fourteen inches in diameter, low enough so that they did
not get in the way when FDR slid from his wheelchair to a sta-
tionary chair. His wheelchair was without arms; the wheels were
without brakes, and there was only a small platform to hold his
feet and keep them from dragging on the ground. Roosevelt seldom sat for long in his wheelchair. Rather, he used it to scoot
from his desk chair to a couch, from the couch to the car. He
used his chair as a means of movement, not as a place to stay.

Roosevelt's chair was small, not much bigger than the original kitchen chair. It was narrow and went through almost any
width door. Because the big wheels were in front, it was able to
turn in a very small circumference. It was not difficult to carry
him up and down stairs in it. Most important, the chair could
be carried in the backseat or the trunk of a car. The chair he
designed was a thoroughly practical contrivance, which made
it possible for him to do the extensive traveling by train and car
that political campaigning requires.

Even so, FDR did not want the public to be aware that he was
forced to use a wheelchair. Sometimes he was really quite decep-
tive in reply to direct questions. For example, in answer to a
newspaper editor who had charged that Roosevelt was still
wheelchair bound, FDR said, "As a matter of fact, I don't use a
wheelchair at all except a little kitchen chair on wheels to get
about my room while dressing . . . and solely for the purpose of
saving time."[5]

What with twice-weekly press conferences, entertainment,
office appointments, and the innumerable delegations visiting
the White House, the President was able to see and be seen over
the year by a large number of people. In addition, he often
broadcast radio messages to the nation. These were not only
formal addresses and fireside chats, but also short statements
on the occasion of various drives and programs. Through these
talks and the press conferences, FDR was able to dominate the

news media from the White House throughout his presidency.

With his magnificent radio voice and his artfully crafted talks, FDR was able to project his presence into every living room. When FDR took up the complicated subject of banking, said Will Rogers, he "made everyone understand it, even the bankers."[6] Using props as an actor does, he was able to project his personality to the audiences who came to hear him speak and, by means of the newsreels and newsphoto magazines, to the nation as a whole.

He used his cigarette holder to suggest confidence and good cheer; his old-fashioned pince-nez glasses reminded people of their schoolteachers and of Woodrow Wilson. They bespoke stability, responsibility. His old fedora campaign hat was as familiar as an old shoe; his naval cape expressed dignity and drama. The complete package of props, together with the characteristic tilt of the head, the wave of the hand, the laugh, the smile, made FDR seem to the American people as familiar, as close as a family member.

When Roosevelt left the White House, his excursions were very carefully planned by the Secret Service. The White House imposed certain rules, which were always obeyed. For example, the President was never lifted in public. If it was necessary to lift him in or out of the car, this was done in the privacy of a garage or behind a temporary plywood screen constructed for the purpose. He was never seen in public seated in a wheelchair. Either he appeared standing, leaning on the arm of an aide, or he was seated in an ordinary chair. He required that the chair be solid enough to support his full weight as he pushed himself up to a standing position. Speakers' podiums had to be solid and bolted to the floor. Once, in the 1932 campaign, this was not done, and the podium and the candidate crashed to the floor. Although reporters were present, the incident was not mentioned in the press nor were pictures taken of his fall, although it was seen by photographers.

This was so because FDR had made it a rule, during his first campaign for governor, that photographers were not to take pictures of him looking crippled or helpless. His actual words, said to some newsreel cameramen taking his picture as he was being helped out of a car in 1928 were, "No movies of me getting out of the machine, boys."[7] And from then on, remarkably, no such pictures were taken. It was an unspoken code, honored by the White House photography corps. If, as happened once or twice, one of its members sought to violate it and try to sneak a picture of the President in his chair, one or another of the older photographers would "accidentally" knock the camera to the ground or otherwise block the picture. Should the President himself notice someone in the crowd violating the interdiction, he would point out the offender and the Secret Service would move in, seize the camera, and expose the film.

This remarkable voluntary censorship was rarely violated. A photograph was published by *Life* magazine in 1937 of the President in his chair being pushed across a field. The picture was taken at great distance, however, and went largely unnoticed. Even so, the fact that it was printed at all angered the White House press office.

Reporters as well as photographers went along with the injunction. According to John Gunther, throughout FDR's career, "News stories seldom, if ever, mentioned that he was a cripple; and the fact that he used a wheelchair was never printed at all." As a result the vast majority of the American people were not aware that their president was dependent upon a wheelchair. Gunther reports that correspondents newly assigned to the White House were startled when the President was wheeled into the room in a chair. He himself found it unsettling to see the President of the United States being carried in arms. "The shock," said Gunther, "was greatest of all when he was carried; he seemed, for one thing, very small."[8]

The voluntary censorship extended even to political cartoonists. FDR was their favorite subject for over twelve years, which is not surprising, for in a way he was larger than life. But never once, so far as is known, did they portray him in a wheelchair, on crutches, or as otherwise impaired. Instead, he was often shown as running, jumping, or even fighting in a boxing arena.

"It's not a story," the President's press secretary, Steve Early, would say when asked about the President's handicap.[9] He was wrong, of course. It was a story, an important one. It was, however, a story the President did not choose to have broadcast. Such a deception as this—practiced by both the President and the press—would be quite impossible in the age of television.

Steve Early, and through him the President, kept close tabs on the numerous rumors concerning the President's health that were common in Washington throughout his administration. The White House went to extraordinary lengths to deny and quash the allegations and innuendos every way they could. There seemed to be an almost hysterical quality to many of the stories. It was said that the polio had affected FDR's brain; that he was permanently institutionalized in a lunatic asylum somewhere on the Georgia Warm Springs Foundation grounds. It was said that certain reporters had certain friends who had seen the President being smuggled into the Mayo Clinic for a major cancer operation. It was said the President had suffered a heart arrest during a Cabinet meeting, but that the Cabinet had decided to keep it secret.

No one was more alert to these stories, nor more sensitive to their import, than Eleanor. With her extraordinary combination of candor and political guile, she met these stories head on and, often as not, was able to turn them to her husband's advantage. Once, in a question-and-answer period after a lecture in Akron, Ohio, she was asked, "Do you think your husband's illness has affected your husband's mentality?" She read the written question out carefully, without emotion. She replied clearly and slowly, "I am glad that question was asked. The answer is Yes. Anyone who has gone through great suffering is bound to have a greater sympathy and understanding of the problems of mankind." It is said that her audience gave her a standing ovation.[10]

Fellow politicians avoided references to his condition. Al Smith provided guidance on how Roosevelt's handicap was to be handled. In response to a question in 1928 expressing doubt about Roosevelt's physical ability to be governor, Smith said, "A governor does not have to be an acrobat. We do not elect him for his ability to do a double back flip or handspring."[11]

95

Only one man made use publicly of FDR's crippled condition in a political attack. This man was Georgia Governor Gene Talmadge. He said, in 1935, "The greatest calamity to this country is that the President can't walk around and hunt up people to talk to. . . . The only voice to reach his wheelchair were [sic] cries of the 'gimme crowd.'" Talmadge was famous for personal attacks on his enemies. Although immensely popular among his rural supporters, the general view of Talmadge was, in Ickes's words, "one of the most contemptible men in public life."[12] And whatever he said received little credence or attention outside his circle.

This largely voluntary suppression of an important aspect of the President's life was an extraordinary thing. That Roosevelt pulled it off in the 1930s is in part a tribute to the close, harmonious relations he maintained with the working press and to the affection and respect accorded the President by the reporters. In a sense, however, this veil of silence about the extent of the President's handicap required the unspoken acquiescence of everyone—Roosevelt, the press, and the American people.

In a very real way a great nation does not want a crippled man as its President; it does not wish to think of its leader as impaired. Roosevelt was undeniably and obviously a crippled man. Literally millions of people saw him moving down his railroad ramp, bent over like a praying mantis, or hobbling painfully slowly on the arm of his son. Crippled or not, the nation wanted this man, with all his magnificent qualities, as its leader. So an agreement was struck: the existence of FDR's handicap would simply be denied by all. The people would pretend that their leader was not crippled, and their leader would do all that he could not to let them see that he was. The generally accepted line was that FDR had had polio and was now a bit lame; he had been paralyzed, but now he was recovered. He was a "cured cripple." When Talmadge spoke of the President's disability, he was like the boy in "The Emperor's New Clothes," blurting out the truth; but, unlike the boy in the story, his story went unattended. The nation *wanted* to believe its Emperor was clothed, and it simply would not hear otherwise. The thought that America, a nation crippled by the Great Depression, would choose a crippled President to lead it back to prosperity, was unthinkable; so, in the Roosevelt manner, it simply was not thought.

It was the Secret Service's responsibility to anticipate the President's movements across official Washington. Sturdy, permanent ramps for the President's use were constructed at the Capitol, the War State Navy Building (now the Executive Office Building), the farther reaches of the White House offices, and St. John's Church across Lafayette Square. These ramps were maintained for over twelve years until the President's death, at which time they were dismantled.

As President, when he traveled, everything was planned for his convenience as carefully as humanly possible. The Secret Service would map the route, concerned not only with security and safety, but making use of a checklist of details, ensuring complete accessibility for the President's wheelchair—measuring the width of doors, the angle of ramps, the height of toilets.

The President moved quite literally in a ramped world. Wherever he went, the Secret Service went first. They built ramps for his use at every point. These were not merely simple ramps for the President's chair; upon occasion the Secret Service would actually raise the entire level of a street to the level of the building entrance by means of temporary but extensive wooden trestles and scaffolding, as was done at Speaker William B. Bankhead's funeral. This allowed the President to "walk" without undue effort from his car into a building. Such construction was necessary for those public appearances in which the President wished to be seen walking with others. His technique of using a strong man on one side and a cane on the other could be used only on a level surface. It did not work on steps or ramps.

When it was necessary that he walk to a podium, efforts were made to keep the distance as short as possible. When the new President roused the nation at his inaugural in 1933, saying, "The only thing we have to fear is fear itself," he was standing but thirty-seven paces from his wheelchair, according to Secret Service records.

If steps to a speaker's platform were unavoidable and if they were in public view, the President would be lifted up the steps in a standing position. FDR would bend his arms at the elbows, holding his forearms rigid and parallel with the ground. A strong man on each side would grab the President at the elbow and lift. So far as the audience in an auditorium could tell, the President, his agents, and the officials of the welcoming committee had simply crowded together momentarily as they moved up the steps. This relatively simple maneuver required of Roosevelt the strength of a gymnast working out on the rings, for without powerful muscle control he risked dislocating his shoulders, or worse. In all, it was an uncomfortable and risky business.

Whenever possible, he spoke sitting down, from the backseat of an open, seven-passenger touring car. On such an occasion a tray-like affair would be hung across the car to hold the microphones and the text of his address. Ramps were sometimes built for the car itself—somewhat like a roller coaster scaffold—perhaps some ten or twenty feet high so that the President could be seen in his car by large crowds. Roosevelt used a touring car because he had devised an effective means of getting in and out of the backseat: he would "walk" to the door of the open car, and then turn around with his back to the door, grip the sides of the car with his hands, and sit down on the jump seat. He would then quickly throw his arms back to the seat behind, and scoot backward onto the backseat, drawing his braced legs into the car. This was done very quickly, and only the closest viewers, watching attentively, would be aware of the procedure. Under careful Secret Service scrutiny, his car would drive slowly through the throngs of people gathered to greet him. From his backseat he would work the crowd, shaking the hands thrust toward him from all sides. Roosevelt loved this contact with the people fully as much as they did.

Throughout his presidency, the President traveled largely by railroad. He did not care for flying, and flew mostly in the last two years of the war. During his twelve years in the White House, Roosevelt traveled over 544,000 miles by rail, making four hundred separate trips from the White House. In 1944 alone, he traveled more than 50,000 miles by train. He always rode in a private car, attached to which would be three or four additional cars for the Secret Service, reporters, the communications gear of the Army Signal Corps, and a freight car for his automobiles. On most occasions, the presidential party was carried as a private train, with all other traffic shunted aside.

Because he had difficulty maintaining his balance at high speeds, he ordered that the trains travel during the day at no more than thirty-five miles an hour. At night, when he was sleeping, they would make up for lost time. FDR took great delight in watching the passing countryside, noticing and remarking on all that he surveyed. "Look, Grace," he said once to city-born Grace Tully, "a cow!"[13] Unable to move about on his own legs, he used travel by car and by train as a substitute motion, a way of observing conditions and seasons.

Traveling at a sedate speed, Roosevelt was able to see the countryside in detail, but more important, he was able to be seen by the crowds gathered at the stations as his train ambled through town after town. At least once in Arkansas, in the 1936 campaign, he tired of it. "Bill, how would you like to be President for a while?" he asked one of his Secret Service guards. FDR had the man sit by the window. He placed his pince-nez glasses on the agent's nose; showed him how to wave with a cigarette holder; instructed him in the FDR smile; and then said, "Fine! Just fine! Now every time we pass a town, sit there and wave. I am going to take a nap."[14]

Roosevelt loved campaigning by train, speaking from the back platform at the whistle-stops along the way. The railings on the back platform were specially elevated for his use. Once the train was halted and the crowd gathered, FDR would "walk" out onto the platform, leaning on the arm of a son. After brief remarks, introducing the members of his family and joking with his son, he would say good-bye. As the train pulled out he would remain, waving on the platform. Once out of sight he would return to his bedroom, and his valet would remove his braces—until the next whistle-stop.

Roosevelt was never quite at ease in public. His son-in-law, Curtis Dall, recalled going to church with him back in the twenties at St. James Episcopal, the Hyde Park church of which FDR was the Senior Warden. "He was unable to stand to join in the singing of the hymns with the congregation, and from his fidgeting, I could see that the situation was embarrassing to him, though he covered it with an assumed attitude of indifference." After the service FDR waited until the congregation had left the church. He then pulled himself to a standing position. Dall steadied FDR with his arm as another member of the party handed him his crutches, one by one. "Outside the church," reported Dall, "a few of his old friends from the neighborhood who knew how sensititive he felt about his walking in public, waited to greet and converse with him."[15]

Roosevelt, of course, learned to mask his feelings pretty well behind this "assumed attitude of indifference." Should something unexpected occur in the rehearsed routine—a slip-up or a fall—the mask could slip, and FDR's feelings would be revealed, if only for an instant.

Clifton Daniel, *The New York Times* correspondent and official, remembers such a time as FDR was attending the Senate funeral of Idaho Senator William Borah in 1940. Reports Daniel: "His [FDR's] eyes blazed with anger when Jimmy didn't take his arm quickly enough to help him rise and walk out at the end of the service."[16]

Similarly, White House reporter Merriman Smith recalled a time he saw the President fall. FDR was at the Capitol to address the Congress. His car had pulled up at the private entrance under the steps of the House of Representatives. The only people present were the Capitol police, the Secret Service, several members of Congress and pool reporters. The President's chair was brought to the door of the car so that he could transfer directly from the car to the chair. Someone neglected to hold the chair steady and as Roosevelt shifted to the chair, it slid out from under him and he slipped to the ground. According to the memory of people to whom Smith told the story, for a split second he saw the President's face twist with fury. But it was only a second before FDR regained his composure and took control—putting people at ease, telling them what to do, how to lift him, and the like.

Of course, in the privacy of Warm Springs or at Hyde Park, while with family and close associates, FDR was more relaxed about how he was helped and handled. There was always a good deal of joshing and banter with his sons and guards as they were hoisting him about. He was a big and well-built man, and there was nothing fragile about him. FDR would cry, "Alley-oop!" as Secret Service Chief Mike Reilly would literally heave the President onto the front seat of his little car. Sometimes, FDR would roughhouse with his attendants, pulling them down on top of him with his powerful arms.

The President's cousin Nicholas Roosevelt recalled once standing "on the verandah watching his son Elliott and Gus Gennerich . . . carry him down the steps and place him in the car. As they turned and left him, he lost his balance . . . and he fell over on the car seat. I doubt if one man in a thousand, as disabled and dependent on others, would have refrained from some sort of reproach, however mild, to those whose carelessness had thus left him in the lurch. But Franklin merely laid on his back, waved his strong arms in the air and laughed. At once they came back and helped him to his seat behind the wheel. . . ."[17]

Roosevelt became quite skillful at moving about on his braces. It took much concentration and hard work. The braces caused him pain, and the effort and the concentration made him sweat profusely during the ordeal of standing and walking. Walking was always dangerous and, in spite of all precautions, Roosevelt fell in public at least three times. These falls were not reported by the press, in accordance with the unspoken understanding.

The most serious accident occurred at the 1936 convention. Roosevelt had been renominated by acclamation, and he went to Franklin Field in Philadelphia to deliver his acceptance speech. A temporary platform and podium had been erected at one end of the stadium, and row upon row of temporary seats had been set up on the playing field. The stadium can hold well over 90,000 people, and that night in June every seat was taken.

The President's car drove to the rear of the platform. FDR emerged from the car on the arm of his son James with Gus Gennerich, his bodyguard, in front of him, and Mike Reilly, then second in command of the Secret Service, behind. The platform was crowded with celebrities, party dignitaries, police, and Secret Service agents. Slowly, the President made his way through the crowd, smiling, nodding, waving, occasionally shaking hands with acquaintances as he passed. He came upon an old man with a long white beard. This was Edwin Markham, a well-known poet of the day. Markham's poems praised the dignity of the hardworking poor and railed against "continued poverty in a land of plenty." The acceptance speech the President was to give that night was certain to warm Markham's heart. Roosevelt stopped to greet the poet.

Roosevelt's first term had concentrated on economic recovery. With an almost warlike mobilization, the government had rushed emergency measures. These were intended to provide food and work for the unemployed, to stimulate demand, and thus to regenerate the American economy. Now, for his second term, Roosevelt intended to propose not recovery, but reform and, by implication at least, radical reform. The party's platform for the 1936 election, largely dictated by the President, said, in part: "We hold these truths to be self-evident—that government . . . has certain inescapable obligations to its citizens"—among which are equal opportunity for all and federal assistance for those overtaken by disaster. The platform pledged to "rid our land of kidnappers, bandits, and "—in the same sentence, using the words of Teddy Roosevelt—"malefactors of great wealth." This night, the last night of the convention, before the crowd of nearly 100,000 people and a radio audience of over 100 million more, Roosevelt intended to take on these "malefactors." In perhaps the strongest speech of his career, he would attack the "economic royalists" who dominated the American economy. It was this speech and this campaign that confirmed the Eastern establishment in their belief that FDR had betrayed his class. It is undeniable that in this speech he seemed to declare war against the power and many of the values of the class in which he was born and raised. For if there were economic royalists, the Roosevelts were certainly one of the royal families.

Under such circumstances it is not surprising that the President would reach out his hand to Markham, the poet of the poor. And considering the intensity of emotions stirred by renouncing the values of one's parents and asserting one's own values, it is not surprising the President was thrown off balance, emotionally and actually. Slowly at first, FDR began to twist off center. As he swiveled past a certain point, his hip joints buckled. Under the pressure, a knee lock on his brace snapped, and down he sprawled. The text of the President's speech was scattered across the platform under the feet of those assembled there. Instantaneously, his aides moved into action. Mike Reilly caught FDR's armpit with his shoulder as the President fell. Gus Gennerich quickly seized the other arm. Together they lifted the President to a standing position, holding him aloft while another agent struggled to straighten and relock the knee brace. Reilly always remembered how the President looked when he was down. Grim-faced, between clenched teeth, FDR had snapped, "Clean me up." As the brace was relocked, the President regained his balance on son Jimmy's arm. His cane was returned to him. The agents quickly collected the pages of the speech and handed them back to the President. His composure regained, the President stayed for a moment to reassure the badly frightened Markham that all was well, and then moved on to the podium.

As he began his speech, he found the text jumbled, the pages out of sequence. As he spoke, he rearranged the pages into some sort of order with his right hand. FDR's delivery seemed somewhat halting at first, but soon he was in full stride. Alone and upright, in the glare of a thousand spotlights, he called out to the nation to follow him in a great struggle equal to that of the American Revolution. It was a struggle, he said, to insure all citizens not just the right to vote, but the right to work and the right to live. He condemned his own class: "These economic royalists complain that we seek to overthrow the institutions of America. But they really complain that we seek to take away their power. Our allegiance to American institutions requires that we overthrow this kind of power." He declared war on the overprivileged. He denounced the "resolute enemy within our gates," and he closed in words remembered throughout the century. "There is a mysterious cycle in human events. To some generations much is given. Of other generations much is expected. This generation of Americans has a rendezvous with destiny."[18]

The cheers of 100,000 people rang out in the warm night air. The President returned to his open car. Slowly, it twice circled the field as FDR received the cheers of the standing, stamping crowd. In later life, Mike Reilly wrote that the cheers he heard that night were the loudest and strongest he had ever heard in a lifetime spent protecting Presidents.[19]

Any presidential fall is a serious matter; for FDR it was plain dangerous. As he fell, his twisting body put such tension upon his braces that the lock of one snapped open. Such tension could easily snap a leg bone. FDR was fortunate that he was only bruised. Falls, of course, are also politically dangerous. Gerald Ford once stumbled at the foot of an airplane ramp in full view of the television cameras. In spite of the fact that Ford was a well-coordinated athlete, the fall brought him the reputation of being something of a stumblebum, and this caused him serious harm and cost him votes. Roosevelt, who really was physically helpless, had convinced the American people he had the strength and stamina to be President. A full fall in public, even without serious injury, would have done great harm to his political image.

And that night in June 1936, the President was not seen as a helpless cripple. In fact, his fall was *not seen* at all by the majority of the people in the audience that night. His agents and his son had rehearsed many times what to do in such a situation. As the President had moved through the hubble-bubble of the welcome from the committee of dignitaries on the platform, he was loosely surrounded by his men. As FDR went down, they closed in, forming a tight circle, blocking the President from view. To the unsuspecting in the crowd it appeared the President had been momentarily engulfed by the welcome he was receiving. Only a very few of the people on the platform were aware of what had happened, and they did not talk about it. The pool reporters were aware of the accident, but as usual did not report it. The entire nation listening to the live broadcast on the radio were told nothing. It was a nonevent.

No one knows what Roosevelt felt as he lost his balance and lay momentarily helpless before the party and the nation he was pledged to lead. It is not recorded that he ever mentioned the incident to anyone.

XI
Recreation

The President certainly
carries his liquor well.[1]
—HAROLD L. ICKES

THE President was fifty-one years old when he entered the White House. He was a vigorous, healthy bull of a man, muscular and strong in the upper torso. He was quite capable of working long hours. Occasionally he would work late, long into the night, and he could function well for days at a time with little sleep. By and large, however, he paced himself well and maintained a schedule similar to the one he had followed as governor. He awoke sometime between eight and nine in the morning, had breakfast in bed, and for the next hour or so read the papers, scanned memoranda and reports, and conferred with his personal staff from his bed. He would get to the office around ten-thirty and have appointments, usually at quarter-hour intervals, from then until lunch at one. Usually he would eat at his desk with one or two guests—a senator, an ambassador back from overseas, the author of a current book. If he had no guests, Missy LeHand would eat with him. After lunch he would dictate to Missy or to her assistant, Grace Tully. Once a week he would have a Cabinet meeting; usually twice a week he would have a press conference.

In the late afternoons, around four or four-thirty, the President might go for a ride through Rock Creek Park or back to the family quarters for tea. If he was still in his office at five-thirty or six, he would call in those of his personal staff who were available for the "family hour." Drinks would be mixed, and with drink in hand, feet up, they would talk about the news of the day and gossip about personalities and politics.

Early in his first year, through the efforts of a New York newspaper, the children of America contributed their dimes and nickels so that an indoor swimming pool might be built for the President's use. This pool was of great value to Roosevelt. During the peacetime years he swam several times a week. A swim was followed by a massage from Petty Officer George Fox. Dinner was at eight. At least two or three times a week, a movie would be shown after dinner in the second floor hallway. After the film, the President might work an hour or two at his stamp collection, or go through the various and endless reports and papers that flow to a President. Once in bed, he would read a mystery or a thriller before putting out the light. The President seldom stayed up late, and usually slept more than eight hours a night.

Like all paraplegics, Roosevelt found dressing to be a bothersome business. Normally he wore a double-breasted navy blue suit throughout the day, with an ordinary four-in-hand tie at his neck. If his dinner was to be a dinner-jacket affair, the President simply exchanged his four-in-hand for a black bow tie and went as he was, without bothering to change suits. For outside wear in winter, he used his naval cape because it was easier to put on and take off in a sitting position than was an overcoat.

The Roosevelts entertained constantly. They brought people from all walks of life, all professions, all races, and all sections to the White House. This was, of course, of great value in terms of politics; it also served to educate and stimulate the President—to expose him to new ideas and developing issues.

In addition to the annual round of formal receptions and banquets, the Roosevelts had guests for virtually every breakfast, lunch, and dinner. These guests would be politicians, actors, authors, scholars, and, during World War II, royal refugees. Dinners were relaxed; the conversation was lively, and the President mixed the martinis himself.

At a typical dinner, guests would be escorted up to the family quarters of the White House into the oval study where they would find the President already seated in an armchair with a tray of bottles and drink mixes beside him. As other guests arrived, and Eleanor and the other family members who were home at the time appeared, the President would make drinks for all.

After the cocktail hour, dinner was announced. Mrs. Roosevelt would then rise and ask the ranking guest to escort her down to the family dining room on the floor below. Mrs. Roosevelt and her escort would lead the way in leisurely fashion, the other guests following. On the way down the stairs Mrs. Roosevelt would stop from time to time, pointing out a portrait, explaining the history of this or that aspect of the White House. Meanwhile, as soon as everyone else had left the study, the Filipino houseboys would bring in the President's wheelchair. He would be transferred to it and be wheeled to the elevator. Once on the first floor, he would be pushed to the dining room, where a solid chair with firm arms was placed at the head of the table. The President would transfer over to this chair, and his wheelchair would be removed from the room. As the dinner guests entered the dining room, they would find the President already at the head of the table, calling out a cheerful welcome. Most were not aware of how he had moved downstairs and probably didn't think about it.

The dinner guests and the White House visitors always had a wonderful time and, when they got home, they would talk about their visit in local radio interviews, in the newspapers, and to their friends. Over the years this extensive entertaining served to make the Roosevelts seem like close family friends to a great many Americans.

At these affairs the President had one or, at the most, two cocktails before dinner. He was, by and large, a moderate drinker, a social drinker. However, at an evening party when he was having a good time, he could put away rather large amounts of alcohol. At a party on the lawn of Harold Ickes' house, in the summer of 1936, the President appeared to have a wonderful time. He had two cocktails before dinner; he was served a claret and a champagne at dinner; there was coffee with liqueurs after the meal had been cleared. Tommy Corcoran then played his accordion and led the assembled group in songs and, according to Ickes, FDR "must have had five highballs after dinner. He drank gin and ginger ale, but he never showed the slightest effect. . . . The President certainly carries his liquor well."[2]

During the White House years, the President went out to such informal dinners only rarely. He was a member of a penny ante poker group, which met haphazardly, informally, without the knowledge of the press. The group would meet in one or another of its members' houses, but more often than not, in the White House. Here, beer would be served; and it was not unusual for the President to have more than several over the course of the game. On all these occasions, the intoxicating element for FDR was the presence of the people. He reveled in the camaraderie, for he was, under his cheerful exterior, a lonely man. The liquor simply served to hasten and heighten the camaraderie.

The President was often away from the White House. He took weekends as often as possible at Hyde Park; he took overnight and weekend cruises often in the summer months. He was at Warm Springs in the spring and the fall as his schedule allowed, and several times he took lengthy ocean cruises aboard one or another of the Navy's capital ships. These were a mixture of inspection trips, diplomatic visits, deep sea fishing, and rest and relaxation.

FDR was a man of the sea. He loved the Navy, and he traveled by ship whenever it was possible. When Roosevelt spoke of the Navy, he said "we," and the Navy took care of its own. It had two sets of presidential "cruise gear"—as befits a two-ocean Navy. One set was stored at Norfolk on the Atlantic; the other on the West Coast. The gear would be installed on board whatever ship the President chose to use. Within a day of notification, holes would be cut through the decks of the ship and an elevator installed. On board throughout "President's Country," ramps would be built over the coamings and gunnels so that he could wheel about the deck in his chair. An extra-length bed would be installed. A bathtub with steel railings would be installed, as would a toilet with the seat raised to the level of the wheelchair. There would even be a flowered shower curtain hung because the President was said to dislike government-issue canvas ones. All of this would be done whenever the President put out to sea, and all of this would be removed as soon as the cruise was over.[3]

During his vacation cruises, the President attended to business. There were daily mail drops of White House mail and, of course, the President was in constant radio contact with his advisors. Official business, however, did not take up much time. Daytime hours were devoted to such activities as deep-sea fishing; evening hours were spent at cocktails and poker games. On one typical voyage, the President spent the month of October 1935 aboard the cruiser *Houston*. He sailed from San Diego, fished off Baja California, and proceeded through the Panama Canal, stopping at various points of interest, fishing along the way. The cruise ended at Charleston, South Carolina, and the President returned to Washington by train.

On this cruise, the President's fishing launch had two seats mounted on the stern and he would ask one of the members of his party to go along on an afternoon's fishing. Also always present would be Captain Brown, the officer in charge of the cruiser. With him was a sailor who had been specially selected by the Navy because of his previous deep-sea fishing experience. Harold Ickes, who was along, recalled in his diary:

> When the *Houston* anchored, a companionway was lowered from the leeside of the ship and the President's fishing launch was brought alongside the little platform at the foot of the companionway. Then two men would carry him sideways down the companionway. They would hand him over to Captain Brown and the other man I have referred to, who would swing him around into his armchair. There he would sit and fish. Especially when the water was rough, as it was sometimes, I was a good deal worried about this transshipment of the President to and from his fishing launch. Any misstep or any sudden lurch of the launch might have caused an acci-

dent resulting in serious injury to him. But he never seemed to mind. [See photo.]

On this whole trip I have marveled again and again at his high cheer and at his disposition. Never once did he act self-conscious; on no occasion did he seem to be nervous or irritated. Cheerfully he submitted to being wheeled up and down the special ramps that had been installed on the *Houston* for his use, or to being carried up and down like a helpless child when he went fishing. He was an avid fisherman and, with his strong arms and shoulders, he was able to give a good account of himself if he once got a fish on his hook. Fortunately, he was a lucky fisherman also.[4]

The President liked deep-sea fishing. And so, even though his handicap made it difficult and awkward, he went fishing. This led to happenings that occasionally were something less than presidential. In the summer of 1933, FDR was sailing, with his sons, aboard the *Amberjack II*, off the coast of New England. He was, as always, escorted by various vessels of the U.S. Navy. The Secret Service followed along behind in a chartered vessel, as did the Washington press corps in their own charter. The *Amberjack* was a small vessel; its passageways were narrow. Its companionway was both narrow and steep. In the morning after breakfast, Roosevelt liked to sit out on deck. Later, when it was necessary for him to relieve himself, he would go below decks again to the head, after which he would return to the deck for fishing. This meant he had to be carried up and down the narrow staircase several times. This was an awkward business; it is not easy to carry a six-foot-three, 190-pound man in narrow quarters. It was hard work for those doing the carrying, and it was uncomfortable and undignified for the one being carried. So it was not surprising, one foggy morning, as son James recounts, that Roosevelt "suggested that, in light of the special circumstances of fog, a triangular extension on the stern could perhaps serve as a toilet seat; he could simply do what had to be done right there." With the President thus positioned, James went up to the flying bridge to give his father privacy.

"No sooner had I reached the bridge," said James, "than I realized the fog was lifting. And there coming asteaming up on us, were several ships of the convoy. As they closed in Father was bound to be visible. I shouted a warning." Shouting for his brothers below decks, James rushed to his father. "They can't see the President like this," said FDR. With that, FDR's sons picked him up, with pants down, and hustled him down the companionway.[5]

XII
Relations

. . . The persons of kings are invariably attended by a great number of people concerned to see that diversion comes after affairs of state, watching over their leisure hours to provide pleasures and sports so that there should never be an empty moment. In other words, they are surrounded by people who are incredibly careful to see that the king should never be alone and able to think about himself, because they know that, king though he is, he will be miserable if he does think about it.[1]

—PASCAL

ROOSEVELT had a most enigmatic personality, and nowhere is this more apparent than in his dealings with others. Roosevelt functioned intuitively, and he can only be understood by intuition. His character can be expressed, to some degree, by a series of paradoxes. FDR was a loner who was never alone. Throughout his life, he seemed emotionally dependent on no one, yet he was always emotionally close to his mother. It was a relationship of great emotional love and even greater social reserve. Roosevelt had a devoted wife who was not really a wife, and a lover who was not really a lover. Although he was surrounded by friends—thousands of friends—he was, in the ordinary sense, quite friendless. Paradoxically, the farther away he was from people, the closer he was able to be to them. For millions of Americans, FDR's voice on the radio conveyed his genuine and intimate concern. Yet to his children, he was a remote, even at times uncaring, father.

Central to all this was the principal paradox of FDR's being: this man who seemed to be so little crippled by his handicap was, in fact, most severely emotionally crippled. Unwilling, unable as he was to share with anyone his feelings about being handicapped, his life ultimately was an artificial one lived on its surface. The image he presented to other people was one he had carefully constructed and artfully maintained. His feelings, to the extent he was aware of them, he kept to himself. This caused him to live a life of emotional isolation. Alone and crippled, he was a prisoner to his emotions. "You do, surely, bar the door upon your own liberty," warned Shakespeare, "if you deny your griefs to your friend."[2]

Roosevelt had been a lonely child. Loved dearly by his parents, encouraged always to follow his interests, he lived, however, quite isolated from other children. At fourteen, when sent away to prep school at Groton, according to the judgment of his daughter Anna, "He no more knew how to get along with the boys his own age than the man in the moon."[3] In fact, Anna reported that her father had always been "a lonely man . . . wanting terribly to be one of the boys."[4] He never was—not at Groton, not at Warm Springs, nor in the White House. He tried too hard. With others, he was always cheerful, always entertaining; people loved to be with him. Raised by a loving yet reserved mother, he found it difficult to be intimate. He was taught by his mother to keep his feelings to himself. Unwilling to discuss unpleasant things, he did not share his feelings with others. This inadequacy—for so it was—served as a barrier and kept him from genuine intercourse with others. As a man, after polio struck, he was still alone—suffering the hurt and grief caused by paralysis, not expressing any of the anger he must have felt.

Roosevelt was always faithful to the personal values taught him by his parents and, as he did not share the feelings stirred by polio with anyone, he also denied them to himself. FDR was, like Pascal's king, surrounded by people—never alone, constantly diverted, to avoid the pain of being alone with his thoughts.

This tendency was supported, even exaggerated, by his paralysis. After polio, FDR was in some ways physically helpless, and he could not, in fact, safely be left alone. As a result, it was necessary that there was always be someone within hearing distance of his voice.

One night, FDR's son John returned to the White House late and noticed that his father's light was still on. Going into the presidential bedroom, he found Roosevelt in his chair. The President had rung repeatedly for his valet, Irvin McDuffie, for help to get to bed. McDuffie, who liked his drink, had had too much, fallen asleep, and had not responded to the bell. FDR was stranded, unable to care for himself. John helped his father to bed, and Roosevelt decided that McDuffie must be fired. It was typical of the Roosevelt personality that he could not bring himself to perform this unpleasant task. In this case, FDR did what he did so often: he had Eleanor do it. She told McDuffie he was fired at a time when FDR was out of town. "I just couldn't take the chance it might happen again at a bad time," FDR explained.[5]

It is but one more apparent contradiction in the Roosevelt personality that he used to complain about the Secret Service and his loss of privacy and solitude. He said once: "You know . . . I can never be alone. I cannot even go out and walk alone under those trees. Always someone has to be with me or near me. I am never alone."[6] This is an example of his complaints. He did not mean them. Presidents always complain about the restrictions imposed upon them by security, and the demands made upon their time by the Congress, the press, politicians, and the like. Roosevelt was no exception. The evidence, of course, is that he loved the attention.

The modern presidency fit Roosevelt as though it were a coat that had been tailor-made for him. He and his family moved into the White House as though it had always been their family home, which it became over the years of the Roosevelt occupation. FDR lived surrounded by staff and family, appointees and reporters, Congressmen and dignitaries. The house was always full of people, and FDR was always the center of attention. He lived in the center of this hurly-burly with great zest. It was diverting. Because of his disability, he could no longer walk alone in the woods he loved. But with people, events, and duties, he kept himself entertained—fending off, denying even, any thought of what he could not change—his disability.

MOTHER

In September 1941, FDR's mother, Sara Delano Roosevelt, died at the age of eighty-seven. FDR was an only son. Throughout his life he was completely devoted to his mother. Her death, even at an advanced age, was a severe blow to him. The funeral was held in the small parish church, St. James Episcopal, at Hyde Park. Although this was for him a moment of intimate grief, it was still the duty of the Secret Service to accompany the President to the very graveside as he saw his mother buried. This intrusion was too much for Mike Reilly, the head of the White House Secret Service unit. At the gate of the cemetery he turned to FDR's son James and said, "You watch out for him, Jimmy. I don't think we belong in there, even if Congress says we do."[7] Even without the Secret Service, because of his handicap, Franklin Roosevelt went to the interment of his mother's body carried on the arm of his son.

Throughout her life, Sara Delano Roosevelt was a central figure—perhaps *the* central figure—in her son's life. In fact, the two lived out their lives together—he survived her by only three years, dying himself in the spring of 1945. The President saw as much of his mother as he did of his wife. Sara had her room at the White House. In Manhattan, Franklin and his mother had adjoining townhouses on East Sixty-fifth Street. At his beloved Hyde Park, she was, of course, the matriarch. Widowed in 1900, she ran the estate for over forty years. At Hyde Park, she always sat at the head of the table, with Franklin at the foot and Eleanor seated in between. After meals, they sat in the library in their chairs flanking the fireplace—Mother to the left, FDR to the right, Eleanor, often as not, perched on a footstool at her husband's feet. At Hyde Park, Sara was *the* Mrs. Roosevelt, and

Eleanor was always referred to by the staff as "Mrs. Eleanor."

After FDR's polio attack, he lived largely confined to quarters. He could not go out with ease, and his old style of life was denied to him. He could not live the life of the New York banker/broker/lawyer—a life of business lunches, workouts at the club, drinks on the run, dinner, theater, golf at the country club. If people were to meet with him, they had to come to his house. This meant FDR spent far more time at home than most men do. So, in a physical sense he lived closer to his mother than most men do. For years he saw her every day. Sara was deeply and fully involved with the life of her son and, as the years went by, her grandchildren. In a psychological sense, perhaps, it can be said that Roosevelt never really completed his separation from his mother. She was a person of great strength, formidable in the style of Queen Mary. Her behavior was eminently correct, her values were those of her time, class, and station. She was reserved in the display of emotion. She did not hold with expressing one's feelings. She believed that unpleasant things should not be discussed. Still, she was not a cold person. In this complex family, Sara was both a pillar of Victorian propriety and a warm, demonstrative mother. She gave her child, and later her grandchildren, great hugs and kisses—physical signs of love and affection. FDR's daughter, Anna, remembered how she and her brothers, when very small, would crawl in early morning into their grandmother's bed to receive passionate hugs to her ample bosom. "Hugs which were," remembered Anna, "quite literally smothering."[8]

Sara's life was fully as dedicated to helping her son's political career as was Eleanor's. Hyde Park was in constant use for political purposes. Sara had guests under her roof she would never have dreamed of receiving but for her son's political needs. She found Huey Long to be an appalling person, but he was her guest at luncheon in her home. She found many of these people—politicians, labor leaders, social workers—strange and incomprehensible, but they were of value to Franklin and she made them welcome. She was always rather fond of Mussolini because he had feted her on her visit to Italy. It was said of Sara that the only political visitors FDR brought to Hyde Park of whom she thoroughly approved were the King and Queen of England, and she had, of course, known the King's mother.

Whatever FDR was to the world, to Sara he was always simply her adored son. In the middle of his second term as President of the United States, FDR was working at his correspondence on the terrace at Hyde Park. From a window above, his mother (then in her eighties) called out, "Franklin, put on your sweater, or you will catch your death of cold."[9] The President laughed at this, but he sent a Secret Service man to fetch a sweater.

FDR was raised by this passionate woman who believed passion must not be shown, but rather repressed, guided into carefully controlled channels, or more often than not, denied totally. She had encouraged him to keep his fears and his hurt to himself—for example, when his teeth had been knocked out at Campobello. This was a lesson FDR had learned well. How FDR interacted with his mother is nicely illustrated by a letter Sara wrote at the time describing her first meeting with Franklin after his attack of infantile paralysis. Sara had been in Europe when he got sick. Upon her return she went straight to his bed at Campobello. She found her son paralyzed from the waist down, "those beautiful legs quite, quite useless." She was most distressed. She said of this first meeting with her paralyzed son, "I realized that I had to be courageous for Franklin's sake, and since he was probably pretending to be unworried for mine, the meeting was quite a cheerful one."[10] Sara said once that her son, in fact, had *never* talked to her about his paralysis. Most likely, this was a true statement, and it serves to illustrate how very isolated and repressed FDR was in his emotional life. His mother was capable of great love and comfort. He knew this from the care she had lavished on him as an infant. Yet, as an adult at a time of need, of hurt and loss, he could no more ask for love and comfort from his mother than could she volunteer it. They shared the same standards, and these standards served to keep them isolated even as they were together.

WIFE

Like everything else in his life, Franklin Roosevelt's relations with his wife are extraordinarily well documented. In a way now unlikely—and perhaps now impossible—the Roosevelts continued to lead active and most complicated private lives after they had moved into the White House. They were a large and complex family with many interests and concerns, maintaining old traditions and trying new adventures—all under the glare of the intense publicity attendant upon the President and his family. During their lifetime the newspapers chronicled their daily activities. Now, books and articles, biographies and memoirs, letters and diaries provide great additional detail and depth on the life of the man and his family.

From this evidence, it seems clear that FDR's relationship with his wife was a stable one during the White House years. Each had admiration and respect for the other. There was a strong, unquestioned mutual trust. Having similar backgrounds, similar values, and a similar sense of social consciousness and responsibility, they saw the world much the same way. They were—each in his own and her own way—consummate politicians. Theirs was a business partnership, effective, efficient, and successful.

The "trial by fire" at Campobello in 1921, when Eleanor nursed her husband through polio, had something to do with the forging of this solid relationship. In the wake of FDR's affair with Lucy Mercer in 1918, he and his wife had agreed to continue the marriage both for the benefit of the children and so as not to endanger his political career. FDR's life previous to that time had been a whirlwind of activity and movement, drama, adventure, and high expectation. Eleanor was quite shy and withdrawn. She had felt herself useless, almost a burden to her handsome husband. With polio, the roles were dramatically altered. His movements were now severely restricted; she was now forced out into the world on his behalf. At this juncture she could not mistake her importance to her husband, nor could he. Their daughter, Anna, said, "I always felt that the polio was very instrumental in bringing them much closer into a very real partnership."[11] With the vital insistence of Louis Howe, who worked sometimes as a catalyst, sometimes as a go-between, Eleanor and Franklin evolved the system of shared responsibilities and support that allowed him to continue in politics. It was during the period of recovery and rehabilitation that Anna remembered her parents as having "real discussions" for the first time.

Eleanor was deeply moved by the plight of her paralyzed husband throughout the rest of his life. She worried constantly about the state of his health and his physical safety. She was fearful that he might be dropped when he was being carried, or that he would fall in public doing injury to himself, perhaps, but surely doing injury to his public image. This is a concern about which she spoke only by indirection. Early candid photos and home movies clearly reveal her concern, even agitation. In her autobiographies she speaks of her husband's paralysis as a "blessing in disguise," finding that he developed from it a greater understanding of the tribulations and suffering of others, and that it taught him a patience that he had not had heretofore. It was in her character to find value in suffering, to seek growth from adversity. It was, however, also her character to see things clearly, and to call things as they were without flinching. Consequently, she never considered Franklin's affliction anything but "a tragedy." She once wrote, "Though he learned to bear it, I am afraid it was always a tragedy."[12]

Polio altered the dynamics between them. No longer was it only Eleanor who could be hurt and humiliated. No longer was Franklin the only one whose life was expanding and growing. It is possible to catch a glimpse of the effort that went into the evolution of their marriage relationship. Marian Dickinson and Nan Sussman lived on the Roosevelt estate at Hyde Park. They were friends of Eleanor's who, at Eleanor's insistence, became friends of Franklin's as well. In Marian's memoirs, as told to Kenneth Davis, Davis writes:

> Ordinarily, when he [FDR] was at the big house at Hyde Park, Eleanor stayed there, too—but one summer evening she left

him there and came, distraught, to the cottage. The "mis-
understanding" that time was serious. She "remained
closeted with us for three days," as Marian vividly remembers. Finally, Nan telephoned FDR at the big house and spoke
with some sternness.

"If you are wise, you will come over here," she said, "and
right away!"

"But will she talk to me?" he asked.

"You come."

He did, in the Ford with hand controls . . . But once there,
he could only sit and wait helplessly . . . She went out to
the car. She sat with him there for a long time—more than
two hours, Marian believes—but then she went back to the
big house, and the quarrel was not mentioned again.[13]

Roosevelt had led a fortunate childhood; he had not confronted the feelings of abandonment and helplessness experienced by so many children. Yet here in mid-life, in such situations as this, he found himself helpless, the object of pity.
Nothing in his experience had prepared him for the feelings such
conditions produce. It is very hard to repress these feelings, but
indications are that repress them he did, on all occasions.

Eleanor was his partner in the family business, and the family business was politics. She served him in many ways. She was
his inspector, moving with great energy and a keen perception
across the length and breadth of the land. She was his contact,
developing and maintaining communications with an immense
network of people and organizations. She was his conscience,
urging him on and never allowing him to forget the social purposes of the New Deal. She was his advisor, giving him her political judgment, always as perceptive as his own—often more
sensitive and aware.

In this political partnership, Eleanor was an equal. FDR trusted
her to handle matters of extraordinary importance and delicacy.
For example, at the Democratic Convention of 1940, the delegates were close to rebellion over the third term issue and FDR's
selection of a running mate. FDR sent Eleanor to speak before
the seething delegates. Her intuitive political shrewdness en-
abled her to quell the revolt to a degree that FDR himself could

not have done. He always trusted her to give him hard counsel, honest and direct. For example, in 1944, she reported to her husband that his health and fitness had become a serious issue. She is reported to have told him that if he wished to win the election, he must put his leg braces on and appear in public, standing as a strong and healthy candidate. This was grim news for the weak and failing FDR. But he did as she advised. She was, until the end, perhaps the only one who spoke the unvarnished truth to FDR.

The bond between these extraordinary people was strong and lasting, providing them with trust and confidence, but little in the way of love and comfort. Eleanor sought these emotions elsewhere. Eleanor's own appraisal of their relationship is exactly typical of the woman: honest, self-deprecating, discreet, yet with a strong sense that there is more, much more to be said. "He might have been happier with a wife who was completely uncritical; that I was never able to be, and he had to find it in other people. Nevertheless, I think I sometimes acted as a spur, even though the spurring was not always wanted or welcome. I was one of those who served his purpose."[14]

CHILDREN

Roosevelt's relations with his children were proper and traditional. They loved their father dearly, respected his talents and his achievements immensely, and helped him as best they could whenever possible. For his part FDR was an affectionate, if distant, father. Between the father and his sons there was much good-natured bantering. The Roosevelts were always a comfortable, open family, the members thoroughly at ease with each other. Easy as they were, however, FDR was no more open about sharing confidences with his children than with anyone else.

As the children were growing up during World War I, their father seemed a glamorous, remote figure. As a junior member of the Woodrow Wilson Cabinet, FDR was very busy and very involved in his burgeoning political career. During the week the children were cared for by governesses and nannies, their frazzled mother and, occasionally, by their doting granny. They saw their father for any length of time only on the infrequent Sunday when he would lead them out to adventure: yachting, swimming, picnics with roughhouse games, and exciting chases. It was no wonder they adored him, but they wished he would have more time for them.

In 1921, when FDR came down with polio, the situation changed. Suddenly, the glamorous man with the crowded schedule was housebound and physically paralyzed. During the following months and years of convalescence, the children saw, on an intimate basis, their father's struggle to regain his career. Their love and admiration for their father grew and, for the first time, they were able to be of genuine help to him. Roosevelt needed to be lifted in and out of cars and carried upstairs. His four sons, strong and healthy boys, were pleased, and even proud, to serve their father in this way. When the time came for FDR to reappear in his public role, he could do so only with long leg braces and a cane, while leaning on the strong arm of an aide. In the early days of his return to active politics, this aide was in most circumstances one of his two older sons. At Warm Springs, James and Elliott worked out with weights so as to develop their arms to be steady and secure. Now the boys were needed, and what is more they *knew* they were needed. Thus, as polio strengthened the bond between Eleanor and Franklin, so, too, did it strengthen the ties between FDR and his children.

Yet this did not mean that confidences were exchanged; far from it. Late in life, his daughter, Anna, reflected on the means by which her parents had "made me increasingly reticent about talking . . . about any and all types of difficulties as they rose in my life." She saw clearly the paradox in her father's life and the impenetrable isolation it caused him: the further he was from intimacy, the more intimate he became. "To the farmer in the area to the east of our house at Hyde Park, Father related with obvious warmth and sincere interest. On the radio, his voice radiated the same warmth and personal interest to the extent that people have often told me they felt his words were specifically directed to them as individuals." And yet, she summarized, "it has always seemed to me that the greatest contradiction in my parents was, on the one hand, their supreme ability to 'relate' to either groups of people or individuals who had problems, and on the other hand, their apparent lack of ability to 'relate' with the same consistent warmth and interest to an individual who was their child."[15]

FDR'S CIRCLE

FDR lived confined to a chair. He could not ride horseback across the countryside like Ronald Reagan, nor could he jog in the morning along the towpath like Jimmy Carter. More than most Presidents, FDR was a prisoner in the White House.

Only very occasionally did he go to a private home in Washington for a dinner or a party. He never went to the theater or concerts for pleasure—not because he was not interested, but because of the physical difficulties involved. At the theater, he had to wear his hated braces all evening in order to "walk" to his orchestra seat, or else he would have to be seen by the audience riding in a wheelchair or being carried to a box seat. He never went out to the movies, but had regular screenings of current films in the second floor hallway of the White House. FDR's usual recreation was, like Woodrow Wilson before him, to go for a drive in the backseat of a White House car through the byways of Rock Creek Park and the gentle countryside around Washington.

Although Roosevelt's White House office, study, and bedroom were air conditioned—thanks to his predecessor, Herbert Hoover—he was unwilling to make use of the newly developed convenience because he believed it aggravated his sinus problem. On summer evenings, to escape the oppressive Washington heat, he would board the presidential yacht, *Sequoia*, and cruise slowly down the Potomac. Roosevelt spent quiet hours working over his stamp collection, and he always had a stack of paperback mysteries at his bedside.

Such were Roosevelt's simple relaxations and pleasures.

However, his principal interest and recreation were people, always people. They entertained him, diverted him, flattered and attended him. And they occupied his time. He needed to have people around him from morning till night. At the White House he assembled a group of associates about him that can best be described as courtiers in the court of Pascal's king. Not just their working days, but their entire lives centered on Roosevelt and the White House. They had virtually no private lives of their own other than their service to Roosevelt.

The makeup of FDR's inner circle varied over the years, but at one time or another, it included: Louis Howe, Roosevelt's confidential advisor; Missy LeHand, his secretary, advisor, and often hostess; her assistant and successor, Grace Tully; Harry Hopkins, his trusted, ailing, wartime advisor; Major General Edwin "Pa" Watson, military aide; Gus Gennerich, private bodyguard, attendant, and family helper; Judge Samuel Rosenman, speech writer and advisor; Louise Hackmeister, the President's personal telephone operator; Toi Bachelder, secretary and fellow polio; Marvin McIntyre and Steve Early, press secretaries.

These people were available to the President at any time, for whatever purpose. They were close to him during the working day, but they were with him at other times, too. When he traveled to Warm Springs, they went with him. During the war, under the cover of a press blackout of the President's movements, FDR went to Hyde Park almost every weekend, and they went with him aboard his private train. When he went on a picnic, so did they. When he went on an evening's cruise, they went along. Often as not, they would share lunch at his desk, take dinner with him in his study, enjoy the cocktails he whipped up at the regular "Children's Hour" get-together at the end of the working day.

The atmosphere in the Roosevelt circle, whether in business hours or out, was efficient but informal, sometimes casual in the extreme. The President had special nicknames for his cronies by which they became exceedingly well known. Attorney Thomas Corcoran was always "Tommy the Cork"; Secretary of

Treasury Henry Morgenthau was "Henry the Morgue"; Hopkins was "Harry the Hop"; Grace Tully was the "Countess of Abbey." With one and all the President was relaxed and at ease. He was, of course, always clearly the President, always in charge; no one except Missy LeHand ever called *him* by a nickname. No one, outside the family, addressed him by his first name. He was "Mr. President" to them all.

These people were present at family gatherings; at table at informal White House dinners; guests at State dinners. They were presented to kings and queens, senators, and Supreme Court justices. They understood much of what was going on, and they were aware of what FDR was saying and thinking—or, at least, what he seemed to be thinking. They were informed and they had access; this made them important people in the nation's capital. They were courted and feted by columnists, ambassadors, and congressmen. Such people as Joseph Kennedy and Felix Frankfurter knew that the way to get a message to FDR was to take it to Missy. Letters which the authors intended to be seen by FDR were routinely addressed to Missy and Grace, and replies from these ladies were taken as expressions of the President's opinion.

As a result these people—Missy, Harry, even the President's telephone operator "Hackie"—became celebrities in their own right, reported on in the gossip columns and news magazines. It was a unique situation. At no other time have the President's personal assistants had such national prominence.

Louis XIV was the center of court life at Versailles. His courtiers left their palaces and chateaux, their families and activities, to devote their lives to the service of the King. Louis devised a complex set of court rules and activities that served to keep his courtiers occupied and himself diverted. Life with Roosevelt was, of course, not exactly like life at Versailles, but certainly there were parallels.

People who entered service with the Roosevelts were like those who ran away to sea—they were lost forever to their family and friends. Missy and Grace Tully devoted their lives to their boss; they were on call at any time, day or night, for dictation or, per-

haps, just quiet conversation. FDR's closest advisors actually
lived with the family—Missy, Harry Hopkins, and Louis Howe.
Howe, who had a wife and children, installed his family upriver
from Hyde Park and saw them only on an occasional weekend.
"They took away my father," his son once complained.[16]
Eleanor's driver and friend, State Trooper Earl Miller, actually
left his wife and came to live on the Hyde Park estate. He was
sued for divorce; his wife charged desertion and named Eleanor
as corespondent. These people did more than work for the Roosevelts; they were swallowed by them.

The life of a staff member in the Roosevelt circle was exciting; it meant participation in important decisions and historic
events, meetings, famous people. It was also great fun; FDR made
certain of that. There were office pools and poker games and
gin rummy by the fire, insider gossip and practical jokes, party
skits and reading aloud. The house was always full of guests.
Many of the world's most interesting, entertaining, or colorful
people visited the Roosevelts to liven up the cocktail hour or
stimulate the dinner table. This was all carried out in an atmosphere that was both corny and sophisticated. The White
House, for the twelve years they were there, had a thoroughly
"lived-in" quality that belonged unmistakably to the Roosevelts.

A point must be made about this happy group surrounding
Roosevelt. He was, in an unspoken way, their master. They
served his every need, responded to his every mood—laughing
when he laughed, staying silent when he frowned. His laughter
rang through the halls. His great head thrown back, he would
exclaim, "I love it! I love it!" He dominated every conversation
with his unending flow of facts and figures, anecdotes and history. He told fascinating stories, and he told them very well.
His people adored listening to them, even if they had heard some
of them many times before.

These people were not of his class or background. Many of
them were not particularly *interesting*, either in terms of experience, intellect, or training. They were, in a sense, trivial
people. FDR, with his subtle, quick mind, his vast range of in-

terests and experiences, could not have found intellectual stimulation or satisfaction from his circle. They were no challenge to him; their job was to be there, and this they did well. They were always available. They were easy to entertain, gaining much of their pleasure simply from being in his presence. They were not, however, in the usual way, friends. Friendship carries with it an implication of sharing, hopes, disappointments, feelings. Roosevelt did not share these things, and so these constant companions could not provide the emotional comfort and support that genuine friendship conveys.

They entertained the President, served him, did his bidding, ran his errands, monitored his calls, scheduled his days, drafted his speeches, and reported on gossip and strategy. They made it possible for this crippled man, seated at his desk, to carry forward his policies and his career. They served to make him an effective force, and so became invaluable to him. Eleanor said, toward the close of her life, in evaluation of the role she had played for FDR in the White House, "I was one of those who served his purpose."[17] And that is what the others did—Tommy and Mac and Hackie and Pa and all the others—they served his purpose. They were not, in the accepted sense, friends. Missy, who was closer to FDR longer than any person outside the family, summed it up when she observed, "He was really incapable of a personal friendship with anyone."[18]

Louis XIV was renowned for the courtesy he extended to his subjects, whatever their rank. Whether addressing a duke or a duke's gardener, the King was unfailingly polite. In fact, so far as the King was concerned, there was but one social distinction of any importance—that of the King himself. And those who were not of royal blood were, in the King's eye, more or less equally inferior and more or less equally deserving. Thus, he was equally courteous to all.

There was, in a sense, something similar to this attitude in Franklin *and* Eleanor's relationship with others. They had been raised in the belief that the Roosevelts were American nobility. To a unique extent they believed in, indeed dedicated their lives to, the public service implicit in the principles of *noblesse oblige.*

Their kindness and courtesy were unfailing: The Roosevelts made no distinctions—all persons were treated with equal interest. Some people—Dean Acheson, for one—were made uncomfortable by this attitude.

While most of Washington's society and politicians looked for opportunities to be received into the Roosevelt circle, not everyone did. Acheson, himself a man of good family and no small ego, remarked that the circle reminded him "of the relationship implied in a seventeenth-century levee at Versailles." Observed Acheson:

> The President could relax over his poker parties and enjoy Tom Corcoran's accordion; he could and did call everyone from his valet to the Secretary of State by his first name and often made up Damon Runyon nicknames for them . . . ; he could charm an individual or a nation. But he condescended. Many reveled in apparent admission into an inner circle. I did not. . . . To me it was patronizing and humiliating. To accord the President the greatest deference and respect should be a gratification to any citizen. It is not gratifying to receive the easy greeting which milord might give a promising stable boy and pull one's forelock in return.[19]

XIII
Sex

I could not help thinking, too, how odd
was the whole arrangement.[1]

—FULTON OURSLER

FRANKLIN D. Roosevelt appears to have been celibate from the age of thirty-six until his death twenty-seven years later. This is an important aspect of FDR that should not be ignored. This celibacy was due in part, but only in part, to his handicap. What effect sexual abstinence had upon FDR's character and behavior is debatable, but that it had an effect cannot be denied.

Man's sexual drive and function are central to his being. If one is to fully appreciate and evaluate a man, what he does and how he thinks, one must know something about his sexual habits and values. John Adams becomes more human in the light of his lifelong love and trust of Abigail, while Thomas Jefferson seems even more elusive when the mystery of his emotional life is explored. Similarly, a knowledge of Roosevelt's sexual life is integral to understanding the man.

Much of the evidence concerning FDR's sexual activity is circumstantial. Some of it is suppositional—the musings of his family and associates after his death. Although the evidence is not overwhelming in support of FDR's celibacy, it is at least significant that there is no piece of evidence, large or small, which counters such a conclusion, while the available evidence clearly suggests it. And a careful analysis of FDR's character and his reaction to his paralysis, considered within the context of his society's view of the handicapped, gives the conclusion overwhelming support. Celibacy is consistent with Roosevelt's denial of his handicap.

When he entered the White House at the age of fifty-one, Roosevelt was healthy, vigorous, and enthusiastic. He was handsome and well built, and his upper trunk, arm, and shoulder muscles were strong and powerful. Although the motor skills of his leg muscles were severely impaired, his sensory perception was normal. Normal, too, was the functioning of his sexual organs. This was acknowledged in veiled fashion in the doctors' report of 1931 on FDR's health. There were, said the doctors, coyly, "no symptoms of *impotentia coeundi.*" Roosevelt was capable of an active sexual life.

FDR had ceased conjugal relations with Eleanor by mutual agreement in 1918. In the 1930s, sexual activity outside marriage was by no means as socially acceptable and, most probably, by no means as common as it is today. Adultery certainly was strongly condemned. Public knowledge of it could wreck a political career. FDR, whose personal values were those of his mother and his headmaster, was no rebel when it came to sexual mores. He was, if anything, more conservative than the standards of the day. He did not approve of the sexual license of others. Did he apply such standards to himself?

Clearly, his children are uncertain whether their father was sexually active. Said James of FDR, "I traveled the world with him and slept in the same room with him at times. From my observation it would have been difficult for him to function sexually after he became crippled from the waist down by polio. He had some use of his lower body and some sensation there, but it was extremely limited."[2] James later told biographer Richard Thayer Goldberg that his father would have been "too embarrassed" to have tried sexual relations.

This sounds odd. FDR was not "too embarrassed" to have risked falling flat on his face as he gave the "happy warrior" speech of 1924. Nor was he "too embarrassed" to have been carried aboard Winston Churchill's flagship, the HMS *Prince of Wales*, at the 1941 Atlantic Conference. FDR was not easily or often embarrassed.

Although Roosevelt's values were those of his mother, his behavior was always his own. So far as his own activity was concerned, FDR was no conformist to other peoples' rules. Throughout his entire life, he did as he wished, whether it was allowed by the rules or not. He married Eleanor in contravention of his mother's wish; contrary to law he commandeered a Navy destroyer to transport his children; he drank liquor on shipboard even though it was against Navy regulations to do so; and, of course, it was FDR who broke the no-third-term tradition. "He lived his life exactly as he wished," Eleanor once remarked.[3] If Roosevelt had desired sexual activity, no perceived difficulty, embarrassment, or conventional morality would have stood in his way.

The closer one gets to the intimate aspects of Roosevelt's life, the sadder one feels. Certainly, the cheerful, socially well-behaved boy became a cheerful, socially well-behaved man. As a child, Franklin was lonely, but uncomplaining; he was the same as an adult. Nevertheless, Roosevelt, the most ebullient and entertaining of men, was afraid of being alone—alone with himself. And he was afraid, too, of fire, of being consumed by the flames that his paralyzed body was helpless to resist.

Roosevelt was dependent on those who had to assist him in the ordinary tasks of daily living. If he dropped his glasses, someone had to fetch them for him. If he wished a book, someone had to get it down from the shelf. He needed help to dress himself. A strong man had to lift him from one place to another. He was, perhaps, even more dependent on a psychological level. People had to be with him at all times to do his bidding and run his errands, but more important they just had to be there to divert him from the strong and powerful feelings that were the inevitable companions of his paralysis. These were feelings of loss, of loneliness, of anger, which he denied, and which he struggled to repress. Perhaps the strongest of these suppressed feelings was his sexual frustration.

It must be emphasized that Roosevelt was not asexual. He was extremely fond of women and they adored him. He carried on, in banter and flirtation, with secretaries, actresses, and princesses. But, aside from his lifelong love of Eleanor, he had but two lasting affairs of the heart. One was with Missy LeHand; the other with Lucy Mercer Rutherfurd.

MISSY LeHAND

From 1921 through the next twenty years, until the end of her life, Roosevelt's most intimate associate and comrade was his private secretary, "Missy" Marguerite LeHand. There is no one word in the English lanugage to describe Missy's relationship with FDR. Perhaps the closest word would be partner; perhaps it would be lover.

In 1922, FDR turned forty; Missy was twenty-three. She was slim, graceful, and five feet seven inches tall. Although not beautiful, she had striking good looks: fair skin, deep blue eyes, dark hair prematurely streaked with gray. She had, said Fulton Oursler, "a lovely throaty voice . . . a strange secret smile composed of cunning and innocence forever baffling."[1] She had an easy and an infectious laugh.

There was a comfortable, easy warmth between these two people. They trusted each other. Their relationship, fun and exciting, was somewhat similar to those in the sophisticated comedies of the 1930s. Dean Acheson, as a young man, accompanied Felix Frankfurter on a spontaneous visit to FDR in the Oval Office. In his memoir, *Morning and Noon*, he catches something of Missy's style with FDR.

> We drove to the police box at the north gate and, to my surprise, the officer let us through despite our absence from his authorized appointment list, since FF was a constant caller. Similarly, the head usher let us in on our assurance that "Missy," as Miss Marguerite LeHand, the President's secretary, was known in the White House, would take care of

us. When she appeared, she was greeted in the future Justice's buoyant style. . . .

"Why, oh why, did this have to happen today?" she complained mournfully. "We're an hour behind schedule; and more coming every minute. I'll tell him and try to keep you out, but this isn't my lucky day. Remember, fifteen minutes and not a second more." She took us into the President's office the back way, through the Cabinet Room. . . . After half an hour Missy LeHand came (back) in.

"You two have got to get out," she ordered. "There's such an uproar going on in here that the customers know he isn't working."

"Five minutes more, Missy," pleaded the President. After ten, she drove us out the way we had come in and sent us home in a White House car.[5]

Fulton Oursler, author of *The Greatest Story Ever Told*, made notes of a White House weekend in 1935. Printed in his memoirs, they give a sense of how Roosevelt and Missy spent their evenings.

Presently we were called to join Missy in the President's upstairs study. She explained that Mr. Roosevelt had gone on a hunting and fishing trip and was expected home around seven-thirty. She was just proposing a drink when suddenly we heard a great hullabaloo at the south entrance right beneath our windows. Looking down we could see a cavalcade of twenty motorcycle policemen and a long train of cars and already we could hear the booming laughter of the President. There never was another laugh like Franklin Roosevelt's. Over the chasm of the years I can hear it now clearly and distinctly—as joyous, hearty, rolling, thunderous laughter as ever was heard on this sorrowful globe.

It was spring twilight in Washington and a red light gleamed up on top of the monument to warn away the aviators, and the birds were chirping sleepily, and through all that serene and lovely scene came that booming laugh of the crippled executive home from his fishing. Presently, we heard the President entering the corridor and a moment later he was wheeled in to us in his chair. Tired as he must have been, he held out his hand in hearty greeting and roared that he was glad to see us again.

Missy explained that we were about to have a drink and he said: "Why not let me mix it?" She said: "Oh, but we are having Martini cocktails." He said: "Oh, no we're not." And by telephone ordered his own fixings. A table was set in front of him with gin, cocktail shaker, and orange juice as he pontificated in high spirits. While mixing the cocktails he told us about the fish he had caught on the spillway—ten trout and a quarter. The quarter he said was a fish two inches long which he named after one of his political enemies, Ham Fish. Then he served the cocktails, which were excellent. But Missy refused them. She insisted on scotch and soda. There was a little tiff between them because she declined his cocktail and he at once offered to make her a Martini. She insisted that she would have the scotch and soda and nothing else.

Looking at her then I thought how lovely she was in the same light blue evening dress which she wore when she had visited our home at Sandalwood. She told us that she did have another dress but that it was at the cleaner's, and laughed very heartily and blushed a little, and the President did not seem to like the trend the conversation had taken.

I could not help thinking, too, how odd was the whole arrangement. The President admitted that he did not know where Mrs. Roosevelt was that night. Here it was near the muggy depths of summer . . . and the President burdened with heavy affairs of state. Yet his only companion was Marguerite LeHand. And what did Marguerite think of that, I wondered. She was young, and attractive, and should have been off somewhere cool and gay on a happy weekend. Yet month after month and year after year she gave up date after date—and she was in the beginning plagued with dates. But a little later she was not asked anywhere very often by people all too willing to understand—here she sat with her knitting, keeping company with a very lonely man, who, so she told me once, was really incapable of a personal friendship with anyone.

Nevertheless the conversation was gay and light. It was clear that Missy had told the President all about her recent visit to Sandalwood and she described our adventures the day before at the Pimlico Race Track when Omaha had won the Preakness and the White House car which had taken her to the race track had broken a crankshaft. The President was complaining about the poker game which he had sat in on the night before; he declared that Vice President Garner had insisted on table stakes and had frozen him out of several hands by betting the entire stack of chips. "I consider this," he said, "the most unsportsmanlike thing I ever heard of and I have no use for such damn poker. I believe there should be a fixed limit. I don't think Garner has any limit on anything."[6]

Missy was a member of the family, recognized as such by all the Roosevelts. Where FDR lived, there lived Missy—whether at Warm Springs, in the governor's mansion, or in the White House. Throughout the business day, Missy was at the President's side. She had control of his schedule; determined what letters and papers crossed his desk; monitored his calls and policed his appointments. She had strong opinions, and she expressed them freely to FDR. Her judgment of character was sound, and FDR paid attention to what she said. When he wrote a letter of which she did not approve, she would hold it back and ask him to reconsider it the following day. It was said of Missy that she knew what the President was thinking even before he had thought it.

When FDR lunched at his desk, she ate with him. When he went for a drive in the afternoon, she would go along. She sat in as the only woman at important political meetings. She hosted many of FDR's political dinners. She invited her guests, he invited his for evening cruises on board the presidential yacht. When bridge was played, they were partners. When he worked on his stamp collection, she sat with him, reading. She thought up ways to keep him amused; she sought out new people who would entertain him. She had no private life to speak of; she had few dates and no love life; for stretches of months and years, she had no home other than her rooms with the Roosevelts. She was loyal; she was trustworthy; she was discreet and perceptive. She was, as Anna remarked, "a very, very astute little girl."[7] Missy and Missy alone called the President "F.D.," and members of Missy's family always believed that, in fact, she loved him very much.

They were, in fact, as intimate as lovers. Biographer Bernard Asbell has performed some interesting calculations. Using family diaries and letters, he has reconstructed Roosevelt's schedule over four of the years of rehabilitation from 1925 through 1928. During this period of 208 weeks, FDR was away from New York for 116 weeks. Of this time Eleanor was with him for 4 weeks, his mother was with him for 2. Missy was with him night and day for 110 weeks.[8] For several years before Roosevelt discovered Warm Springs, he wintered in Florida aboard the houseboat *Larooco*. FDR used the large stateroom; Missy used one of the two smaller staterooms; the other was reserved for guests. They shared a bathroom. For weeks at a time they were the only people living on board. In one of the cottages FDR lived in at Warm Springs, Missy had to walk through his bedroom to get to their shared bathroom. In the governor's mansion at Albany, FDR and Missy had adjoining bedrooms with a connecting door. Eleanor's bedroom was down the hall. At the White House, Missy lived in a suite of rooms on the floor above the President. For twenty years there were many opportunities and enticements to sexual intimacy.

Roosevelt was a bit more open with his intimate feelings with Missy than he was with anyone else. This cannot be surprising as Missy was the only one who had shared with Roosevelt his long convalescence. Although from the first he presented a face of good cheer and confidence to his family and to his guests, he apparently did not always do so with Missy. She was with him in the early years on the houseboat on those cruises to nowhere when nothing worked—neither the muscles of his legs nor the therapies designed to restore them to mobility. Missy saw him then and without his mask, and she saw his struggle to hide his feelings from others. She had confided once to Frances Perkins, "There were the days on the *Larooco* when it was noon before he could pull himself out of depression."[9]

The fact that he did not, maybe could not, hide these intense feelings from Missy made their time on board the houseboat, and their first stays at Warm Springs, very special times for her. "Missy's eyes filled up when on occasions she reminisced about those days," recalled her friend Grace Tully.[10]

Nevertheless, it seems almost certain that FDR was not sexually intimate with Missy. His mother would not have tolerated such an affair under her roof. It would have hurt his wife deeply, and son James certainly would have known about it. Of course, such a liaison would have been very dangerous politically. More than that, it would have threatened Roosevelt's self-image.

It is, of course, impossible to be sure of the particulars; one can only surmise. Each person must cope with being disabled in his or her own way. Nevertheless, the basic facts of Roosevelt's case are common enough. By illness or accident a vigorous, virile, and narcissistic man finds himself a paraplegic. Perhaps, like Roosevelt, he had been successful and popular; admired by men, adored by women. And, perhaps, like Roosevelt, he had always been uncomfortable with naked emotion and feeling. The loss of muscle power is a blow to a man's self-esteem. The strength of the blow is, indeed, fearful. The feelings generated are hard to repress or deny. The man then finds a woman who, by intuition, understands the loss, the pain, the fear. She responds with love, with caring and service. They develop a loving relationship. She learns all the little tricks to help him make his way in social situations—ways to make others feel at ease; ways to make him feel less disabled and dependent by anticipating his requests, knowing his habits. For her it is a career of service, a vocation of love—almost like a nun. And, too often, she is like a nun in another way. There is no physical expression of their love. This becomes the unspoken, unyielding fact of their relationship.

He has been humiliated with the loss of his ability to climb mountains, run races. The impact of his charm and sexual appeal has been severely weakened. His body, once handsome and responsive, is so no longer. He can still make love, but not as before. In the sexual act, he will be vulnerable to hurt and humiliation. More important, and more frightening, is that he will be naked to himself—forced to acknowledge and confront the full extent of his loss and to cope with the fury engendered by that loss. And this some men cannot, will not, do.

Many times, the woman cannot accept this as a condition of the relationship. If she forces the issue, she risks losing all. There are men who have lost a lover rather than confront the truth of their feelings about their disability. There have been other cases, however, in which the woman accepts the terms offered by the man she loves. She represses her carnal desires as the price she must pay to remain with her lover.

And this appears, more or less, to describe the FDR–Missy relationship. They lived in private as they lived in public: entertaining each other, caring for each other, but never risking sexual intimacy. Roosevelt was simply unwilling to confront his feelings. It was not his practice to think unpleasant things. Consistently, throughout his whole life, he simply did not want to know the reality of things he could do nothing about. As he never once complained to his wife or mother about the loss of movement in his legs, so, in the last year of his life, with his health failing rapidly, he never once asked his doctors about the results of their tests of his physical condition.

Missy chose to stay with FDR. She stopped dating and lost interest in other men, for certainly no other man could offer her the life she shared with FDR. Missy came to know kings and queens, newsmakers and movie stars. She was present at most of the extraordinary events, and she took her part in the making of policy during those years of domestic crises and world war. She dedicated her life to the care and well-being of the man she loved. She enjoyed to the hilt the glamour and excitement of life in the White House, but never for a moment did it come ahead of her concern for FDR. She had opposed FDR's acceptance of the nomination for governor in 1928, believing he needed more time for his rehabilitation at Warm Springs. She opposed his acceptance of the third term nomination in 1940, believing he deserved a restful private retirement.

She loved him. They were not intimate, and this cannot have

been easy. The price of a life of repression and denial comes high. Her first nervous breakdown occurred in 1927, when she was twenty-nine, at Warm Springs. FDR was with her, and he monitored her care and treatment. Missy's health failed again in 1931. This time, her treatment seemed to be under the eye of Eleanor, who reported Missy's recovery in letters, day by day, to FDR. In June 1941, Missy's health collapsed totally. At the age of forty-two, she suffered a stroke, and, ironically, now she, too, was paralyzed; her left arm and leg and her speech were affected. She was under medical treatment from then on, at the White House, at Warm Springs, and at her family's home in Somerville, New York. After her stroke, Missy was often despondent, and she attempted suicide at least once. Finally, on the evening of July 30, 1944, she went to the movies to see a newsreel of the failing FDR. She was shocked by his ravaged appearance. She became highly agitated, and she died soon thereafter of a cerebral hemorrhage.

FDR found Missy's stroke and paralysis unbearably painful. Although he did see her from time to time during her last three years, the visits were awkward and of short duration. Roosevelt avoided either seeing or talking with her. And this, too, was completely consistent with his powerful reluctance to confront what he could not change.

So FDR's closest relationship, his most intimate, was to the last unconsummated, even most probably unacknowledged. Missy was, indeed, the lover who was not his lover.

In occupational therapy at Warm Springs, FDR had made by hand a small wooden bookcase. He gave it to Missy in the early days. She treasured it, and in her will she bequeathed it to her beloved niece. FDR, who was to die less than a year after Missy, also left a will. It had been written after Missy's stroke and before her death. In it he directed that up to half the annual income from his estate be used for the payment of Missy's medical bills. On March 27, 1945, as one of his last presidential acts from the White House, he sent a telegram to commemorate the launching of a ship he had ordered named in her honor, the *SS Marguerite LeHand*. In the wire he expressed the hope that "a craft which bears so honored a name will make many a safe journey and always find a peaceful harbor."[11]

LUCY MERCER RUTHERFURD

Lucy Mercer Rutherfurd loved FDR all the days of her life. Although it is doubtful she was ever his mistress, she was certainly always his sweetheart.

After the discovery of their affair in 1918, Roosevelt had agreed to stop seeing Lucy under the terms of the agreement worked out among Eleanor, his mother, and himself. Lucy soon married another man, the older, wealthy Winthrop Rutherfurd. The Rutherfurds had an unremarkable twenty years together. They summered at their New Jersey estate, Tranquility Farms; they wintered at their South Carolina plantation. Theirs was a life of quiet, ease, and comfort. Winthrop died in 1944 after a severe and lengthy illness.

Throughout the years Franklin and Lucy kept in touch with each other, apparently by letter. He saw to it that she was provided with inaugural tickets, and he received her children at the White House. Probably he did not see her again—no one can be sure—until sometime in 1943. By then Missy had had her stroke. She was away from the White House for treatment in Warm Springs and elsewhere. Even when she was back in the White House, Missy was only a shadow of her former self, given to crying attacks and spells of anger. FDR could not bring himself to be with her for any length of time. FDR had lost forever the support of Missy's company. His mother had died, his sons were overseas, and Eleanor was off on her endless travels. It was at this point, with World War II at its most critical juncture in the planning of the invasion of Europe, that FDR resumed seeing Lucy.

Seated with Lucy in the back of a White House limousine, he would drive for an hour through the rolling farm country of Montgomery County or over the shaded, winding lanes of Rock Creek Park. It is said that occasionally Lucy had dinner at the

White House with FDR, and once at tea there he introduced Lucy to his daughter, Anna. On these visits Lucy was accompanied by one or more of her children. These were cheerful, light-hearted social affairs—no more than that.

When Lucy's husband died, Roosevelt had his train stopped in New Jersey, had himself lifted by the Secret Service into a waiting car, and paid a call on her at Tranquility Farms. She gave him a cup of tea. When Roosevelt was attempting to re-cover his failing health at Bernard Baruch's plantation in South Carolina, Lucy drove over to visit, using Baruch's precious ration coupons to obtain the gasoline for the trip. It seems when-ever the President and newly widowed Lucy were together, there were others with them—friends, children, staff, servants. The entire business, Anna protested to biographer Bernard Asbell, was "so open, aboveboard, not hanky-panky or whatever you want to call it."[12]

By 1943, Roosevelt had lost the women who had given him unquestioned love and devotion. These were also the qualities Lucy could offer. She was absolutely uncritical in her adoration of FDR. He was, she wrote in a letter, "one of the greatest men who ever lived—to me the greatest." She wrote in the same let-ter to Anna, after FDR's death, of "the strength of his beloved presence—so filled with loving understanding—so ready to guide and to help."[13] Lucy was content simply to be with Franklin. She did not harry him, as did Eleanor, with unfulfilled commit-ments. She simply sat with him and listened, smiled, and said, "Isn't he wonderful."

Lucy once described a drive with FDR in his little Ford. This was at Warm Springs in 1943, and he had taken her up to his favorite picnic spot, Dowdell's Knob, with its lovely outlook. In FDR's presence she recounted to Anna, "You know, I had the most fascinating hour I've ever had. He just sat there and told me of some of what he regarded as the real problems facing the world now. I just couldn't get over what I was listening to, and then he would stop and say, 'You see that knoll over there? That's where I did this or that,' or 'You see that bunch of trees?' Or whatever it was. He would interrupt himself, you know. And we just sat there and looked."[14]

Roosevelt at Hyde Park in his wheelchair, his dog Fala on his lap. One of two known photographs of FDR in a wheelchair. The little girl is unidentified. (Courtesy of the Franklin D. Roosevelt Library)

This is the second of two known photographs of FDR in a wheelchair. It was taken on the terrace at Hyde Park in September 1937. FDR's doctor, Admiral Ross McIntire, stands in the background holding coat and hat. (Courtesy of the Franklin D. Roosevelt Library)

Roosevelt at Warm Springs in the mid-1920s. Note how he props up his wasted leg with his left arm. Jack Dempsey once said that FDR's shoulder muscles were as powerful as any he had ever seen. (Courtesy of the March of Dimes Birth Defects Foundation)

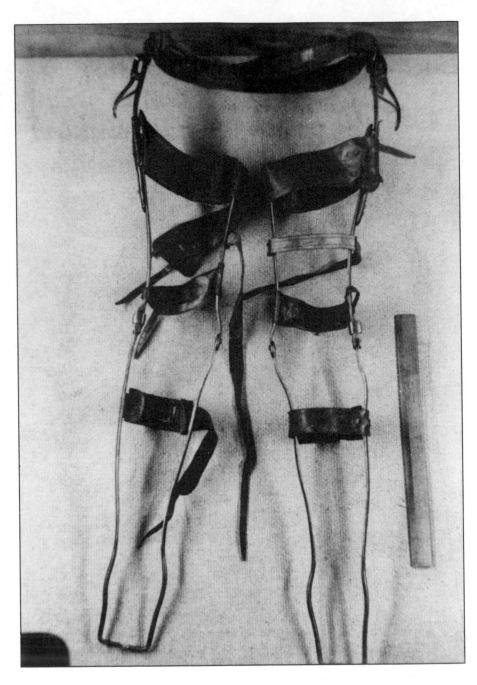

FDR's braces with pelvic band attached. At Warm Springs, Roosevelt stopped using the pelvic band. (Courtesy of the Franklin D. Roosevelt Library)

A picnic at Dowdell's Knob at Warm Springs. The President wears his braces over his trousers, as he often did in private. He sits with a fellow polio on a seat pulled out from the car. Notice the crutches in the background. (Courtesy of March of Dimes Birth Defects Foundation)

FDR works out with other polios at Warm Springs in the mid-1920s. (Courtesy of the Franklin D. Roosevelt Library)

This photograph is said to record the day Roosevelt stood without braces. Clearly, his legs are bearing some weight, but the shoulders of his valet and his doctor appear to carry most of the burden. Nor does it appear he will be standing long—that is his wheelchair directly behind him. (Courtesy of the Franklin D. Roosevelt Library)

FDR hosts presidential candidate John W. Davis (center) at Hyde Park, August 1924. Roosevelt realized that crutches made him appear crippled. He worked long and hard to perfect a technique by which he could appear to walk. By 1928 he had learned to "walk" with long leg braces, using a cane and leaning on the arm of a strong man. (Courtesy of Wide World)

A nicely posed publicity photo. FLR maintains his balance by gripping the strut of the car and leaning on his cane. (Courtesy of the March of Dimes Earth Defects Foundation)

A carefully posed study of Roosevelt with law partner Basil O'Connor at Warm Springs, November 1928. Roosevelt leans back against the door for support and uses his cane to create a tripod. (Courtesy of the Franklin D. Roosevelt Library)

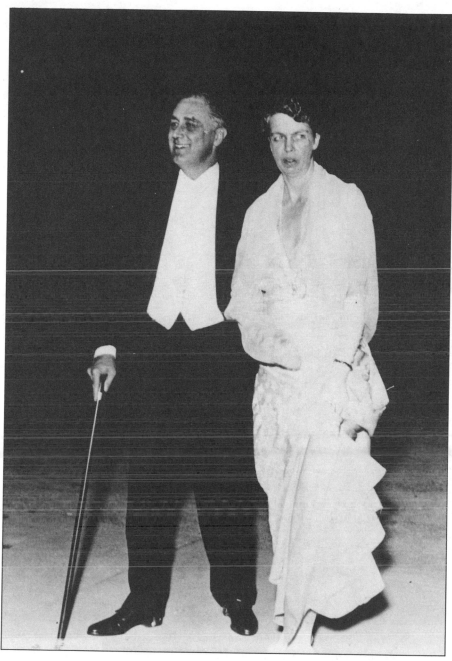

Governor and Mrs. Roosevelt at President Hoover's White House reception. Hoover kept them waiting close to an hour while, "FDR was forced to stand on his braces, gripping Eleanor's arm tightly as his only support. . . . They never forgave Hoover." (Courtesy of the Library of Congress)

FDR enters the lobby of his hotel in Hollywood, September 24, 1932. He walks by leaning alternately on his cane and then the arm of son James, swinging each foot forward in a semicircular arc. FDR thought it important that he and his son should appear relaxed, smiling broadly and trading wisecracks during this arduous progress. James reported that at times FDR gripped his arm so tightly it was bruised. (Courtesy of U.P.I./Bettmann Archive)

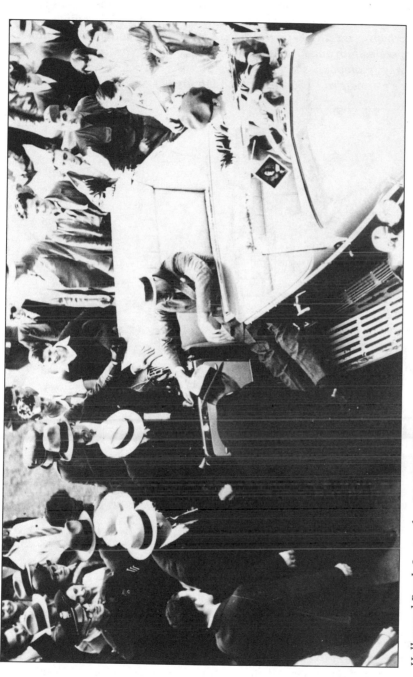

Hollywood Bowl, September 24, 1932: FDR sits on the jump seat of his seven-passenger touring car as a Secret Service man straightens and locks his braces. Son James, his hand resting on the car's back seat, waits to take over as his father's "arm." (Courtesy of Wide World)

These are stills from a home movie taken, perhaps, by family friend Marion Dickerman. The President is being carried ashore by two men, son James on the left, perhaps son FDR, Jr., on the right. According to reporter John Gunther, "outsiders seeing him and his methods of conveyance for the first time were almost always profoundly shocked. . . . The shock . . . of course was greatest of all when he was carried." (Courtesy of the Library of Congress)

"Two men would carry him [FDR] sideways down the companionway. They would hand him over to Captain Brown and the other man . . . who would swing him around into his armchair. . . . Any mis-step or any sudden lurch of the launch . . . ", from the diary of Harold Ickes, Secretary of Interior. (Courtesy of the Library of Congress.)

The President addresses a joint session of Congress. Notice the ramp to the left of the podium, specially constructed for his use. He was probably carried in a standing position up the ramp on the arms of his two military aides. They are wearing white uniforms and are seated, flanking his sturdy leather armchair. (Courtesy of the Library of Congress)

FDR reports to the Congress on the Yalta Conference. "I hope you will pardon me for the unusual posture of sitting down . . . but it makes it a lot easier for me in not having to carry about ten pounds of steel around the bottom of my legs. (Courtesy of the Library of Congress)

Harmony Massage

Shannon Reagan, CMT

2224 J Street
Sacramento, Ca
(916) 541-6767
www.reviveharmony.com

$20 off your first massage!
Option of complimentary hot stones.
(Minimum of one hour)

60 min. - $60 (now only $40)
90 min. - $85 (now only $65)
120 min. - $105 (now only $85)

The President moved in a ramped world. Sometimes the Secret Service would raise the level of an entire street so that FDR could enter a building in the same manner as the other guests. Such was the case at the funeral of Speaker of the House William B. Bankhead in Jasper, Alabama, September 1940. (Courtesy of the Franklin D. Roosevelt Library)

At other times the Secret Service would construct a ramp not just for the President, but for his car, too. This was done in Portland, Oregon, September 1942, when FDR addressed war workers from his open car. FDR is the man in the center car, waving his hat. (Courtesy of the Franklin D. Roosevelt Library)

*Sam Scogna, FDR's tailor, deliberately cut the President's trousers too long;
this was to counter the tendency of pants legs to ride up when the wearer is
seated. This strategy worked well unless, as in this photo with Churchill on
board the USS Augusta, August 1941, FDR was unexpectedly required to put
on his braces and stand for a photograph, in which case the results were
unfortunate. Sam made the pants too long. (Courtesy of the Franklin D.
Roosevelt Library)*

FDR at the first Inaugural. Roosevelt leans on the arm of his son James. Notice that he uses his cane behind his back to stabilize himself. (Courtesy of the Franklin D. Roosevelt Library)

Leonard Baskin's bas-relief of FDR at the first Inaugural, to be placed at the entrance of the FDR Memorial. The cane and the support of son James have disappeared. (Courtesy of the Franklin Delano Memorial Commission)

There would be little to write about this seemingly innocent relationship, were it not for the deviousness with which it was concealed. Anna knew about Lucy and knew of the story, but FDR's sons did not. Eleanor believed, until FDR's death, that he continued to abide by his pledge not to see her. The Secret Service knew of her; so did the White House staff. Hackie, the telephone operator, had instructions to put calls from a Mrs. Rutherfurd through without question or delay. When the President's train stopped on the siding in New Jersey during wartime 1944, the reporters on board were operating under a total news blackout of the President's movements and were unable to report the occurrence. This blackout, considered necessary for security reasons, allowed the President a freedom of movement and activity greater than that given any other modern President—and he used it to see Lucy.

Lucy was present at Warm Springs—actually in the room—when FDR died. She was spirited away before the reporters were called, and it was several years before the public learned of her presence or of her ties with the President. This was so, even though dozens of people knew she was there.

When Eleanor learned of the deception, she was, according to Anna, deeply hurt and very angry. Eleanor's reaction would seem to be inappropriately excessive, considering the relative innocence of the relationship. Eleanor had so many close and loving friends, giving and receiving from them so much love and support, it is difficult to see why she should begrudge her lonely husband his cup of tea with Lucy.

When the question is raised, "Did Franklin have sexual relations with Lucy?" the answer, as in Missy's case, again must be, "Probably not." When their meetings took place in 1943, 1944, and 1945, Lucy had become a "stately . . . person" of "innate dignity," according to Anna.[15] FDR was a sick and exhausted paralytic, charged with the responsibility of leading a great alliance in a great war. In their drives together, she was able to give him a brief respite; some warmth, encouragement, and support; a pat on the arm; a fond remark; and not much more.

Even during the height of their liaison in 1918, there seem to have been no sexual relations. FDR did not seem to be at ease, even then, with such intimacy. At the time Lucy told her close friend Mary Ferrand Henderson there had been "no question of sexual intimacy." By the standards and practices of today this may seem an unlikely assertion. By the standards of 1918, however, given the background and situation of Lucy and Franklin, it could well be an accurate one. Whether or not they made love, the ardor of their caring was intense. Again, according to Mary Henderson, as related to her nephew, "The love of Lucy for Franklin lasted her lifetime."[16]

During the last two years of his life, the President's pleasures were, like his life, subdued. He would take his supper in bed and read a detective story; weekends at Hyde Park, he would have tea with his spinster cousins. He was then carrying responsibility for the world and its future on his shoulders. He could allow nothing to divert him from his task. He needed all the personal strength and support he could muster. Since the death of his mother he sought out and continued the living patterns he had learned from her. There is strength in patterns. He enjoyed and found gentle pleasure in them. He enjoyed the small talk of gardens and weather, pets and relatives—the conversation over the teacups of his mother's era. This was the sort of thing Lucy was able to give him, and he was grateful for it.

In a symbolic sense, FDR had allowed himself to be vulnerable to Lucy in 1918; they had talked of love and need; he had allowed himself to express strong passions. They had risked intimacy, and the result was almost catastrophic—the threatened loss of his marriage, family, and career. In his childhood, strong feelings had been associated with illness. Now, once again, illness in the form of paralysis had followed the passionate expression of strong feelings. Subconsciously, it could be that Roosevelt linked the paralysis as a punishment for the passion. And, of course, with the paralysis there came new powerful feelings, unpleasant, unwelcome ones. These the President repressed. He would not deal with them; he would deny them. To do so he shut down his entire emotional life.

XIV

The March Of Dimes

Call it the March of Dimes.[1]

—EDDIE CANTOR

ROOSEVELT never denied his polio. Although he minimized the extent of his impairment—to himself as well as to others—he always acknowledged it. He had a lifetime interest in the care and treatment of victims of the disease and in research into its cause and cure. As President he was able to further these interests to a quite remarkable extent.

Roosevelt always seemed to know, in his intuitive way, what the mission of the Georgia Warm Springs Foundation should be. It was to be more than a treatment center for polio. It was to be a pioneer, an example for the rest of the country to follow. "You must always remember," he told the patients at Thanksgiving, 1934, "that you who are here   only represent a tiny fraction of the people throughout the land . . . who have infantile paralysis. . . . Even if we were to double in size or quadruple in size, we could treat only a small fraction in this country of the people who need treatment.

"We need to do everything we can to spread the knowledge we are gaining at Warm Springs . . . so that, throughout the country, the facilities for taking care of grown-ups and children who have polio can be vastly improved."[2]

Speaking to a group of surgeons visiting Warm Springs a year later in 1935, FDR summarized: "The important point is that people all over the country know about what we are doing and

145

are following our example in their own communities. My whole objective was to make the country as conscious about polio as it is about TB."[3]

At the time he was elected President, such dreams of a nationwide effort to improve the treatment of polio seemed remote. The country was in the depths of the Great Depression, and Warm Springs was virtually broke. Although professional fund raisers had been employed since 1929, their efforts had been less and less successful as the Depression deepened. Roosevelt's social and corporate friends no longer had the money to give. One wrote to Basil O'Connor thanking him "for the compliment of asking me for $1000. . . . I haven't $1000, and if I did I think there are many cases [at home] that could use a little money very nicely."[4]

O'Connor and the fund raisers were close to shameless in their efforts to get money for Warm Springs, as they were later in their drives for the National Foundation for Infantile Paralysis. Even so, by the summer of 1933, it was clear that a new direction to their efforts was needed. Large givers had all but disappeared. The fund raisers decided, therefore, to shift instead toward a nationwide drive for small contributions from many contributors. President Roosevelt was immensely popular, and they decided to make use of the President's popularity. A New York public relations man named Carl Byoir gets the credit for thinking up the gimmick: a nationwide birthday party for President Roosevelt. A National Committee for the Celebration of the President's Birthday was organized in a great whirl of publicity. Wiley Post, the famed aviator, kicked off the drive by flying from city to city distributing press releases and posters. Local chairmen and local committees were named in every major community. At the beginning, it was difficult to distinguish the polio fund raisers from Democratic Party workers. The ranks of the first drew freely on the ranks of the second. The drive was a thoroughly modern PR blitz, making full use of the usual materials: celebrities, media events, and exploitation of touching photographs of crippled children. On the night of January 30, 1934, President's Birthday Balls were held in cities across the country, including New York, Washington, Chicago, Palm Beach, Cleveland, and Pittsburgh. "This is the happiest birthday I have ever known," said Roosevelt in a radio broadcast to the balls.[5] The effort produced $1,016,443 for Warm Springs.

The Birthday Balls were a splendid idea. They were held annually, and they grew and grew. In 1936, a businessman and presidential friend named George E. Allen took over the planning. He staged a ball in every hotel in Washington, D.C., and one in every major town in the country. It was Allen who thought up the idea of inviting Hollywood stars to come en masse to Washington for the occasion. In 1936, he obtained the services of Jean Harlow, Robert Taylor, and Ginger Rogers. Mrs. Roosevelt, arm in arm with the movie stars, visited each of the gala balls in Washington throughout the night. This, of course, produced spectacular publicity. The movie stars loved it. The following year, some twenty stars arrived, and all were hosted for lunch at the White House by Mrs. Roosevelt.

By 1937, there were over seven thousand balls attended by more than three million Americans. It was that year that Allen, on his way to Hyde Park to present FDR with a check for a million dollars before the newsreel cameramen, had his car break down. He was forced to hitchhike to the occasion. Allen always figured "he was the first hitchhiker in history with a million-dollar check in his pocket."[6]

It soon became apparent to O'Connor—and Roosevelt agreed—that the effort had become too large and too important to be handled informally as an adjunct to the Roosevelt personality. Roosevelt had political enemies, and they were beginning to snipe at Warm Springs. The columnist Westbrook Pegler wrote that the Roosevelt family was profiteering from the Warm Springs operations, and Georgia Governor Gene Talmadge charged that Warm Springs was "just a racket, being disguised under the guise of charity by the President."[7] Roosevelt did not want the fight against infantile paralysis to become the object of political attack.

And so, on September 23, 1937, FDR announced the creation of the nonpartisan National Foundation for Infantile Paralysis.

In setting up the Foundation, Roosevelt outlined an ambitious program of research, education, and care. "The general purpose of the new Foundation will be to lead, direct, and unify the fight on every phase of this sickness."[8] It is an extraordinary fact that, despite controversy and error, this is exactly what the Foundation accomplished during its lifetime. The president of the Foundation would be Basil O'Connor. The Foundation had a Board of Trustees made up of immensely wealthy men of both parties who had agreed to serve at the personal request of the President. These included Jeremiah Millbank, Edsel Ford, Marshall Field, Averell Harriman, Edward Stettinius, James Forrestal, and Thomas Watson. Local committees were set up in each of the nation's more than three thousand counties.

The first ball in 1934 had been so successful that $100,000 of the proceeds was to be set aside to develop polio treatment programs in places other than Warm Springs. In 1935, it was decided that 70 percent of the money raised would remain in the communities in which it was raised, to be used to benefit polio victims and to improve treatment facilities.

O'Connor and Roosevelt hoped that with the continued success of the national fund-raising effort there would now be money available to fund research. This was a controversial matter. An early, amateurish research effort funded by the Birthday Balls had killed six children and generated much harmful publicity. O'Connor was determined that the new National Foundation under his direction would never again risk lives through improper research. To this end he created panels of outstanding doctors and scientists to review all policies and all grant proposals for the Foundation. He and Roosevelt were insistent, however, that full and total control of the Foundation remain in the hands of laymen.

The Foundation was an organization of volunteer citizens. They raised money from their neighbors to fund the fight against a common health hazard. Scientists and doctors would be funded to search for treatment and cure, but they would not be in charge of the Foundation. This extraordinary policy received much attention, a lot of it critical. Even more extraordinary, however, was O'Connor's announcement that the Foundation intended to fund to the fullest extent possible the high cost of patient treatment. Roosevelt had set up a patients' aid fund at Warm Springs from the very first days. He said, "I wouldn't want anyone to be sent away for lack of money."[9] As explained to the families of polio patients, the Foundation was conceived as an organization of neighbors. All the neighbors would be asked to contribute to a common fund. This would be kept ready and available for the use of anyone in the neighborhood struck by polio. The local Foundation would provide financial help to meet the costs of patient care. And it would do so on an as-needed basis, without requiring a means test. The cost of medical care for a severe case of polio was high and the treatment was long and drawn out. Maintenance of a patient in an iron lung was an extremely expensive procedure. The Foundation did not require a polio family to sell off all its assets before providing assistance. It was enough that a family confront paralytic polio; proof of financial ruin was not also required. Conservative medical opinion found this policy to be a dangerous precedent—perhaps even communistic in concept.

Because of the publicity surrounding the Foundation's creation and the great attention given to its program, there quickly developed a huge demand for its services. At that time many cases of polio went undiagnosed because of medical ignorance, and many diagnosed cases went untended because of fear and poverty. Many hospitals were unwilling to take polio patients. Some were willing, but not equipped to do so. Many doctors knew very little about the treatment. Polio-trained nurses and therapists were in short supply. Now that the Foundation intended to pay the cost of needed care, the requests for care increased dramatically.

To begin meeting this demand, the Foundation established various fellowship programs for doctors and scientists. An early beneficiary of such a program was Jonas Salk, later to be a developer of the polio virus vaccine. Training programs were established to teach hospital personnel the latest methods of polio patient care. Treatment centers were endowed in central hospitals. Later, regional respiration centers were set up for patients with severe breathing impairment.

The growth of the National Foundation was quite without precedent. Roosevelt had declared that "the whole attack on this plague should be led and directed, though not controlled, by one national body."[10] The Foundation was, indeed, a national body, but it was also a private organization without access to government funds. How was this national effort to be financed?

The Birthday Balls never raised much more than a million dollars in any one year. Over half of this money had been left in the communities in which it was raised, and most of the rest had gone to finance the operation of Warm Springs. Clearly, the Birthday Ball effort would not be sufficient to finance the Foundation and its work. Said O'Connor in 1937, "This is going to have to be more now than a one-day party. . . . I don't know how much it is going to take, but it's going to take millions."[11]

FDR, like his wife, was never hesitant about investing his name and position in the service of a good cause. The President remained an immensely popular man. Eddie Cantor, the radio and vaudeville entertainer, suggested that an appeal be made, asking people to send money to FDR in the White House to be used in the fight against polio. "Call it the March of Dimes," said Cantor. O'Connor asked the President's secretary to check with FDR and "see if he'll stand for it." FDR reportedly said, "Go ahead."[12] Cantor took his appeal to the radio waves; so did the Lone Ranger. Soon the stars of radio and Hollywood added their names to the public appeal.

The response at first was minimal; a mere trickle of dimes. The President's press secretary, Marv McIntyre, complained to George Allen, "You fellows have ruined the President; all we've got is $1,700.50. The reporters are asking us how much we've got. We're telling them we haven't had time to count it." In desperation, the Foundation officials suggested that listeners be asked to send their dimes to the local Foundation chapter rather than the White House. McIntyre took this suggestion to the President, only to report back, "The damage is done; the President has got his Dutch up and insists he'll see it through." The following day the response began. Twenty-three bags of mail arrived. On an average day the White House received 5,000 letters. That day it received 30,000; the following day, 50,000; the day after, 150,000. The White House was buried under an avalanche of mail. The President's assistants were in the basement opening letters; the President's children were helping; WPA artists and writers were brought in to help count. In the deluge, official correspondence was lost; invitations, RSVPs never found. The White House mail chief reported, "The government of the United States darn near stopped functioning." But according to the Foundation's public relations director, "The President was just tickled pink."[13]

In seven years the amount of money raised through the March of Dimes and associated efforts increased the revenues of the National Foundation by over a thousand percent. In 1938, 1.8 million dollars had been collected; in 1945, 18.9 million dollars had been raised. These were huge sums in terms of the value of the dollar of the day. They were raised by using every available means—every trick of advertising, every public relations gimmick. Not surprisingly, the nation became exceedingly conscious of infantile paralysis. Roosevelt had said he wanted to make "the country as conscious about polio as it is about TB." And he had most certainly succeeded. It is not surprising that the number of reported polio cases climbed rapidly. Parents were now universally on the lookout for polio symptoms; doctors were ever on the alert to make a positive diagnosis. The country became polio-conscious to a degree close to hysteria.

After World War II, the Foundation undertook a massive research effort seeking the development of an anti-polio virus vaccine. As progress was made, O'Connor stepped up the effort. With monomaniacal drive he pursued the research and the fund raising necessary to support it. In the early 1950s, the Foundation raised over fifty million dollars a year. Even these immense sums were not enough, and O'Connor authorized the Foundation to go into debt to finance the final push necessary to prove and produce the serum. The program, of course, was successful. Because of Franklin Roosevelt, the great administrative skill of Basil O'Connor, and the continuing generosity of the American people, infantile paralysis was conquered.

Without Roosevelt, it would not have been done—not then, perhaps not ever. It was done by voluntary contributions, not by government intervention. Because it was done then, there have stemmed from it a vast array of achievements in virology and associated fields to the incalculable benefit of man.

XV

"HI, HO, SILVER!"

Hi, ho, Silver![1]

—FRANKLIN D. ROOSEVELT

ROOSEVELT was never able to spend much time at Warm Springs after his return to elective office. It was always his intent to have a couple of weeks in the spring and a couple of weeks in the fall at his cottage on the Foundation, but duties and obligations elsewhere usually ate into this schedule. In 1941, he spent but one night at Warm Springs, and in the war year 1942, he did not go to Georgia at all. This was the only year he missed, however, and in 1944, he was there for three weeks in the fall, and returned again in the spring of 1945.

The fact that he was not often physically present does not mean that he had less interest in the operation of the Georgia Warm Springs Foundation. He continued to oversee the formulation and direction of Foundation policy until the day he died. He ran Warm Springs in much the same way he ran the government or World War II. He worked *through* others. He sought out energetic people who were good at what they did, and he let them do it, giving them full support and encouragement, yet retaining for himself the direction and ultimate responsibility for what was done. The affairs of Warm Springs he placed in the hands of three persons: Fred Botts, Registrar; C. E. Irwin, M.D., Chief Surgeon; and Basil O'Connor, Treasurer.

Botts, one of the original patients and severely paralyzed, handled admissions policy. After Warm Springs received worldwide recognition, the number of polios seeking admission was always much larger than the Foundation could possibly handle. Botts could be relied upon to be judicious and evenhanded in his selections. Admissions, like everything else at the Foundation, were always under FDR's control. A call from him or from Missy would, of course, cause Botts to provide immediate entrance for the patient endorsed by the President. Botts always had access to FDR, either by mail or in person. They saw eye-to-eye on the kind of place Warm Springs should be. Botts was, in a sense, guardian of the Warm Springs spirit. He reported to the President the patient's view of what went on. So long as Botts represented the interests of the patients, Roosevelt could be sure the patients would retain their preeminence. Unfortunately, after FDR's death, Botts lost his job and the patients lost their preeminence as Warm Springs was taken over by professional medical administrators, who turned it into an institution like any other.

Dr. Irwin and his wife were valued friends of the President. Irwin, able and intelligent, was dedicated to the treatment of polios, his commitment unsullied by personal ambition. He understood and accepted completely FDR's rationale about Warm Springs. With him, FDR had the medical building and surgical theater built, and developed treatment policy. Irwin, like Botts, gained authority because it was general knowledge that he was close to FDR.

Basil O'Connor had been FDR's law partner. He was a shrewd handler of money and a very able administrator. When Roosevelt reentered public life he turned over the principal administrative and financial responsibilities of Warm Springs to O'Connor. He raised the money, paid the bills, set salaries. He was contentious, hard-driving, and tough. Roosevelt practiced consensus politics; O'Connor did not. Many people disliked him intensely. But he was efficient and he was Roosevelt's man.

O'Connor, Irwin, and Botts kept Roosevelt informed. Even through the war years, the President personally received weekly reports on patient admittance, incidence of paralysis, and geographical breakdown. He reviewed financial reports. He worked on and approved construction plans and alterations of policy. Research articles on polio and its treatment were referred to him. He received the monthly mimeographed patients' newsletter, and Missy dutifully and regularly sent one dollar to pay for FDR's subscription to the local paper. A flood of correspondence with Warm Springs regulars, in addition to Botts's and Irwin's letters and O'Connor's reports, kept FDR up to date on the gossip he loved. From the White House, Roosevelt presided over Warm Springs as an absent lord of the manor. Warm Springs received every benefit that presidential attention can bestow.

The Navy built the Foundation's east wing under the terms of a deal approved by Roosevelt. Patronage jobs for various citizens of Meriwether County were arranged by Missy at FDR's behest. Draft deferral requests for essential medical personnel were routed through the Oval Office. The local post office, school district, and town hall received the benefit of his interest. During the war, a troop of sixty marines was based at Warm Springs ("Camp Roosevelt") to provide security during presidential visits. The marines also did odd jobs and favors around the Foundation and livened up the social life of the female patients.

When Roosevelt was governor, he had commissioned architect Toombs to design a permanent cottage at Warm Springs for himself. It was already apparent then that FDR was a presidential candidate, and Toombs designed a rather formal house as befits a President, replete with an octagonal sitting room. Roosevelt would have nothing to do with such pretensions. Working with Toombs, he planned a simple, almost spartan cottage. The building was completed in May 1932, and it served the President as a vacation retreat until his death in 1945. It was known to the world as "The Little White House."

The white clapboard cottage with green shutters was set on the side of a hill facing west. It was deep in the woods under the dappled light of the tall Georgia pines. It was a one-story structure in the style of the other buildings at Warm Springs designed by Toombs. The columned front porch opened onto a small entry hall. This, in turn, opened onto a large living room-dining room area. Full windows on the west wall reached to the floor, and French doors opened onto a porch. This served as a sun deck, receiving sun for more than half the day. The view from the deck of the Pine Mountain ridge and the valley between was gentle and pleasing. To the left of the living room was the President's small bedroom, with a connecting bath to his wife's bedroom. To the right of the living room was a bedroom for the use of Missy LeHand.

The house was paneled throughout with siding made from the local pine wood. It was decorated in the typical Roosevelt way with furniture and effects accumulated over time from here and there. His mother gave him a set of rustic chairs and a table for the deck. The dining-room table and chairs came from Eleanor's Val-Kill furniture shop on the grounds of Hyde Park. The rugs were hand-hooked mementos presented to him by admirers. The paintings and decorations were mostly nautical: ship models, engravings of yachts, and a painting of John Paul Jones. The house contained numerous examples of the odd but folksy gifts Americans liked to give their President. The effect was comfortable, random, and a bit shabby.

FDR's bedroom was spartan. His narrow single bed was covered with a chenille spread. There was a rag rug on the floor, a bedside table, and a wooden chair made for him by workers in one of the New Deal programs. That was all.

About the house there was a sense of comfortable confidence and a simple good taste—which again is typically Rooseveltian. Clearly, the man who lived here had no need for, nor indeed any interest in, the pretentious or the fashionable.

The kitchen had no refrigerator, only an icebox. It was no more than the average kitchen of its day, and it was presided over by Roosevelt's cook and maid, Daisy Bonner. She worked full time for Dr. and Mrs. Irwin, and FDR or Missy would dutifully write before their visits to inquire if Daisy would be available and if the Irwins could spare her for the President. Daisy introduced FDR to such southern specialties as Brunswick Stew and Country Captain. She was a great favorite of FDR and she was in the house at the time of his death. With a pencil she wrote on the kitchen wall, "Daisy Bonner cooked the first meal and the last one in this cottage for the President Roosevelt."

The house, of course, was built with Roosevelt's handicap in mind. The bathroom was designed to be accessible for the wheelchair. The toilet and bathtub were elevated specially for FDR's use. There were no doorsills or steps. The telephone was equipped with a twenty-five-foot wire and could be plugged in to any of seven jacks. This arrangement, unusual for its day, allowed the President to have a phone by his side wherever he might be.

When the President was in residence, a hand-controlled car was kept parked at the front door so that it was available for his use at any time. The car (with its license plate FDR-1) was owned by the Foundation, which paid the insurance and taxes. Botts drove it when the President was not in residence. FDR had an agreement with the Secret Service that allowed him a certain freedom of movement at Warm Springs. The Service protected the *entire* twelve hundred acres of the Foundation. When the President was there, no one could leave or enter the Foundation without passing through the Secret Service checkpoints. The entire Foundation was secured. This meant that on the Foundation grounds, the President was free to come and go as he wished, to drive himself to the various cottages, the Foundation buildings, or along the wooded trails without notifying anyone and without Secret Service escort.

Roosevelt loved driving and the freedom it gave him. Correspondent and pool White House reporter Merriman Smith remembered a day he was riding horseback along one of the Foundation's trails. FDR passed him, driving alone in his little convertible Ford with the top down. As the President drove out of sight, Smith distinctly heard him cry out in that familiar FDR voice, "Hi, ho, Silver!"[2]

The President's privacy and freedom of movement within the Foundation were retained—but not without much struggle against a zealous Secret Service. "I certainly do not want a high wire fence around the Warm Springs cottage!" FDR told the Secret Service in a 1933 memo. If the Secret Service insisted upon some sort of a fence, the President suggested one "placed at least 100 feet away and running down into the ravine, down the bottom of the ravine, and up the other side. . . . I will draw you a picture of where it should go if you want it," he finished help-fully.[3]

These security arrangements meant that the Foundation was off limits for the working press. Roosevelt was the most accessible of modern Presidents. His great popularity was in part dependent upon maintenance of good relations with reporters assigned to the White House. Accordingly, a tradition was soon established with the pool reporters at Warm Springs. On his afternoon drive, the President would swing by the main gate of the Foundation, where the reporters and photographers would be waiting. He would banter with them for a few minutes, tell them what he had been doing, and make what comment he wished on the news of the day.

The regular White House reporters came to love Warm Springs almost as much as did FDR. They made the little hotel their headquarters and eventually came to know everyone in town. FDR, master politician that he was, took an active interest in the local politics. And soon the reporter regulars also began to take an interest: they gave the mayoral candidates advice, both sought and unsought; they staged rallies on the candidates' behalf; and occasionally they made wagers with the President on the election results.

Roosevelt always tried to be present at Warm Springs for Thanksgiving, when a banquet was held to commemorate the founding of the Foundation. All the patients, the staff, reporters, and Secret Service employees participated. The President sat at the head of the table and made a great show of carving the turkey. After the pumpkin pie, skits were staged, and songs were sung. FDR was always in top form. He would give an after-dinner talk filled with jokes, and anecdotes, and reminiscences of the early days at Warm Springs. And at the end of the evening he sat at the door and shook the hand of every person present.

These occasions seemed to mean a great deal to him, as well they might. The Georgia Warm Springs Foundation was his creation. These people were benefiting from it and responded by clearly showing their love for him. It is a commonplace that a politician needs love and attention more than most men. And one of the problems of politics is that displays of love and attention are not that easy to obtain. The affection Roosevelt received at Thanksgiving at Warm Springs was of a magnitude that made it quite special.

It has been said that his polio was FDR's "log cabin." His paralysis softened the handsome patrician, made him approachable, more human. His physical weakness was something people of every class could understand. At some level of consciousness, perhaps, FDR's paralysis served him as a link with ordinary men and women.

In his early days at Warm Springs, Roosevelt had been able to explore and develop this link. His first car was a secondhand, open, Model-T Ford. John Rhile, a local blacksmith, and FDR rigged a set of primitive hand controls. Seated behind the wheel, usually alone, FDR would drive the dusty back roads of Meriwether County. "Hiya, neighbor," he would call as he passed a farmer and his wagon on the way to town. If he saw someone in a front yard, he would pull up for a chat. He would give a lift to anyone, black or white, trudging along the road. He would drive the three miles to Manchester, pull up in front of the drugstore for a cooling soda and syrup, and chat with passersby. FDR talked money with the local banker, county politics with the newspaper editor, weather and crops with the farmers. He even drank home brew with the moonshiners down in the Cove. He developed a wide asssortment of friendships in this depressed rural Georgia county.

Roosevelt was at home in Georgia; he loved his new friends and they adored him. In his four presidential elections he swept Meriwether County with margins approaching fifty to one. After he became President, his freedom of movement was restricted by the Secret Service. He continued to take his drives, but the county people were hesitant to approach the car of the President of the United States and, if they tried, the unfamiliar found their way blocked by burly agents. FDR was a skillful driver, and he knew more about these back roads than did the Secret Service drivers. Once in a while, even as President, he was able to shake his escorts and drive off into the country.

Roosevelt seemed to obtain genuine support from the friendliness of the people he met around Warm Springs. From them he learned firsthand what hardship was like in the Deep South Depression. From observation he learned about marginal farming practices, subsistence living conditions, and race relations. In his car he could move where he wished and be alone with his thoughts.

His favorite run was along the crest of Pine Mountain, stopping at Dowdell's Knob, a rocky outcropping with a splendid view over the river valley. The Knob was the site of many a famous FDR picnic. On his last visit to Warm Springs, in April 1945, he was exhausted and dying, too weak and shaky to drive his own car. Roosevelt had himself driven to Dowdell's Knob, and there he sat alone for two hours looking out across the lands he loved. Even that last time at the Knob, he was not really alone. It was wartime, and immediately below the brow of the hill, combat marines with bayonets drawn, shoulder to shoulder, ringed the hillside, protecting their leader.

During the presidential years, Roosevelt's patterns of activities at "The Little White House" were not much different from what they had ever been before. He would breakfast in bed, swim and exercise in the morning, take a nap and a drive in the afternoon. And at night he would have informal cocktails and dinner with a pick-up group of friends, neighbors, and staff.

There were visits back and forth between the cabins and always a splendid picnic. The President in his wheelchair would visit the patients. Now and then he would dine with them, or have a hand of bridge in Georgia Hall, the center of Foundation activities.

FDR was a man of comparatively simple tastes: He liked old clothes, country cooking, and corny jokes. He was no Thomas Jefferson, and neither a scholar nor an intellectual in the usual sense of the word. He had a magpie mind, and many interests, but he was not deep. He was more intuitive than rational in his thinking. His correspondence is preponderantly trivial. He reveled in gossip, small talk, martinis, and murder mysteries. These he enjoyed at Warm Springs.

Dr. Stuart Raper, then a young doctor, recalls an occasion when the President drove himself to a party—for some reason without his wheelchair. He simply swung with his arms to the ground and bumped his way, legs dragging behind him, up the path and into the cottage. This was an unusual way to navigate, even for Warm Springs. At Warm Springs, paralyzed legs were the norm, and Roosevelt was free to do as he wished. Even so, people who saw the President of the United States dragging his inert body across the ground have not forgotten it to this day.

Once, much earlier in his rehabilitation, Roosevelt miscalculated and did a stunt like this around people who were not as comfortable with the handicapped condition as were those at Warm Springs. The occasion was a dinner given by the Charles Hamlins, family friends. As recorded by Mrs. Hamlin, "He [FDR] was carried into a seat at the dining-room table. He told the men not to return until 9:30. We wondered how he would spend the evening—probably staying in the dining room. Though when dinner was over, Franklin pushed back his chair and said, 'See me get into the next room.' He dropped down on the floor and went in on his hands and knees and got up into another chair by himself. My husband was so overcome at such courage and seeing that superb young fellow so pleased at being able to do this, that on the plea of hearing the telephone he went into his den for a while. . . ."[4] Mr. Hamlin's reaction was precisely the sort of emotion that would have destroyed FDR's career as a politician. Pity is political poison.

As President, Roosevelt always had to be on guard against such occasions, and only at Warm Springs could he relax his guard a bit.

XVI
War

Our greatest War President.[1]
—HENRY STIMSON

An extraordinary effort . . . of willpower over physical infirmity.[2]
—WINSTON CHURCHILL

The Japanese bombed Pearl Harbor on Sunday, December 7, 1941.

That night, Washington was cold and misty, the moon hidden by ragged clouds. In the evening, a crowd numbering more than a thousand people gathered along the Lafayette Square side of Pennsylvania Avenue. Stunned by the news, these people stood silently, watching the official cars—cars bearing generals and admirals, congressmen and senators—move in and out of the White House gates. All night long some two to three hundred persons stood outside the gates as a sort of civilian sentry, while inside the President slept. FDR was awakened early on Monday, after but five hours' sleep. Reports of events and, even more alarming, rumors of events flooded in to the President. Squadrons of Japanese planes were reported flying over San Jose, California. Rumors had it the Japanese intended to bomb Southern California, as they had Pearl Harbor the day before. FDR recieved these messages and more. From his desk in the Oval Office, he was issuing the orders and directives necessary to place the United States in mobilization for total war. Roosevelt was now Commander-in-Chief.

Shortly after eleven, FDR was rolled in his wheelchair back to the family quarters on the second floor of the White House. There, in his bedroom, he was helped onto his bed by his valet, Arthur Prettyman. The valet lifted FDR's legs from the floor and straightened them full-length upon the bed. He removed the President's trousers, untied his shoes, and removed them as well. With the dexterity that comes from practice, he strapped the President's legs into their long-leg braces. These stainless steel calipers had shoes affixed to them, with straps at the knees and the thighs. The mounting of the shoe to the brace was rigid, and this made it rather difficult to ease the lifeless foot of the paralyzed limb into the shoe. Once this was accomplished, however, it was an easy matter to strap the restraining pad over the kneecaps and to buckle the thigh bands. Prettyman took care that the knee pads were properly adjusted—if too tight, they would cause the wearer pain when the brace was straightened; if too loose, the flexed knee might pull the heel out of the shoe when the wearer was in a standing position. As always, the President's shoes were black, his socks were black, and the metal parts of the brace were painted black. This arrangement was intended to camouflage the fact that the President was dependent upon leg braces. Once the braces were affixed, Prettyman skillfully helped the President into a pair of striped pants: each trouser leg had to be carefully worked over the foot and the right angle juncture of the heel and brace. Prettyman rolled the President to the left and back again to the right, easing the trouser leg up over the braces. Once the pants were up, Prettyman pulled the President to a sitting position. With Prettyman lifting the heavy, braced legs, the President was able to heave his trunk back into the wheelchair. Again, with Prettyman's help, he donned his cutaway coat and made ready to leave for the Capitol.

Roosevelt was quite capable of dressing himself. With ingenuity and practice, the paraplegic learns how. Dressing, however, can never be as easy and unconscious a business as it is for the nonhandicapped. It can be done from a wheelchair, but it takes effort, thought, and time. Roosevelt, like any other polio or, indeed, like any other person, had limits to his energy and his strength. He was routinely lifted in and out of bed, in and out of cars, dressed, bathed, and toweled. He stood on his feet only in public, for speeches, receptions, and military reviews. He walked as best he could, whenever walking was required and unavoidable. Over the seven years of his rehabilitation, FDR had shown that he had fully as much motivation to be independent as any other polio. However, he had been raised in a world where butlers, valets, and nannies were available to assist in the monotonous tasks of daily life. Now, as President, faced with virtually unlimited demands upon his energy and interests, he chose not to waste his limited muscle power on things like dressing.

Inside the south portico of the White House, the President stopped his chair. Colonel Starling, head of the White House Secret Service, straightened the President's leg braces, locking them at the knee. Starling and Roosevelt's son James, now a Marine Corps colonel, lifted FDR to a standing position. He stood for a moment at the door, leaning heavily on the arm of his son, his old naval cape draped over his shoulders. Then, walking slowly on James's arm, using the cane as he had learned to do at Warm Springs, with Eleanor at his side, he moved toward the limousine. At the car door he turned away from the car, moved a step backward, buckling at the hips so that he would fall in a sitting position upon the jump seat of the car. Starling unlocked the stiff braces, and the President scooted backward onto the backseat with his strong arms and trunk muscles. Eleanor and James sat beside him, two Secret Service agents faced him on the jump seats with loaded Tommy guns; another armed agent sat next to the chauffeur. After the doors were shut, the car circled the south lawn and moved out of the White House gates at 12:10 p.m.

The President's closed car was flanked on each side by open Secret Service cars. In each were four agents armed with sawed-off shotguns. On each running board were three more agents armed with .38-caliber service revolvers. Security was exaggeratedly heavy because rumors and fears were rife. After the shock of Pearl Harbor, the Secret Service did not know what to expect.

The cavalcade moved swiftly down Pennsylvania Avenue, past military sentries and Metropolitan Police guards stationed along the way. In 1917, when President Wilson had passed along the same route to ask the Congress for a Declaration of War, the streets were thronged with people—merry people excited by the supposed glamour of battle. On this dreary December day in 1941, there was no such joy. The crowds were sparse and silent as the President's car sped by. Americans had seen this war in the newsreels, had heard it on the radio. They knew what it was about. On Capitol Hill the building itself was heavily secured. Marines stood with fixed bayonets at every entrance. The building was ringed by over two hundred fifty local policemen and Secret Service agents. Within the building, a secondary line of Capitol Police stood guard. The building was closed to the public; the great rotunda stood empty.

In the House chamber every seat was taken. The House of Representatives was present, as was the Senate. Along the front row sat the members of the Supreme Court of the United States. Also seated in the front row were the Joint Chiefs of Staff in military uniform. The atmosphere on the occasion of a joint session is usually one of excitement and good humor, with much cheerful bonhomie. But the excitement was muted on that day.

The President's motorcade moved into the Capitol plaza. His own car, followed by a Secret Service car, pulled up to the ground-floor entrance under the great staircase of the south wing away from the eye of the public. The President's chair was brought up from the car behind, and Secret Service agents lifted him into it. Mrs. Roosevelt left the party and was escorted by elevator to the Executive Gallery where she greeted her guest, Mrs. Woodrow Wilson. Roosevelt had asked particularly that the widow of the wartime President be present.

The President's wheelchair, pushed by Colonel Starling, moved up and into the building on the ramp built for his use in 1933. He was followed by son James carrying the speech typed by Grace Tully, bound in a three-ring looseleaf notebook such as students use. The President waited in the Speaker's Room, a chamber just off the House floor. At the word that all was ready, Starling again bent down, seized first one and then the other of the President's legs, throwing them forward, locking the braces firmly into their extended position. With James, he pulled the 190-pound man to his full six-foot-three standing position.

The doorkeeper called out his famous, "Mister Speaker, the President of the United States." The doors to the House chamber were thrown open, and the President, leaning heavily on Jimmy, moved slowly down the side aisle to the Speaker's podium. Jimmy had been at his father's side at the very first public speech after polio, the 1924 "happy warrior speech." He had been at his father's side on many other occasions. He had walked his father to the podium for the first inaugural, for the second inaugural, and for the third. No one in the world knew better how to provide the stability and strength FDR needed; and likewise, nobody in the world understood the importance of appearing to do it smoothly and effortlessly.

On December 8, 1941, Franklin Roosevelt came to the House chamber to ask the Congress for a Declaration of War, a declaration that the United States would lead its allies in a great global confrontation with the enemy. Implied in this declaration would be an unspoken, but vital, pledge of loyalty to Roosevelt as the leader of this great and mighty effort.

The nation's economy had been crippled when FDR assumed the presidency in 1933; now, as he moved to assume the awesome powers of wartime Commander-in-Chief, the nation's military authority seemed humbled and helpless; its great Pacific fleet was at the bottom of Pearl Harbor. As his inaugural address, "Nothing to fear . . . ," had brought the confidence of recovery, so this speech must instill the confidence of victory.

After he had polio, FDR never took an easy step. Each step was an effort, painful, requiring concentration and balance. A false or hasty move would cause him to lose his balance and fall. Slowly, carefully, steadily, Roosevelt moved down the aisle and, with the constant steadiness of son James, to the podium just below the Speaker's chair.

Roosevelt had many things to think about that morning: present defeat and ultimate victory; mobilization; alliances; the organization of an all-out effort unequaled in history. But his uppermost thought at the moment was that he get one braced foot after the other in the right position; that he hold his balance over his hips and pelvis just so; that he shift his great shoulders forward, left, and right just so; that he not fall down. This concentration caused him to break out into a sweat as, indeed, it always did.

Once at the podium, the President grasped the sides of that firm platform, held himself at his tallest, most direct stature; then with firm voice and steady gaze, he began, "Yesterday, December 7, 1941—a day which will live in infamy ..."[3] As they followed his speech on their radios in their homes and offices, the entire nation had confidence in the leadership of their President.

Old Justice Oliver Wendell Holmes had said of FDR once in an oft-quoted comment, "Second-rate intellect, first-rate temperament."[4] Now, with the nation at war, that first-rate temperament met its supreme test.

At Warm Springs, "Doctor Roosevelt" created a rehabilitation therapy and treatment center that changed inalterably the role of the handicapped in society. He always knew what to do next, how to make things happen. Able to motivate others to action, he always retained ultimate control himself.

As peacetime President, Roosevelt called himself "Doctor New Deal." In the White House, the doctor's practice had been much the same as at Warm Springs. He motivated not just the young New Dealers who flocked to Washington, but the Congress, the press, and the nation. And again he was able to get people to act and to get things done. With a sharp instinct he made use of the available economic therapies of the day, keeping what was useful, throwing out what was not.

Intuitively he knew what to do next. During the breathtaking first days of his administration, after Congress, in less than a week, had overhauled and restructured America's banking system, FDR sat back one day and said, "Now it's time for beer."[5] And although Prohibition was still the law of the land, Congress authorized 3.2 beer the next day, virtually by acclamation. FDR's timing was often uncanny, and his self-confidence seemed unshakable.

After Pearl Harbor, Roosevelt informed reporters that "Doctor New Deal" had become "Doctor Win the War." FDR brought to war the attributes he had developed in peace. These personal attributes had a direct and real impact upon the nation's war effort. For example, on the Sunday of Pearl Harbor, the President seemed to know at once what must be done and what must be said. It was the President himself who wrote out the notices that were passed to reporters announcing the attack to the nation. It was the President who talked first to the governor and commanding officers at Pearl Harbor, once a phone line was established. The President conferred with his generals and admirals. He issued the orders and authorized the directives necessary to put the nation on a full wartime footing. He alone dictated his war message to the Congress, and he delivered it exactly as he had dictated it. He called his Cabinet into session, and he conferred with the congressional leaders. "Would it be acceptable" for him to appear before a joint session at 12:30 P.M. the following day, he inquired of the Speaker of the House of Representatives. It would, answered the Speaker. For the first twenty-four hours of war, what was done and what was said by the American government was done and said by the President himself.

As wartime leader, Roosevelt displayed a continued sense of propriety, good judgment, unshakable confidence, and courage. He sought out and appointed to high office men of proven ability. The competence of the men who directed America's war effort, both in the military and the executive, was clearly above the level of World War I or the Civil War. Once FDR had these men in their places, he let them do their job, and ventured into their operations only when clearly necessary. When he had to make a decision, he made it promptly with a judgment and intuition that were a kind of wisdom. Never did he doubt victory, and never did he lose his famous optimism and good cheer.

The President's optimism and confidence were displayed at every turn. In his State of the Union message to the Congress in January 1942, he boosted production targets to absolutely unheard-of levels. He did so, acting on his own intuition. He called for the construction of 75,000 tanks in 1943 and 125,000 airplanes. When questioned, he replied, "Oh, the production people can do it if they try."[6] They did try, and they did do it.

The men he chose to run the war effort were not New Dealers, not political types, nor were they ideologically aligned with FDR. They were bankers, industrialists, members of the Eastern establishment—Henry Stimson, Robert P. Patterson, Robert A. Lovett, James T. Forrestal, John J. McCloy. These men were in Washington to serve their country, not the President. Nevertheless, as they worked with Roosevelt over the war years, they came to have great respect for the man and his personal qualities. Particularly, they were impressed by how he coped with his handicap. Stimson spoke of how FDR "carried his burden with such buoyant courage."[7] Chief of Staff General George C. Marshall, who cared so little for charm, saw FDR's courage and was much impressed.

To a degree difficult to assess, these men saw Roosevelt's wheelchair as a symbol of his character. Associates could see that his life was a daily struggle without comment or complaint. FDR asked for no sympathy from his secretaries or generals. Yet sympathy he received, unspoken yet genuine, and much respect. Clearly, as Perkins had remarked in the 1928 campaign, the handicap, and the very presence of wheelchair and braces worked to the President's advantage in his relations with his peers, and Roosevelt made use of it and built upon it. Even Joseph Stalin responded to it. Stalin was said to have admired Roosevelt greatly. At Yalta, from time to time during the course of the meetings, the Field Marshal would get up from his place, walk around the table, and pat the President on the shoulder appreciatively. Churchill, too, of course, responded to it. As he explained to the Commons when it it met to commemorate Roosevelt's death, "President Roosevelt's physical affliction lay heavily upon him. It was a marvel that he bore up against it through all the many years of tumult and storm. Not one man in ten million, stricken and crippled as he was, would have attempted to plunge into a life of physical and mental exertion and of hard, ceaseless political controversy. Not one in ten million would have tried, not one in a generation would have succeeded, not only in entering this sphere, not only in acting vehemently in it, but in becoming indisputable master of the scene." It was, concluded Churchill, an "extraordinary effort of the spirit over the flesh, of willpower over physical infirmity."[8]

It was, indeed, an extraordinary victory of will over uncommon odds. And as such, it was immensely helpful to FDR. His visible handicap was a badge of courage that men respected and responded to. It was no small part of Roosevelt's magnetism and authority.

The President's life in wartime took on a certain stark simplicity. Sentries stood watch along the White House fence. Most of the gates were chained shut, antiaircraft guns were mounted on the roof, and a bomb shelter was constructed deep in the bowels of the Treasury building next door. Even the President's wheelchair was equipped with a gas mask. The White House was closed to tourists, and many of the routine annual receptions and events were canceled for the duration of the war. The President worked hard, and there was little time for rest or relaxation.

The President's commitment to the prosecution of the war was total. Millions of lives were at risk. Decisions made by him, policies reached, could determine in a very direct sense not just the future of the United States, but of all peoples of the world. His responsibilities as Commander-in-Chief allowed no respite.

The presidency of the United States is, of course, a political office, and a President rules by consensus and persuasion. This requires his constant attendance upon senators and congressmen, political functionaries, and community leaders. Even in time of war, FDR could not totally avoid these matters. He gave them much less time, however, than before. The major part of his day and of his attention was given to the strategy and mobilization of the war effort and the relations among the Allies.

FDR's schedule did not change greatly in war. He worked from his bed in the mornings; was in his office during the middle of the day; had a massage before dinner; and worked in his study in the evening. He continued to mix the cocktails from the tray by his side before dinner and to take drives on pleasant afternoons in the countryside. Often he was away on weekends.

A sophisticated map room was set up in the White House—actually in a little-used ladies' powder room. The President stopped by the map room for the latest briefing at least twice a day, sometimes more often in moments of crisis. Much as Abraham Lincoln used to cross the street to the War Office to read the telegraph dispatches from the battlefield, President Roosevelt kept in touch with war developments through his map room.

The room was staffed and operated by the U.S. Navy. Only six persons had sufficient security clearance to enter. Mrs. Roosevelt was not one of the six. Nevertheless, she stopped by the room one day to check on the battleground location of one of her sons, and the awestruck ensign on guard lacked the courage to bar her entrance. None of the President's Secret Service bodyguards was allowed to enter the room; therefore, the responsibility for pushing the presidential wheelchair went to the watch officer. At one point early in the war, Ensign Ed Carson became so nervous at his solemn responsibility that he banged the President of the United States into a desk. As a result of this episode, regular wheelchair practice was scheduled, at which the Officers of the Day would take turns pushing each other around the room in a spare wheelchair. From then on, the Navy was prepared.[9]

Wartime security measures allowed Roosevelt to move about the country in reasonable secrecy. He made use of this new freedom by spending at least one or two weekends a month at Hyde Park. Other weekends were spent at Shangri La—now named Camp David—his secret retreat close by in the Maryland mountains. In those days the site was not much more than a rustic campground, guarded by Marines.

President Roosevelt traveled a great deal during the three years, four months he served as Commander-in-Chief. He was, in this period, away from Washington more than any recent President. He inspected munitions plants and military bases on a cross-country tour in 1942, and again in a seven-thousand-mile, twenty-state jaunt in 1943, including a conference with the President of Mexico at Juárez. He crossed the ocean for a conference at Casablanca in 1943, and again in 1943 for meetings at Cairo and Teheran. He inspected the Pacific theater of operations on a month-long trip to Hawaii and Alaska in 1944. He was away for six weeks in early 1945 for the conference at Yalta in the Crimea. During this period FDR met with Churchill on nine different occasions for a total of 120 days—at Argentia, off Newfoundland; Casablanca; Tehran; Yalta; twice in Quebec; and three times in Washington.

On these trips FDR was more open about his wheelchair than ever before. For example, at Hawaii, he took the opportunity to visit the many hospital wards filled with wounded American men, including Japanese-American casualties wounded in Europe. The Secret Service advised Roosevelt not to see these Nisei soldiers on the grounds that one of them might prove disloyal to the United States and threaten the life of the President. FDR's one-word response to this was "Nonsense!"[10]

In the past, at hospitals, as at other public gatherings, Roosevelt had allowed himself to be seen in but two ways: standing or seated in an open car. Now in the presence of wounded boys the age of his own sons, FDR did a remarkable thing. He had himself lifted from his car into his wheelchair. And he had himself, President and Commander-in-Chief, wheeled on his wheelchair through the wards of amputees. He rolled slowly so that all could see him. He stopped at many beds, chatting with the men. He was as crippled as they were, and he wanted them to see that.

Roosevelt understood what these men were undergoing. He had gone through it himself. He was, by all reports, deeply moved by what he saw, and so were the men. The President had heard specifically of one man who had amputated his own legs in order to save his life. As he rolled up to this man's bed, Roosevelt said, "I understand you are something of a surgeon." And then, after a pause, "I'm not a bad orthopedist myself."[11]

The security for these trips was extreme. FDR's movements were accorded the highest secrecy. Although pool reporters were with him, they were not allowed to file their stories until the completion of the trip. Otherwise, the remainder of the White House correspondents were as ignorant as the general public concerning the whereabouts of the President.

Of course, wherever the President went, he took direction of the war with him. He was never out of touch by phone, Telex, and radio. Communications responsibilites were handled by the U.S. Army Signal Corps. An entire railroad car filled with transmitters and such was always coupled to the President's train. The presidential map room was routinely packed up and taken along on FDR's journeys.

The Secret Service had located a railroad siding in the basement of the Bureau of Engraving and Printing about five blocks away from the White House across the Mall. This siding was hidden and private. When traveling, the President would be taken to the siding by closed car, with security escort. His car would be driven up onto the railroad platform so that once the President had transferred to his wheelchair, he could be rolled directly onto the train. For the occasions when he was going to sea, the Navy constructed a similar platform arrangement at Newport News. There a track for the President's train was laid along the length of the dock so that his wheelchair could be rolled directly from the train, across the platform, and directly into the ship without taking a step or a bump.

In 1940, the Pullman Company had commissioned a private car, *The Magellan*, specifically built for President Roosevelt's use. This was designed according to the specifications and directions of the Secret Service, and was leased by the company to the country for one dollar a year. *The Magellan* was armor-plated and bulletproof. The steel frame of *The Magellan* had been reinforced and was said to be strong enough to withstand a fall of over a hundred feet from a railroad bridge without telescoping or serious damage. It was not clear, however, what the fate would be of the passengers caught inside during such an accident. *The Magellan* had a bedroom, bathroom, and sitting room, especially designed for the President's convenience. Secure railing bars were installed on the back platform for FDR's use at whistle-stops. At the end of the car there was an elevator so that the portable ramp to the platform no longer needed to be used.

The Secret Service reported that, try as they might to keep the President's trips secret, two things invariably gave away his presence. The first was the construction of the ramps that his wheelchair required. The second was his Scotty dog, Fala, who often traveled with him. Fala, like any other dog, would insist upon being taken for a walk when the train came to a stop. The sight of a closed train standing at a siding, heavily guarded by military sentries, as a Secret Service agent walked a little Scotty dog was a dead giveaway to any American of the 1940s. Fala was as much a celebrity and as well known as any other member of the President's circle. It is no wonder that the Secret Service code name for him was "The Informer." They could eliminate the ramp with an on-board elevator, but they could do nothing about Fala.

During his trips, FDR seized what opportunity he could to see new places and experience new things. He was a man of overwhelming curiosity, and in spite of the constraints imposed by his responsibilities and his handicap, he saw a lot. He inspected the harbor at Bathurst in the Gambia by whaleboat. He visited rubber plantations in Liberia. He toured remote bases in the Aleutian Islands. He looked over the battleship *HMS Prince of Wales* after its battle with the *Bismarck.* He spent an afternoon visiting U.S. troops, sitting on the hard backseat of a jeep, bouncing over the dirt roads of North Africa. His hip bones lacked the cushion protection that healthy muscles provide, and as he remarked to his son Elliott afterward, "Once in a jeep is enough to last quite a time."[12] At Marrakesh, Churchill had recommended the view over the Atlas Mountains from the top of a six-story tower. FDR called for volunteers, and his masseur George Fox and his Secret Service Chief Mike Reilly carried the

President all the way up to the top of the tower and then all the way back down.

Reilly of the Secret Service came up with ingenious ways of getting the President where he wanted to go without carrying him in public. Routinely, FDR reviewed troops from the back of a jeep with a specially raised seat, so that he could be better seen by the men. The welcoming officer and, in one case, Prime Minister Churchill walked alongside the slowly moving jeep. Reilly solved the problem of how to get FDR aboard a ship at sea by placing him in a whaleboat, and then having the entire whaleboat lifted onto the deck of the host ship. At a 1941 conference held at Argentia, off the coast of Newfoundland, Winston Churchill was aboard the battleship *HMS Prince of Wales* and the President was aboard the heavy cruiser *Augusta*. The President was less than accurate when he confided to his press conference upon his return, "It was a little bit difficult for me in getting over on the *Prince of Wales*."[13]

By the end of the war the Air Corps had specially equipped a four-engine C54 for the President's use. This was called *The Sacred Cow* and was the predecessor of the present prestigious *Air Force One*. *The Sacred Cow* had a cabin designed for FDR's wheelchair. The lavatory was accessible; there was a bed for his use, and a particularly large window beside the lounge chair allowed him to survey the territory in flight. A special telescoping elevator device was installed in the belly of the plane so that the President, chair and all, could be lifted up into the fuselage. For reasons of security, the elevator was designed so that from the outside the plane looked just like any other C54.

Although ingenious, the elevator caused many a headache. "The darned thing didn't always work," complained the President's pilot, Lieutenant Colonel Henry Myers. "We sure were worried about that elevator. Every time we showed it to General Arnold [Commanding General of the Army Air Corps], it got stuck. Soon as Arnold's back was turned, then it worked again."[14]

The plane was a part of the Air Corps plan to woo FDR away from his devotion to the Navy. It did not work. FDR thought the remodeled plane a foolish waste of money. All the services were aware that Roosevelt was partial to the Navy. Formally, as Commander-in-Chief, of course, he was in charge of all the services, and he dealt with them all in an equal manner. Occasionally, however, he would slip. General Marshall was once heard saying, almost plaintively, "At least, Mr. President, stop speaking of the Army as 'they' and the Navy as 'us.' "[15]

By late 1943 or early 1944, the President had begun using a practical folding chair designed by the Everest and Jennings Company of Los Angeles, California. Roosevelt used their standard chair, but when Reilly of the Secret Service was working on the design of FDR's plane, he asked Everest and Jennings to build a special chair, compact enough for use on the elevator. The chair as built was indeed compact, without arms and with four eight-inch caster wheels. Larger wheels, it was reasoned, took up additional space and would be unnecessary as the President would not be wheeling himself on board.

Although Roosevelt presided as effectively over the nation at war as he had in peacetime, the demands of war placed an extraordinary strain upon his resources, both mental and physical. Over the years, these were to take their toll. FDR moved through his first term with great enthusiasm and gusto. He thrived on being President; he loved it. His polio-weakened muscles lost little, if any, of their strength, and at the end of the term he was as healthy as at the beginning. The third term—the war term—was quite different.

FDR's doctor, in a move of quite exceptional folly, suggested to the President that he drop his daily exercise routine for the war's duration. The doctor was trying to relieve the President of as much stress and effort as possible in his daily life. Out went the swimming; off came the braces. Because of the controlled nature of his limited public appearances, the President was able to put aside his hated, painful braces and, in fact, FDR did not stand erect from some point early in 1943 until his speech at Bremerton, over a year later, in August 1944. So complete was FDR's hold over reporters assigned to him that there was not one comment in the press that the President had not been observed standing for some time.

The President's failure to exercise or to keep fit is understandable. The fatigue experienced by the leaders of World War II was exceptional. Winston Churchill, who suffered from no major physical complaint, was so exhausted by the end of the war that he had himself regularly carried up and down stairs. Roosevelt, whose body was seriously weakened by polio, was forced to garner strength in every way possible. It was, however, false economy for Roosevelt to drop his exercises. The exercising had kept the President's muscles in good condition. Now, his muscles began to deteriorate.

At the beginning of the third year of America's participation in World War II, FDR began to lose significant muscle strength and function. From January 1944 until his death, the President's decline continued ever more markedly. The results of this decline would be of worldwide importance.

XVII
Depression

It finally crushed him. He couldn't stand up under it any longer.[1]
—ROBERT E. SHERWOOD

UPON Roosevelt's return from the first Big Three conference at Tehran in December 1943, he had contracted a severe case of influenza. He never completely recovered his health or sense of well-being. He suffered several bouts of severe stomach distress; his sinuses caused him constant difficulty; and he suffered, off and on, from a persistent, aggravating cough. He became increasingly fatigued and disinterested. His breathing became labored, and his complexion took on a deadly ashen hue.

Roosevelt's physical condition over this period underwent a marked deterioration. FDR always took a certain pride in the physical skills that he had developed. He could transfer his body from wheelchair to office chair with a quick and tidy efficiency. He loved to drive his own car and to mix the cocktails himself for his guests. Gradually, during the war years, he had stopped doing such things, allowing others to do them for him. He allowed himself to be lifted everywhere all the time. Roosevelt was no longer even semi-independent. He was truly a crippled man.

Presidents, like kings, usually receive a poor quality of medical care. They are ministered to by not one, but many doctors. And medical committees are not notably more efficient or decisive than any other kind of committee. The eminence of the

Presidents' doctors is often dependent upon their skills at politics and publicity rather than doctoring. They are "important" doctors because they have an important patient. They hold their place of eminence at the pleasure of their patient; and often as not, they tell him what he wants to hear.

The President's principal doctor was Admiral Ross McIntire, Surgeon General of the Navy. A long-time friend of the President, McIntire was an ear, nose, and throat man of dubious ability. He had been with the President since 1933. Before that he had served for over fifteen years as an ordinary Navy doctor. His speciality had determined his selection as the President's physician. As was explained to him at the time, "The President is as strong as a horse with the exception of the chronic sinus condition that makes him susceptible to colds. That's where you come in."[2] And in fact, through the years, the only doctoring McIntire ever did for his eminent patient consisted of dosing him on a daily basis with nose drops and sinus sprays, irrigating his sinuses with saltwater douches, and experimenting with one of the more extreme treatments of the day: cauterization of the sinus tissues by means of red-hot wire loops stuck up the nose. Ironically, the years of dosing with drops brought the President only marginal relief, while at the same time it served to increase his already elevated blood pressure.

With his selection as the President's physician, McIntire found himself an instant celebrity. As the years of Roosevelt's presidency went by, McIntire rose through the ranks, retiring finally as a vice admiral. In 1938, the President appointed him Surgeon General of the Navy. During World War II, the medical department under his direction consisted of over 175,000 doctors, nurses, and professionals, 52 hospitals, and 278 mobile units. McIntire came to hold no small position in the order of things. This position, however, was dependent upon the favor and indeed the presence of the President. Should Roosevelt no longer be President, it was certain McIntire would not much longer be Surgeon General. Thus, it was clearly in McIntire's interest to keep Roosevelt in good health and in the White House. Furthermore, like all others, doctors like to bring good news. They have as much difficulty as others with bad news, particularly as it impinges upon their own life and well-being. It was, in a sense, McIntire's duty to keep the President well. The family, the press, the nation turned to him for reassurance. His professional position—indeed his very self-esteem—was involved in this responsibility.

Doctors do not minister to their own loved ones for fear their emotional ties will cloud their professional judgment. This is what happened to McIntire. He was so dependent upon Roosevelt's being in the White House that it altered his judgment. This was of no great matter so long as the President was healthy. In 1944, it would matter very much.

McIntire had every incentive, and no doubt desire, to believe the President was well. By the end of March 1944, McIntire was worried. Something was clearly wrong with the President's health. McIntire arranged for FDR to undergo a complete physical examination at the Bethesda Naval Hospital by a young cardiologist, Howard G. Bruenn. Bruenn's diagnosis was as unexpected as it was incontrovertible. The President was suffering from hypertension, hypertensive heart disease, and some degree of congestive heart failure. His blood pressure was highly labile; that is, it was extremely responsive to emotional variations and physical changes. These conditions, while not necessarily immediately life-threatening, were serious. They were continuing and progressive; and, given the limited medical skills of the time, they could be monitored, but not much altered.

Dr. Bruenn was a young man, a junior officer in the U.S. Navy Medical Corps (Reserve). Throughout the months he attended Roosevelt, Bruenn reported to Admiral McIntire and not to the President. He was under specific orders to discuss the case with absolutely no one—not with other doctors, not with the family, not even with his patient. McIntire was in command and Bruenn did as he was told.

When Bruenn informed McIntire of his findings, McIntire acted in a very peculiar fashion. He did nothing. Bruenn recommended that the patient receive what was standard treatment of the day for heart disease: immediate bed rest for several weeks, digitalization, a light diet, sedation as needed for sleep, and codeine for the cough. These recommendations McIntire rejected out of hand because, according to Bruenn, "of the exigencies and demands on the President."[3] Instead, McIntire simply told the President to get more rest, and he prescribed a codeine cough syrup.

In the face of a continuing decline in the President's condition and after continuing remonstrations from young Bruenn and various additional consultations with specialists convened under the highest security conditions, McIntire at last relented and placed the President under a restricted regime, which he was to follow with various modifications for the remaining months of his life.

FDR's daily activity was greatly curtailed. He was to work in bed in the morning, spend only a few hours in his office in the afternoon, and eat in his quarters by himself in the evening. His social activities were virtually eliminated. He was required to rest for at least an hour after each meal. He was no longer allowed to swim in the White House pool. His diet was to be limited to 2,600 calories a day. It was to be low in fat and salt-free. A chain smoker, his cigarette ration was to be greatly reduced. Mild laxatives were prescribed as needed, and sedatives were available for sleep. The President was to sleep at least ten hours a day, if possible. Digitalis was to be administered on a regular basis.

It must be a matter of some amazement that while living under the constraints of this regime, President Roosevelt was able to successfully direct the conclusion of World War II. Over the following months he maintained close contact with his generals in both the Pacific and European theaters. He approved the grand strategy for the war in the Pacific. He conferred with Churchill on European policy as the war with Germany reached its climactic stage. He also waged a brilliant and successful re-election campaign and he was inaugurated President for the fourth time; he met at Yalta with Marshal Stalin and Prime Minister Churchill, where the future shape of Europe was negotiated, the principles of operation of the United Nations were decided, and Russia was brought into the Pacific war. These were all matters of the greatest importance, and they were handled by a crippled man in failing health, operating under a regime his doctors euphemistically called "modified bed rest."

Throughout these last sixteen months, FDR was, by and large, cheerful and uncomplaining. It is McIntire's extraordinary testimony that he told his patient nothing whatever of Bruenn's findings. FDR simply did as his doctors directed, and he never once questioned their directions or asked about his condition. He never once asked cardiologist Bruenn why he was present on a daily—sometimes twice daily—basis, checking, testing, and monitoring his health. This made Bruenn's job a lot easier, but he could not help thinking it a most unusual situation. Patients generally ask many questions, seeking knowledge and reassurance as to their condition. This Roosevelt did not do.

The fact that he never inquired about his condition is significant. During FDR's rehabilitation years, he took great interest in his condition. He personally conferred with every leading specialist on poliomyelitis in the United States and he carried on an extensive correspondence with doctors and fellow victims concerning the care and treatment of post-polio patients. At Warm Springs, he actually devised a system of treatment. He supervised exercises and insisted upon regular testing of muscle power to measure progress. Occasionally, he himself gave the exercises and performed the muscle tests. Now, "Doctor" Roosevelt was subjected to a multitude of tests and medicines on a daily basis, and he never asked why. This radical shift in personality behavior puzzled his doctors. They were puzzled because they did not see what he went to some lengths to keep them from seeing—that he was, in fact, in the grip of a severe depression.

The immense burdens of the modern presidency take a deadly toll. In the last months of his administration, Herbert Hoover was so deeply depressed he found it difficult to function. He found it hard to focus upon individuals. Speaking, the very act of forming words, was a struggle; and Cabinet meetings with President Hoover, as Secretary of State Stimson reported, were like taking a bath in black ink. Now, at the end of World War II, President Roosevelt was similarly depressed. His character, of course, was quite different from Herbert Hoover's. Roosevelt's early training, his pattern of behavior, emphasized good cheer, positive thinking, the denial of unpleasant truths, and no complaints. This training held, and Roosevelt's superficial behavior traits remained consistent. Closer examination, however, reveals physical symptoms and altered behavior patterns that clearly indicate depression.

Roosevelt was a lonely man, as his children have said. "Of what was inside of him, of what really drove him, Father talked with no one," said son James.[4] FDR had no way of relieving his feelings, no one with whom he could talk about his anguish, his frustrations, his essential sadness. Although his White House doctors did not seem particularly cognizant of the fact, Roosevelt had an extremely sensitive and vulnerable personality.

One of his earlier polio doctors, George Draper (incidentally, a schoolmate), had understood FDR's makeup. Wrote Draper of FDR's post-polio treatment, "The psychological factor in his management is paramount. . . . He has such courage, such ambition, and yet at the same time such an extraordinarily sensitive emotional mechanism that it will take all the skill we can muster to lead him successfully to a recognition of what he really faces without crushing him."[5] Now, in the twelfth year of his presidency, the burdens, which Hoover had found so heavy, had grown tenfold heavier. FDR had guided the nation through the Depression and the war. No man had ever had such sustained responsibility, such unrelenting duty. And as a result, FDR's "extraordinarily sensitive emotional mechanism" was being crushed under the burden.

Dr. McIntire always denied that this was the case. He viewed his patient as superhuman, without flaw, capable of anything. FDR, said McIntire, never indulged "in so much as a moment's self-pity." Furthermore, said McIntire, "Periods of depression, if any, were hidden and never at any time shadowed the smile with which he faced the future."[6]

FDR's depression may have been hidden, but its existence was revealed in various changes in personality and behavior. Roosevelt's loss of interest in the management of his health was one clear change. Another change in behavior was the development of a curious indecision. He had always been a man who had no problems making a decision. He made up his mind quickly and intuitively. Now he seemed to have trouble with decisions. For example, he wavered back and forth in the selection of a running mate. In 1940, he had known precisely whom he wanted for vice-president, why, and how he was going to get him. In 1944, he did not seem to know or even to care. "The whole thing doesn't matter a damn," he told his son James.[7] Even on some aspects of war strategy, he was vague and wavering, he did not know when or where, or indeed whether, the Big Three should meet again. And for the first time he had distinct difficulty in organizing his thoughts in the preparation of his report to the Congress upon his return from Yalta.

Although never particularly interested in great substance or much detail, Roosevelt had always maintained a masterly understanding of the matters that came before him. Now, he no longer seemed much interested in things. He no longer scanned reports and dispatches. He took no interest in briefing papers prepared for his use; he barely thumbed through them. He took no briefings. In meetings his mind would wander, his attention would lapse. And, often as not, he would stare off into space, his jaw falling slack. He had seldom confided in others, and now he did not talk about his policy or strategy with any of his advisors. He spoke of his intentions only in bits and pieces to others.

In fact, during the last sixteen months of FDR's life he was very seldom in the White House at all. He spent over a month in the Pacific; Yalta and travel time consumed another month. He spent a month resting in Warm Springs, another month convalescing in South Carolina. He made political campaign journeys to Chicago, Cleveland, Philadelphia, New York, and Boston; and he spent virtually every weekend at Hyde Park, or at his new retreat, Shangri La.

During the last months of his life, when he was in declining health, Roosevelt was actually very seldom *seen* in public. The few appearances he made were carefully arranged, widely publicized, and heavily photographed. His skillful press assistant, Steve Early, made full use of releases, statements, short press conferences, and radio talks. As a result, Roosevelt continued to dominate the news throughout the war. He continued to exercise his leadership and influence over public affairs, but he did so from outside the public eye. So far as his own condition and activities were concerned, the press saw only what he wished them to see. Thus, over the sixteen months of his decline, only a very few persons on his immediate staff were aware of how marked it had become. And they were reluctant to admit, even to themselves, how serious it was.

The somatic symptoms of FDR's depression were classic: In the spring of 1944, he began to complain of frequent headaches; he suffered from chronic fatigue without apparent cause; his appetite, always hitherto good, became poor; he lost interest in his food and found it to be tasteless; he had chronic indigestion; he had various aches and pains throughout his body. He had a continuing weight loss. At the beginning of 1944, he weighed 188 pounds. His doctors placed him on a diet to lose weight and reduce the strain on his heart, and lose he did. Once begun, the weight loss could not be stopped, and at the time of his death he weighed 165. He had constipation. Most unusual for him—he had always under any circumstances slept well— FDR found it difficult to sleep: "Now that's a new one," he said.[8] These symptoms are the signs of depression; they are not the symptoms of heart disease.

It is notoriously unwise to diagnose the mental state of persons one has never known, who are long since dead. Nevertheless, in the case of Franklin Roosevelt, it seems undeniable that depressive neurosis—a state of reactive depression—was a condition of the last year and a half of his life. Depressive neurosis is a common complaint which, as melancholia, has been recognized since ancient times. According to the *Encyclopedia Britannica*, it has a relatively high frequency "among the more sophisticated, educated, mature, and intellectually favored groups of people."[9] In the case of a reactive depression, there is, as the cause or at least the trigger, an external precipitant. This can be the loss of a loved one, permanent injury, major career or financial reverses, or some combination thereof. Commensurate with the external loss is a loss of self-esteem brought on in part by a sense of helplessness and weakness in the face of the external shock. Accompanying this loss are feelings of grief, anger, and aggression. For some persons these intense feelings, directed toward those most loved and closest, are frightening and unacceptable—and so they are repressed. Diagnostic manuals warn, "Although in most individuals the depressive affect is prominent, it must be remembered in some the somatic complaints overshadow the emotional, leading the unwary physician to a mistaken diagnosis of physical illness."[10] This most certainly was the case with Franklin D. Roosevelt.

Roosevelt's aides and doctors were, with perhaps one exception, good men. They were as vulnerable to self-deception as other men. They did not want to see their leader, the man who had led the nation through crisis and war, seriously sick, failing in strength, or mentally ill. By and large, they blinded themselves to what was happening to FDR. The Boss was tired, they would say. He needed a little rest. A few days at Warm Springs will fix him up and he will come bouncing back, they said. Eleanor, daughter Anna, his secretary Grace, his staff, his generals, his Cabinet, congressional leaders, the reporters who saw him weekly—they reassured each other that the Boss was fine.

Yet clearly the Boss was physically ill; the symptoms were obvious enough. What was not so obvious was the fact that the President was seriously depressed. And as the doctors were reluctant to acknowledge even to themselves the severity of the President's physical illness, so they were unwilling, perhaps even unable, to see his depression. Not only did he have the usual symptoms but he *looked* depressed: he sat in a slumped posture, his body limp, his eyes dull. He also *sounded* depressed: he seemed preoccupied; his conversation was no longer animated; there seemed to be an apathy and an emotional deadness about him. Perceptibly, too, his behavior had changed. He took little interest in the political and presidential activities that had brought him such joy in the past. He seemed even more emotionally removed from those about him who loved him so dearly.

The etiology of FDR's depression in 1944 is subtle and complex. It seems probable that the primal cause was his attack of poliomyelitis in 1921, and its resultant paralysis. Roosevelt's loss of motor power, as traumatic to the person as a double amputation, had generated anger and aggression, which he had repressed and turned inward upon himself. He had refused to deal with his feelings. He had denied them, and over the years diverted himself and the nation with his extraordinary display of leadership. During the third year of World War II, the cost of this denial finally caught up with him.

As previously noted, the onset of depression requires an "external precipitant." In Roosevelt's case the principal cause was over twenty years old. There were, however, external precipitants—three of them—at work in the spring of 1944:

Roosevelt was shouldering a crushing load. It is no exaggeration to say it was greater than that borne by any man in history. Grace Tully recounts that many times she heard her boss say to a complaining Cabinet officer or general who was too tired, too busy, or possibly inadequate to perform a task, "All right, send it over to me. My shoulders are broad. I can carry the load."[11] This confidence in his own ability was part of FDR's leadership style. This had been his style in peace and it continued in war. He was able to carry the load. In war he made the mighty decisions without ducking or flinching—the A-bomb, D-Day, priorities between the war zones, proprieties among the Allies. Roosevelt had a sure and certain sense of his role and his nation's role. It was his responsibility to make great decisions. This was a very heavy burden—one no man could sustain for any great length of time.

The second external factor in Roosevelt's depression was the absence of joy. A current handbook on mental illness describes the "inner desolation" experienced by those in depression: "What once were gay, vibrant, meaningful surroundings become bleak, sunless, and lifeless."[12] This could be taken as a description of the change that gradually overtook the wartime White House. At first, in the thirties, Roosevelt had great fun with the presidency. There were picnics and weekend trips, fishing expeditions, the twice yearly journeys to Warm Springs. There was much laughing, no little drinking, song singing, and other innocent activities. The President always had Missy with him. His sons were in and out of the White House constantly. His close advisor, Louis Howe, was in many respects replaced by his new confidant, Harry Hopkins. There were the New Deal regulars, the New Deal clowns, the gossip, the glamour, the crises, and the outrages. It had been fun. Now, in the third year of this war, fun was put aside for the duration. Louis and long-time attendant Gus were dead. Missy lay victim to a stroke on her deathbed. Harry was sick. All four sons were in the service in war zones a long way across the world. Eleanor was constantly away, working around the clock when she was present. And, perhaps most important, his beloved mother had died at the end of 1941. Roosevelt was lonely and, of course, night or day, wherever he was, the responsibilities of the wartime President never let up. They were inescapable.

Perversely, FDR's doctors removed, step by step, what remaining pleasures were left to him. FDR enjoyed a swim in the afternoon. In water he could move about in a way he could not on land. In water he was more nearly a whole man, able in somewhat limited fashion to swim and to compete at water polo. His doctors ordered an end to the swimming. FDR had been a lifelong smoker. He smoked some two packages a day. His doctors ordered that he cut down from over forty cigarettes a day to fewer than half a dozen. Roosevelt had always loved his food and had much pleasure from his dinner. Now he suffered from indigestion after meals. He now had gallstones. His doctors ordered a bland diet, salt-free, fat-free, the evening meal to be eaten by the President alone in quarters before an early bedtime. The doctors directed that the President was to have only such social life as was absolutely necessary. The man who once had found so much pleasure and nourishment in talking with persons of all interests, from all walks, was now, in the supposed interest of his health, restricted to a diet of milk toast, on a tray, with Grace Tully as his only companion. Miss Tully was an estimable person, a crackerjack secretary, but she was no conversationalist. Tully was a dull soul, and the President can have gained little nourishment from her company. The duties of war, and the deprivations caused by death and illness, pretty much erased the joy of White House life. And what the war made grim, the doctors had made worse. They did not seem to understand the truth of what Roosevelt at Warm Springs had known instinctively: successful treatment requires a positive psychological environment.

The third external factor in the President's depression was the loss of strength he experienced as his polio-ravaged muscles began to weaken and decay. There is substantial uncertainty about what happens to polio-affected muscles over the life of the patient. Some doctors believe there is a sort of premature aging that takes place as the decimated anterior horn cells of the nervous system give up their efforts to service the muscles. These doctors believe that short circuits develop as the system deteriorates. Whether or not this is an accurate description of the process, it is generally true that polios face significant loss of muscle power as they grow older. Sometimes this loss can be great and sometimes it comes quickly. Roosevelt's loss was both quick and great. Polio expert Dr. Lauro Halstead has characterized this loss as post-polio syndrome.

FDR's hands had been paralyzed at the onset of the disease. Quickly, however, they had recovered virtually their full strength, and he had regained normal use of them. Now, by the end of 1944, even his hands refused to function. They had always been shaky, but now he found them unable to hold a cup and saucer. Occasionally, he found the grasping of a pen between thumb and fingers to be difficult. His writing became tortured. Over the last months, he was at times unable even to light a cigarette for himself. His valet, Arthur Prettyman, attended to an ever-larger degree of personal nursing care for the President. Prettyman dressed him as he lay in his bed, and shaved him because his hands were not steady enough to shave himself. Prettyman bathed the President in his tub and attended to him on his toilet.

The decline in FDR's muscle power became marked. Eleanor became concerned when at Hyde Park he asked her to drive him, whereas before he had always taken such pride in his own driving ability. He asked her also to mix the cocktails, a task he had always reserved for himself. Eleanor did not approve of FDR's drinking, and it can have given him little pleasure to have asked her assistance. Similarly, Eleanor was a poor driver. Franklin used to taunt her for her lack of skill. His was a pathetic request.

The decline was undeniable, obvious, and serious. The impact on Roosevelt's self-esteem was heavy. He was a sensitive and vain man, interested in his appearance, and always aware of the impact he was having upon others. The old campaign fedora, the admiral's naval cloak, the cocked cigarette holder— these were props he used to produce a calculated effect. As few men ever have, FDR carefully re-created his physical appearance during the rehabilitation years. In a conscious way, he had to think about and decide how he would sit, what he would sit in, how he would get up, how he would stand, how he would walk, how he would enter a room and leave it. As much as any actor, he rehearsed his appearances in order to achieve a polished performance. It is not surprising that he once told Orson Welles he considered the two of them to be the finest actors in America.

FDR's reconstruction of his public image had taken seven years of effort, and in the years since then it had never become easy. It had always required careful concentration and coordination. Now he could do it no longer. Roosevelt had never fully acknowledged his paralysis, either to others or to himself. His wife remarked once that, in fact, he had never admitted he could not walk. For years he had kept himself going with the assumption that he would regain full mobility—perhaps not immediately but soon, perhaps not this year, but next. By the end of 1944, this assumption had long since passed away. FDR had defied polio; his reconstruction of himself and of his person was based upon his confidence that he could lick polio. Now polio was licking him. This was an absolutely deadly blow to his self-esteem.

Roosevelt carried the seemingly endless and inescapable burden of leading the world's attack on Nazism. His loving confidants had departed, and he was without the emotional support he needed. His body no longer had the strength or stamina needed to respond to the demands he placed upon it. It was all over: FDR was a sick, tired, and crippled man. In what sounds a unique and a genuine *cri de coeur*, the President complained to Eleanor, "I cannot live out a normal life span. I can't even walk across the room to get my circulation going."[13]

Eleanor wrote to a friend that she was afraid FDR had given in to "invalidism." She was a great humanitarian, with great sympathy for the suffering of distant peoples. She and her husband, however, lived by a far more spartan value system. She judged her husband too severely. The two had struggled years ago to deny FDR's paralysis and to rebuild his political career. Now it seemed to her that he had given up the struggle. She was wrong. He had not given up the struggle; he had lost it.

XVIII
Farewell

The fox knows many things but the hedgehog knows
one great thing.[1]
—ARCHILOCHUS

I T was clear that 1944 would determine whether the Allied powers could break the Axis enemy. The planning was underway for the invasion of Europe, scheduled for the summer. The Japanese advance in the Pacific had only just been halted. The policy disputes and the personality differences among the leaders of the Allied great powers were threatening their unity of action.

In 1932, FDR made a pact with the American electorate. In a sense, both agreed to pretend the President was not handicapped. For his part, he would do all within his power to give the appearance of being unimpaired; for their part, they would simply deny that he was. Now, in 1944, this pact had become a trap. Roosevelt must decide whether to stand again for reelection for the fourth time as President of the United States. It was the very height of World War II, and FDR was as close to irreplaceable as any man had ever been. Like Franco or Mao Zedong, he seemed immortal. For many young Americans, FDR was the only President they had ever known. To them it was unthinkable the man should step down. To the armies slogging through Europe and the Navy on the high seas he was the unquestioned Commander-in-Chief. To the nation, to the Allies, indeed to America's enemies, he was the very embodiment of the United States and what it stood for.

Eleanor opted out of the fourth-term issue. "I wouldn't discuss it with him," she said, "because I hated the idea and he knew I hated it. Either he felt he ought to serve a fourth term and wanted it or he didn't. That was up to the man himself to decide and no one else."[2] Eleanor had opposed his running for the third term. When he ran in 1940 against her wishes, she accepted his decision, giving up all hope of his having a life after the White House. That he should now run for a fourth term she accepted as a foregone conclusion, only checking first with his doctors. They of course assured her, as they assured the family and the nation, that with care and rest he should live and govern for many a year.

Not everyone was as sanguine. Several of the President's men feared Roosevelt was too enfeebled to last out another term. Undersecretary of State Stettinius and several others determined to face the President and tell him he was to ill to run. In the event, they lost their nerve and failed to do so. Tommy the Cork Corcoran was another who decided to meet with the President to urge him to step down. He did, in fact, meet with Roosevelt, but when push came to shove, he also lost his nerve. He could not tell the great leader to his face that he was too ill to carry on. Only one of his advisors told him he should step aside. That was Ben Cohen, and he did it by memorandum— which Roosevelt simply filed without comment.

FDR made the decision to run as he made most of his decisions in his last year—on his own, without discussing it with others. He did later comment to son James that "he had run again so as to maintain a continuity of command in a time of continuing crisis." Said Roosevelt to his son, "The people elected me their leader and I can't quit in the middle of the war."[3]

The President told the nation he would run, but added he would not campaign "in the usual sense" because of his duties as Commander-in-Chief in time of war. Actually, he could not have campaigned in the usual sense even if he had wished to.

He was not strong enough. Roosevelt probably spent less time on his campaign in 1944 than had any President since George Washington. He opened the campaign with a speech in Washington; he spoke twice from the White House; he spent a day in New York; part of a day in Philadelphia; and he gave speeches in Chicago and Boston. He campaigned in an open car in Dutchess County, New York, the day before the election. Altogether, he spent less than five whole days on the trail.

As always, his sense of timing and his political intuition were flawless. His strategy was clear, and it was effective. Roosevelt told reporter Merriman Smith that as there were no burning issues, no great public interest in the election, so there would be a low voter turnout. A low turnout would favor the Republicans and his opponent, Governor Thomas E. Dewey. Accordingly, what he planned to do, FDR confided to Smith, was to fire up the campaign.

And fire it up he did.

With one of the great speeches of American political history, Roosevelt took control of the campaign and made it his. There really was only one issue: was FDR a good Commander-in-Chief or was he too old, too weak for the job? Roosevelt's speech to the Teamsters was designed to answer that question.

In the speech he demonstrated without question that he was a master of the craft of politics at the top of his form. This is how he did it: As a political leader, he reminded the New Deal coalition of the achievements of the past twelve years, and he invoked their shared commitment to social progress. As Commander-in-Chief, he spoke of war and the victory to come. And for his opponents he had but scorn and a comic derision—the Republicans, not content with attacks upon him and his family, had now turned upon "his little dog, Fala." With this speech Roosevelt demonstrated he was, indeed, still in command. His audience loved the speech; they shouted, and cheered, and wept to have their old leader leading them into battle one more time.

This time, for the first time in his political career, however, the President spoke sitting down. He did not have his braces on. He was rolled into the hall before that large banquet audience in his wheelchair. His hand was seen to shake as he ate his meal, and smoked his cigarettes in the famous holder. At the beginning of the speech his voice quavered a bit with a degree of uncertainty. Daughter Anna was worried; "Do you think Pa will put it over?" she murmured. "If the delivery isn't just right, it'll be an awful flop."[4] She need not have worried. The delivery was perfect, the speech was anything but a flop. The President gave a masterful performance.

Three weeks later, the President took his campaign to New York City. At the height of wartime, in the midst of rumors and fears of Nazi infiltration and spying activities, the President broke his security cover and announced that he would ride through the streets of New York in an open car, rain or shine, to be seen and to greet all those who had come to see him. In a cold and driving rain he did, indeed, drive through more than fifty miles of the streets of the five boroughs of New York City in a ride that took more than four hours. President Roosevelt was seen by millions of people. Through the day he was cheerful, animated, conversing, waving, throwing his head back in that famous contagious laugh. The pictures and press coverage were stunning. With this tour de force, the President put to rest, for the campaign at least, the rumors that his strength was ebbing, that his health was failing, that he was a dying man. It seemed evident to all that day in New York that he was as strong, as resilient as ever.

It was an extraordinary performance for a healthy man, let alone a sick and ailing one. Neither the press nor the public knew that at points along the parade route the Secret Service had commandeered garage space. As the presidential cavalcade passed the garage, the President's car was turned out of the parade into the warmth of the heated building. Secret Service agents quickly lifted the President from the car and stretched him out full length on blankets laid on the floor. They removed his clothes down to the skin. He was toweled dry and given a rubdown. He was redressed in dry clothes, brandy was poured down his throat, and he was lifted back into the car. The pit stop was quickly done, and the President was soon back in the cavalcade.

Roosevelt demonstrated his skill as Commander-in-Chief simply by continuing to command, and by allowing closer press coverage than hitherto. He took a much publicized "secret" inspection trip across the United States in the summer of 1944. He visited military bases, defense plants, and shipyards. He was seen by hundreds of thousands of people, and he spoke informally on many occasions. He continued to Hawaii for the meeting with MacArthur and Nimitz and returned by way of Alaska, inspecting naval bases on the Aleutians. Upon his return to the continental United States, he addressed the nation on the progress of the Pacific war, speaking from the deck of the destroyer tied up at the Bremerton Navy Yard. In the following month, on September 6, he met once again with Prime Minister Churchill at Quebec. This was but one of the ongoing series of summit conferences by which World War II strategy was decided. These meetings were critical, indeed essential; they were also glamorous. Roosevelt appreciated this. He was extremely effective in his role as Commander-in-Chief, impressive and well photographed. It is no wonder the dispirited Republicans took to calling him the Democratic Commander-in-Chief.

Back in August 1943, after the first Quebec conference, FDR, wearing his braces, almost fell to the ground. He was in the process of taking leave of Churchill. He was standing by his car, turning, and preparing to sit down on the car seat. As he turned, he lost his balance. Mike Reilly was at his side. Reilly caught the President as he fell and pushed him backward, so that the fall appeared to be no more than an abrupt entry into the car. FDR had always hated his braces. According to Reilly, from that point on the hate turned into a phobia. FDR did not put his braces on again until the 1944 campaign. His wife, who had been doing much traveling across the country, returned to the White House concerned about GOP candidate Dewey's increasing popularity. She felt that if Roosevelt wished to win reelection, he must get out among the people, be seen, and be seen standing on his own two feet. In this he was supported by his advisors, Judge Samuel Rosenman and Robert E. Sherwood, the playwright. And so the President donned his braces for the speech at Bremerton. It was probably the worst speech of his life, poorly written, poorly delivered. His leg muscles were tight and the braces did not fit. They caused him agony. The President's balance was uncertain; the deck of the destroyer was not stable; he gripped the podium, his fingers clenched with fear and apprehension. As he spoke, he felt spasms of pain radiating from his heart. He burst into a sweat, and his delivery became confused and imprecise. That great, clear tenor voice became muffled. Afterward, his doctors found he had suffered an attack of angina—a severe pain caused by a restriction of the arteries bringing blood to the heart.

Desperate and painful as this experience was, the President persevered with his determination to appear standing on his own two feet during the campaign. He had been dieting on doctor's orders. The diet had caused him to lose close to twenty pounds. His clothes hung loosely from his frame. His face looked gaunt in repose. His legs were tight, and it was necessary that the muscles be stretched so that the braces could be locked at the knee. It is a powerful and sad thought that President Roosevelt, saddled with the responsibility of mounting and directing the largest military operation in the history of man, also felt it necessary to struggle to regain his footing—just so that he could be photographed in a standing position for political purposes. Judge Samuel Rosenman was a speech writer, a close advisor, and a friend to FDR. He wrote of the 1944 campaign,

> At no time during my long association with him did I feel more admiration for his fortitude and perseverance, or more deeply grieved by the sight of his severe physical handicap than during this campaign. One day in September, before he gave up the idea of standing during his speeches, I went into his bedroom and found him with his braces on, walking up and down, leaning on the arm of Doctor McIntire. He was literally trying to learn to walk again! . . . In spite of the almost overwhelming amount of work that faced him daily in late 1944, he had made up his mind that he was

going to learn to walk again—and he did. I never saw such a display of guts.[5]

Roosevelt *did* appear standing several times during the campaign. Furthermore, he began to take a real interest in what was going on. He developed a genuine antipathy toward his opponent, and he attacked him with gusto. FDR's appetite improved; he slept soundly. His blood pressure went down. The President loved campaigning and, at least temporarily, this love lifted him out of his depression. By Election Day Dewey was soundly beaten. Roosevelt pulled 432 electoral votes to Dewey's 99. As he rolled off to bed on election night, FDR was heard to mutter about his opponent, "I still think he's a son of a bitch."[6]

By the end of 1944, Roosevelt was again depressed, exhausted, in failing strength and health. Throughout the year, the tides of war had turned. The invasion of Europe at Normandy had been successful and the total defeat of Germany seemed imminent. MacArthur's masterful island-hopping strategy in the Pacific against Japan was well and successfully launched. Planning had begun for the postwar world.

Roosevelt's abilities and character were not changed by his depression. He was as capable, as shrewd, as skillful as ever— but with a difference. He could, as required, raise himself from melancholia, sometimes for days at a time. He was certainly fully active and about on his July 1944 inspection trip to the Pacific, again during the election campaign, and later at Yalta. He was able to "get up" for Cabinet meetings and press conferences. But afterward he would slip back, relapse again into the muffled grayness of depression. It was like an additional burden he must drag along with his paralyzed body.

Roosevelt was depressed, and a depressed patient is vulnerable. The state of the emotions has a direct impact upon physical health. Recovery from illness, resistance to infection, strength, resilience, and vitality—all are influenced by the emotional state.

At the dawn of 1945, Roosevelt's physical strength was ebbing away at an accelerating rate, and his emotional state was such that he would not—and soon he could not—do anything to stop the decline. In the past, with his extraordinary will as the crucial ingredient, he had been able to surmount the reality of his handicap. Now, even that crucial ingredient was failing.

Roosevelt took the oath of office as President of the United States for the fourth time on January 20, 1945. The war was in its final stages. America had over sixteen million men and women in uniform, many of them overseas. America's interest and energy were focused upon winning the war with a concentration never before equaled.

Inauguration Day was gray and dreary. Snow had fallen the night before. Roosevelt had eliminated all the pomp and fanfare from the occasion. There would be no parade. "Who is there here to parade?" he asked.[7] The ceremony, he decided, would be held on the south portico of the White House and would be simplicity itself—a prayer, the National Anthem, the oath of office, and the Inaugural Address. The address itself would be but five minutes long. The President no longer had the strength to stand erect upon his braces for any longer than that.

Son James, now a Colonel in the Marine Corps serving in the Pacific, had been Roosevelt's "arm" at each of the previous inaugurations. Roosevelt asked him to return to Washington to stand again beside his father at this, the last inauguration. Before the ceremony, the President talked privately with James about what should be done after his death. FDR outlined the contents of his will, adding that his father's signet ring—which he had always worn—should pass to James as the eldest son. James later recalled in his memoirs, "The first moment I saw Father I realized something was terribly wrong. He looked awful and, regardless of what the doctor said, I knew in my heart that his days were numbered."[8] Numbered, perhaps, but James did not realize how few the numbers were.

FDR himself seemed to have had some sort of realization. He insisted that all thirteen of his grandchildren be present for the ceremony. The White House was jammed with Roosevelts of all ages. The President had taken to spending much time with his personal effects, sorting them, labeling and explaining them, deciding to whom they should go upon his death. Items with personal and sentimental meaning were selected for each of his secretaries and assistants, for his children, and there were particular mementos for each of the grandchildren.

On inauguration morning, FDR had the hated braces strapped to his legs so that he might stand for the oath of office and the address. It was the last time he would stand erect as leader before the American people. He walked on James's arm the few paces from the door to a waiting chair. Without coat or hat, he appeared solemn, grave, almost gaunt. Seated throughout the prayer and the National Anthem, he was lifted to his feet by James and a Secret Service man. He took but one step to the lectern. This was a far cry from the thirty-seven steps he had paced with James in 1933, when he had proclaimed, "There is nothing to fear, but fear . . ."

This time, it was not fear but pain. As the President began his speech, his upper body experienced pain. A spasm radiated from his heart, causing his entire body to shake. James, standing behind, was afraid his father would be unable to hold on to his manuscript, let alone proceed with the speech. This attack may have been another episode of angina, similar to that which FDR experienced delivering the speech the previous summer in Bremerton, Washington.

Roosevelt was a man who knew his duty. As a boy he had learned to bear his pain "without fuss." He did so now. He read his speech quietly and with a gentle dignity. It was a simple homily of the sort Dr. Peabody, his headmaster at Groton, had often preached. FDR said, "The only way to make a friend is to be one."

The impact of the speech and its delivery was one of confidence and reassurance. American faith and hope still reigned; American morals and values still governed. In the midst of global death and destruction the President insisted with firm, simple confidence that, "The great fact to remember is that the trend

of civilization itself is forever upward."⁹ It was a comforting
message in a world full of horror and shame.

And it was to be in a true sense FDR's personal valedictory,
not just to his own family but to the American people. FDR was
helped to his seat, and the ceremony was over. He was too ill,
too fatigued to take part in the rest of the day's festivities. Two
days later, he sailed for Yalta.

Roosevelt never stood upon his braces or walked again. He
lived to serve but eighty days of his fourth term. Throughout,
he was weak, tired, depressed, and ill. He had come to the White
House some twelve years before as a great bear of a man, robust, exuding health and vigor. He was now a pale wraith, with
no more than an echo of his old robust vigor.

Twelve years before he had been the wily fox—alert to everything, involved in everything. He had been the center of all activity, the only star of the only show in town. By 1945, he was,
instead, a tired hedgehog with but one great thought in mind.
He took little interest in anything but his one thought. Politics,
Congress, home front matters such as strikes, profiteering, and
black markets he left in the hands of others. Roosevelt's sole
and single concern was to bring the war to a swift conclusion
and to provide a structure for the peace.

Roosevelt had served in the war Cabinet of Woodrow Wilson.
He had observed at close quarters the collapse of Wilson's dream
of an international rule of reason through a League of Nations.
Now, in 1945, Roosevelt's great concern was a very simple one:
"Twenty-five years ago, American fighting men looked to the
statesmen of the world to finish the work of peace for which
they fought and suffered. We failed them then. We cannot fail
them again, and expect the world to survive."¹⁰

Roosevelt wished to lay out the foundation of the peace, the
base upon which a postwar world could build. To bring this
about, he believed it necessary to maintain the Great Alliance
of Russia, Britain, and America; to bring the entire force of the
Alliance to bear upon Japan after the fall of Germany; and, finally, to commit the great powers to participate in the associ-

ation of nations to be established after the war.

In the last months, Roosevelt made his point repeatedly: "This time we are not making the mistake of waiting until the end of the war to set up the machinery of peace. This time, as we fight together to win the war finally, we work together to keep it from happening again."[11] With the tragedy of Versailles in his mind, he insisted, "There can be no middle ground here. We shall have to take the responsibility for world collaboration, or we shall have to bear the responsibility for another world conflict."[12] It might be difficult in the postwar years to work with the Soviet Union within an organization of the family of nations, but it would be almost impossible to cope with a renegade Russia operating beyond the pall.

Roosevelt led a delegation of more than two hundred officers and officials to Yalta. He sailed on the USS *Quincy*. During the day he sat on deck staring out to sea. He became animated during the evening cocktail hour, and after dinner he watched movies. Briefing papers and such lay largely unattended. When advisor James Byrnes expressed his concern to FDR's daughter, Anna, about the way Roosevelt sat slumped and slack-jawed through the films, she reassured him, saying that her father was fine; he was simply breathing through his mouth because of an old sinus condition. When Anna in turn expressed *her* concern to FDR's doctor, Admiral McIntire, she, too, was reassured— again. And so it went with the American delegation.

When the Americans met with the British delegation, the British were far from reassured; they were alarmed. Churchill and his doctor, Lord Moran, were convinced Roosevelt was a dying man. As Churchill recalled in his memoirs, "At Yalta I noticed that the President was ailing. His captivating smile, his gay and charming manner, had not deserted him, but his face had a transparency, an air of purification, and often there was a faraway look in his eyes. . . . I must confess that I had an indefinable sense of fear that his health and his strength were on the ebb."[13]

Moran was struck by how much the President had deteriorated since their last meeting. Moran noted in his diary, "To a doctor's eye, the President appears a very sick man. He has all the symptoms of hardening of the arteries of the brain in an advanced stage, so that I give him only a few months to live. But men shut their eyes when they do not want to see, and the Americans here cannot bring themselves to believe that he is finished. His daughter thinks he is not really ill, and his doctor backs her up."[14]

Stalin too, noticed the change. He is reported to have remarked after seeing the President at Yalta that had he known how frail Roosevelt had become, he would have been willing to travel to the United States for the summit conference. Considering the xenophobia of the Soviet leader, this was a rather remarkable statement.

FDR's main concern at Yalta was that there could be no publicly perceived break in Allied unity so long as the war continued. General Marshall and his military advisors insisted that Russia be brought into the war against Japan, so that a new front on the Asian mainland would divert the enemy as the American invasion of the main island of Honshu took place. Even with the diversion of a Russian front, this invasion was expected to yield upward of a million casualties. Equally important, Roosevelt believed, was bringing the Soviet Union into the new organization of nations. Without the participation of the great powers, the organization was doomed before it had begun—like Wilson's League before it. There were large areas of disagreement: Stalin and Churchill had agendas quite different from Roosevelt's. It would not be possible to resolve the disagreements at Yalta, perhaps not possible to resolve them at all. But with participation in the United Nations, with participation in a continuing process of communication and compromise, there was at least the possibility of resolution; if not now, then in the future.

The strain upon the ailing President was immense. He was away from Washington for more than five weeks. To get to Yalta and back, he traveled 14,000 miles by ship, airplane, and automobile. At Yalta he met for eight days in formal sessions with Stalin and Churchill and their delegations. He met with his own staff innumerable times; he negotiated privately with both Stalin and Churchill; and he participated in the social exchanges involving lunches, dinners, and dozens of toasts of Russian vodka.

From start to last, FDR was the senior personage, acknowledged as such by all. Throughout the conference his mind was clear. The minutes show he ran the meetings with decision and dispatch. As in the reelection campaign, he was able to rouse himself from his depression so as to function effectively at the conference table.

The President's schedule was limited and strictly kept. He was in his quarters each day until noon, largely unavailable to his secretaries or his advisors. In the mornings he slept late, was bathed and dressed by his valet, and saw his doctors. He would lunch and meet with the various members of the American delegation after lunch. He would then take an hour's nap and convene the summit each day at four. For Roosevelt's convenience, the meetings were held in the Livadia Palace, his residence at Yalta. These meetings normally lasted some three to four hours. At the conclusion of these meetings, there would be an hour's recess—during which the President would have a massage and rubdown—and then the conferees would come together again in the state dining room for the evening meal, which was hosted alternately by the three leaders. These dinners, usually featuring Russian cooking, hard drinking, and pointed persiflage, were perhaps the most taxing part of the Yalta Conference.

Roosevelt weathered it all without evident harm to his system. It was noticed that he tired quickly; at times, his color would turn ashen; and at one point during the lengthy, impassioned quarrels over Poland, Roosevelt's doctor detected for the first time in his patient what is called "pulsus alternans," a symptom of impending heart crisis. Increased rest was prescribed, and the symptom disappeared. It is of interest that throughout the conference the President was taking digitalis for his heart, terpinhydrate and codeine for his cough, nose drops for his sinuses, phenobarbital for his blood pressure, and sleeping pills as needed at night. The cumulative effect of these medications could have deepened his depression and could well have contributed to the shakiness of FDR's hand and the occasional wandering of his thoughts.

The Yalta Conference and its results have been the subject of intense controversy ever since. In essence, it is charged that Roosevelt at Yalta was a sick and tired man, which is true. It is further charged that as a result of his infirm state, he failed to take the measure of the Soviet's aggressive intent and thereby acquiesced to the Soviet takeover of Eastern Europe without a struggle. This is decidedly untrue.

There is no reason to believe the results of the Yalta Conference would have been different had Roosevelt been at the top of his form. The Polish issue was the most debated item on the agenda. The reality was that the Russians were already in physical possession of two-thirds of Poland. They were unlikely to be moved by anything less than force, and the Western allies, for a host of reasons, were unwilling to use force. This left Roosevelt and Churchill with little choice other than to lean hard on Stalin, and in the communiqué to paper over the differences with what Alger Hiss calls "rubber words"[15]—which is what they did.

The Russians were already in Europe, and in hindsight, it seems that nothing short of war would have removed them. And the West, drained by the Second World War, was not then willing to launch a third. So far as the occupation of Eastern Europe is concerned, Lord Gladwyn, who was a member of Churchill's party at the conference, was probably right when he concluded some thirty years later, "If there hadn't been any Yalta Conference at all, the result would have been much the same. I think history would have fulfilled itself, Yalta or no Yalta."[16]

The Soviet Union's agreement to enter the war against Japan was considered an important matter by General Marshall, and he was extremely pleased by the outcome at Yalta. Roosevelt, of course, obtained what was his highest priority: a Soviet commitment to participate in the United Nations.

As Roosevelt had hoped, the Soviet Union remained a member of the United Nations. Throughout the harrowing years of the

Cold War, relations between the United States and the Soviet Union were always difficult, at times desperate, but they were never broken. Major armed conflict between the nuclear powers was avoided. With the collapse of communism and the breakup of the Soviet Union, the United States and Russia, side by side on the Security Council, have the opportunity to work together to make the United Nations an effective force for peace.

Taken in all, the Yalta Conference was best summed up by Roosevelt himself. On the first morning of his return to the White House after the conference, FDR remarked to A. A. Berle, "I didn't say it was good, Adolf. I said it was the best I could do."[17] It was, indeed, the best he could do; and at that time and that place, he was the only one who could have done it at all.

XIX
Apotheosis

We never, ever thought of the President as handicapped,
we *never* thought of it at all.[1]

DOROTHY BELSLEY

President Roosevelt reported the result of the Yalta Conference in person to the Congress. For the first time he was
rolled into the House chamber in his chair and transferred to an
armchair. He gave his address sitting at a table in the well of the
House.

Also, for the first time, in speaking to the Congress, the President made reference to his crippled condition: "Mr. Vice President, Mr. Speaker, Members of the Congress, I hope you will
pardon me for the unusual posture of sitting down during the
presentation of what I wish to say, but I know you will realize it
makes it a lot easier for me in not having to carry about ten
pounds of steel around the bottom of my legs [laughter] and also
because of the fact I have just completed a fourteen-thousand-
mile trip [applause]."[2]

A New York congressman told his son after the speech, "I have
just seen the President; he is a dying man."[3] Yet, in spite of the
obvious, the press and radio reports continued in their reassuring
self-denial. The President appears "tan, well rested," said *The
New York Times*.[4]

He was not well rested; he was exhausted. The following day
FDR went to Hyde Park for a week, hoping to regain some of his

energy and strength. He was no better on his return, and he made plans to go to Warm Springs to rest "for as long as it takes." Even at this late stage, FDR had not given up hope of regaining strength in his paralyzed muscles. A month before his death, FDR began work with an unlicensed therapist who claimed exciting results with a new technique.[5]

At the railroad depot in Warm Springs, Secret Service Chief Reilly lifted the President into his car. Even though FDR had lost much weight, he seemed to Reilly terribly heavy—all "dead" weight. Reilly had lifted FDR thousands of times and only once before, when the President was sick with a tooth infection, had he seemed so dead heavy. This alarmed Reilly. Even faithful Grace Tully could no longer deny the collapse of the President's condition. He could rouse himself for short periods, speaking and acting in a bright, animated manner; but then, as in one case, she reported, "We had been waiting for the Boss in the Oval Study and when he was wheeled in I was so startled I almost burst into tears. In two hours he seemed to have failed dangerously. His face was ashen, heightened by the darkening shadows under his eyes, and with his cheeks drawn gauntly."[6]

For ten days at Warm Springs, the weather was fine. It was early spring—a warming sun, dogwood in bloom, the winds gentle in the high Georgia pines. The President sat quietly with his chosen house guests: his two maiden cousins. Lucy Rutherfurd came to visit. As they chatted and she knit, he played solitaire, went over his stamp collection, or worked at a small table on the speech he would give to open the first session of the United Nations.

One afternoon FDR had himself driven once more to Dowdell's Knob, his favorite spot on Pine Mountain, where there had been so many jovial picnics in the past. For two hours he sat lost in thought, looking over the softly rolling Georgia landscape. Two days later, on April 12 at 1:15 p.m., President Franklin D. Roosevelt suffered a massive cerebral hemorrhage. He was pronounced dead at 3:35 p.m.

Every American adult alive in 1945 remembers what he was doing at the moment he learned of the death of President Roosevelt. That Roosevelt was both mortal and dead came as a genuine shock, and the impact was universal. With tears and grief, memorial events and services were held across the nation.

The ramps constructed in the White House and other places across Washington for the use of the President's wheelchair were soon taken up. It is ironic that, as the injured veterans of World War II returned with their wheelchairs and crutches, the ramps that would have provided them access to official Washington were removed. Even St. John's Church, the church of Presidents across Lafayette Square from the White House, removed the small ramp from the two steps at the church's entrance.

Roosevelt had willed the house at Hyde Park and its furnishings to the nation. These were placed under the care and maintenance of the National Park Service. As part of its refurbishing, the Park Service removed the ramps that had made Hyde Park accessible to FDR, thereby making it inaccessible to the handicapped persons who would come on pilgrimages to the home of one of their own. Not until passage of the 1968 Bartlett Act, which required that all Federal buildings be accessible, were FDR's ramps restored at Hyde Park.

FDR's little kitchen chair wheelchair was put on exhibit in the small museum next to the Roosevelt house, along with the campaign memorabilia, the state gifts, and the curios and knickknacks that once littered his desk. For a time, his leg braces were exhibited also—well worn, painted black at the ankles so as to escape detection against FDR's black socks and shoes. Museum curators, however, upon consideration, decided with exquisite sensibility that visitors might find this graphic evidence of the President's infirmity "offensive," and so the braces were removed from public view "as a matter of taste."' Recently, a more open attitude toward the handicapped has caused the museum to put them back on view.

Within a month of his death the U.S. Mint began the process leading to the striking of a new coin, the FDR dime. The dime was selected because it was so closely associated with Roosevelt's fund-raising activities on behalf of the National Foundation for Infantile Paralysis, "The March of Dimes." The coin was released on Roosevelt's next birthday, January 30, 1946. With Roosevelt on the dime, joining Jefferson on the nickel, Lincoln on the penny, and Washington on the quarter, it seemed that Roosevelt's place had been secured in the pantheon of American heroes.

Such was not the case. During the following decade a widespread feeling developed that a suitable memorial should be erected in Roosevelt's honor in Washington, D.C., and in 1955, the Congress set aside land for such a tribute. The spot chosen was the last major site along the noble axis of the national memorials to Washington, Jefferson and Lincoln. A commission was created to devise a suitable structure. It has taken forty years of controversy but—at long last—the construction of the Franklin Delano Roosevelt Memorial is under way. There have been major practical and political reasons for the delay. There is a psychological reason as well.

Roosevelt's place in American history is secure. The overwhelming national reaction to his death proves Roosevelt's importance to rank-and-file Americans was as great as any leader's in our history. Even so, over the years since his death, the ambiguity in the public perception of the man lingers on: The man himself seems somehow illusive.

It is this perception that makes the public uncertain about him as a hero, uneasy about his place in history. And, of course, this uneasiness, this ambiguity has its origins in the deception practiced about the President's handicap while he was in the White House. A deception which—a half century after his death—is still being practiced.

Construction of the FDR Memorial is now underway. If appropriations are forthcoming, it is scheduled for completion in 1996 at an estimated $49 million—commensurate with the costs of the other great memorials. As designed by landscape architect Lawrence Halperin, it will be impressive yet low key, almost informal in the Roosevelt tradition. There will be a long, rambling granite wall backed by a landscaped berm, forming various gardens and open sided "rooms." The memorial will be fully accessible to disabled visitors.

At the entrance to the memorial there will be a heroic scale bas-relief by Leonard Baskin depicting FDR at the First Inaugural, top hat and all. Baskin used a contemporary photo as reference. In the photo, the President stands gripping the arm of his son James, using his cane behind his back as a tripod to steady himself. In the bas-relief, the President stands alone, without cane or support of any kind. Thus, the deception continues. The statue is historically inaccurate. Roosevelt could not stand alone. [see photos]

In their statues, the ancient Romans idealized the features of their emperors, actually turning them into gods. This tradition lingers. We like to have our heroes in heroic scale — the bronze general in the park, sword held high, mounted on a great bronze steed. Idealization is fine. Emphatically, however, this does not give license to alter the basic physical characteristics of the subject. Abraham Lincoln was tall and skinny; Senator Stephen A. Douglas was short and tubby; Senator Robert Taft was plain with glasses. This is how they are portrayed in their statues.

FDR was a hero. FDR was a paraplegic. The one does not contradict or cancel the other. Certainly, FDR should be portrayed in heroic mode, but he should not be portrayed as able-bodied.

There are more than 30 million disabled Americans. It is a source of pride to them that the great American hero of the century was a disabled person. It is important to them—and important as a symbol of how American society perceives its disabled people—that the image of Franklin Delano Roosevelt at the Roosevelt Memorial in Washington D.C. depict the man as he was: tall, strong, heroic, crippled.

As the biographies and memoirs began to appear, the denial continued in a curious way. The memoirs generally acknowledged the President's handicap; some even occasionally mentioned his wheelchair. None, however, acknowledged that the handicap was of any importance. In fact, only Frances Perkins,

FDR's Secretary of Labor, admits to having thought much about it at all.

Roosevelt's associates had been mesmerized by this great man they had known, and they continued to be. In later years, when they were asked about FDR's condition, their answers were quick and emphatic. "The President never gave his handicap a thought, never," said Rex Tugwell in the 1970s.[8] In the 1960s, Grace Tully assured, "Why, it never bothered him at all. He was a wonderful, wonderful man."[9] At the Washington dinner in 1983 commemorating the fiftieth anniversary of the New Deal, Dorothy Belsley, whose husband was in the White House in the first term, looked her questioner in the eye and said, carefully underlining every word, "We never, ever thought of the President as handicapped, we *never* thought of it at all."[10] This was the official position. One sensed that any variance, any thought or investigation of his condition would not be permitted. And this surely was how the matter was passed from the White House staff to the Congress, to the press, and so on throughout the country.

Until the appearance of this book, Roosevelt's biographers tended to treat his paralysis as an episode—with a beginning, a middle, and an end. By their accounts, Roosevelt gets polio, struggles through his rehabilitation, and then overcomes his adversity. End of chapter. The handicap is never mentioned again. It is viewed only as one of the stages through which FDR passed in preparation for the presidency. The biographers appear distinctly uneasy, perhaps embarrassed, by the continuing reality of FDR's affliction.

As has been described in this book, FDR arranged his appearances so that the public would not be confronted with the true extent of his paralysis. In a sense, he conspired with the public to present the image of the President as vigorous and physically fit. Now, after his death, the biographers continued this conspiracy. They simply accepted the image of Roosevelt as he presented it to the public, and they made no effort to assess the extraordinary cost in energy and thought that went into maintaining this image throughout twelve White House years of peace and war.

In a triumph of will, FDR had convinced his family, his party, the press, and the country that his paralysis was unimportant. Furthermore, he had convinced himself of this. Strengthened by that conviction and blessed with that first-rate character perceived by Justice Holmes, FDR built a life of mighty achievement. No matter how much he denied it—to himself and to the world—he was, indeed, a crippled man. The attack of polio that caused his condition was the central event of his life; his illness and lengthy rehabilitation shaped and altered his character. It is important, therefore, to understand *how* it did so. It is difficult, perhaps even foolhardy, to attempt to assess a man's character. With FDR, a man with a "perfectly ruthless, highly versatile, superior but impenetrable mind," as psychiatrist Carl Jung said, it is probably impossible.[11] Certainly, however, polio had an impact, and certainly this impact involved at least such matters as the following:

It is not unusual in man or animal for one faculty to become stronger as compensation for the loss of another. In this sense, the charm and power of Roosevelt's personality were magnified after the paralysis of his legs. By means of various tricks that actors use, acquired both consciously and unconsciously, Roosevelt was able to project from his wheelchair a personality that dominated all others. He radiated a warmth that filled even the very corners of a room. The characteristic tilt of his head; the famous smile; the infectious, hearty laugh; the jaunty cigarette holder; the military cape; the old, floppy fedora—it was by such means that he was able to project and enlarge his presence.

Trapped in a chair, he had to rely upon others to do things for him. Thus, whether to order, beg, or cajole, he was caused to be manipulative to get things done, to enforce his will. Trapped in his room, he was dependent upon the reports of others to find out what was happening in the land, and dependent upon the gossip of others to learn what was happening within his administration. Repressed as his frustration might be, it surfaced in the occasional sadistic pleasure he found in stirring up bureaucratic disputes for his own entertainment, such as first egging on irascible

Ickes and then nudging forward Harry Hopkins, Ickes' foe. The paralyzed President in his chair in the Oval Office was—to a degree and in a sense—like an invalid, confined to his bed in a sickroom, taking pleasure from an ant colony. It is surely not surprising if, now and then, the invalid took a stick to poke up a little action in the colony.

Roosevelt's paralysis was his one and only major experience with failure. From it he learned about humiliation and loss. This appears to have helped make him a more compassionate person. During the pre-polio 1920 vice-presidential campaign, some found the young FDR to be cocky and arrogant. His campaign swing out West was not a success. After the seven-year struggle with his rehabilitation, his interest in others and his appeal to the voters seemed genuine and strong. People sensed his identification with them in a way that had hitherto been lacking.

During those seven years, Roosevelt had the time and the opportunity to meet, talk to, and become friends with people of a sort that he had never met before. Struggling on his braces and crutches down to the end of the driveway at Hyde Park, FDR came to meet the local citizens—the mailman, the delivery boys, neighboring tenants. He met them not as the lord of the manor passing in his limousine, but as a human being, visibly struggling with his problems as his neighbors struggled with theirs. So, too, in Warm Springs, driving his open Ford about the back roads of rural Georgia in the severe agricultural depression of the 1920s, FDR came to understand the problems and fears of the farmers, the tenants, the poor whites, and the blacks of red-clay Georgia. FDR would never have had this leavening experience had he continued the life of a New York society attorney/broker with a career in politics.

And, of course, this seven-year hiatus from public life served to buy time. When he contracted polio in 1921, FDR was already a national figure and clearly a coming presidential contender. The enforced seven-year rehabilitation period was used by FDR, his wife, and Louis Howe to build a nationwide network of correspondents, friends, and supporters. Without polio, FDR's career would have peaked much earlier. Timing is all when it comes to obtaining a party nomination and winning the presidency. The presidency is like the brass ring on the merry-go-round; it must be grabbed as it comes round. Without polio, Roosevelt might have been forced to run for the presidency in the 1920s, a period of Republican ascendancy. His illness and his rehabilitation allowed FDR a valuable flexibility in planning to become president.

Polio, and his efforts at devising a helpful rehabilitative therapy, also helped him to develop the management techniques he used to bring the nation through the Depression and the war. FDR always saw himself as his own chief orthopedist. He was delighted when they called him "Doctor Roosevelt" at Warm Springs. He consulted with all the experts and tried, in turn, all the existing therapies. Keeping that which was helpful, he discarded that which was not, and he did it all with a contagious bravado. This was precisely the technique he used as President. It is no accident that in the White House he became "Doctor New Deal," or that after Pearl Harbor, he traded the title in for "Doctor Win the War." "Doctor Roosevelt" had struggled against imponderable odds in his own rehabilitation. The odds for the rehabilitation of the nation after the Depression or for prevailing in war were no worse. And his confidence was no less.

These were some of the effects that polio had on FDR. Perhaps the greatest effect of all was caused by the deception that FDR found it necessary to practice. Given the social attitudes of the time, the deception was necessary if he was to get elected. And it made his leadership role easier to carry out. The deception was not easy—it drained FDR's energy, diverted his attention and, emotionally, it served to enforce his isolation. It became, in fact, a barrier that no one could pierce.

When he was alive, the power of his presence and his marvelous personality overwhelmed all doubts. After his death, the memory of his personality faded and the doubts surfaced. The image of the inspiring President, the great wartime leader, endures—how could it not?—but a curious, sometimes cynical public seeks to look within, to find the inner man—and it seems no one is there.

However, as the full extent of Roosevelt's physical handicap is acknowledged and its impact upon him is detailed, then the very human being who was Franklin Roosevelt comes alive and develops believability and integrity. Roosevelt's splendid deception—and it *was* splendid as, indeed, was everything else about this man—can then be seen as but a part of his defense mechanism, behind which was a good man whose emotional life was as withered as his legs. His character, behavior, and motivation no longer appear so enigmatic. FDR is seen, not as an unreal political wizard, but as a genuine suffering human being struggling with a lifelong problem.

Appendix
The Muscle Test Charts
of Franklin D. Roosevelt

When I was a patient at the Georgia Warm Springs Foundation in 1953, Dr. Robert Bennett, the medical director, informed me that I would never walk again. He said, however, that with training I should be able to learn how to function from my wheelchair in an independent manner. Bennett suggested that I become acquainted with the cofounder of the Foundation, Mr. Fred Botts. Botts, who was as paralyzed as I, lived an independent and satisfactory life. Bennett thought I could learn a lot observing Botts, and he was right. I did.

I once asked Botts how it was that his friend FDR had been able to use his braces in a functional way and even appear to be walking, while we could not. In reply Botts suggested that I look at FDR's muscle test charts. And so, with the help of my therapist I studied FDR's charts carefully, comparing the President's pattern of paralysis with my own. It was a heartening experience—even inspiring. I learned what muscle weaknesses the President had and how he managed them. The chart made clear to me that FDR experienced the daily struggle and frustration of paralysis. I was not the only patient to see FDR's muscle records. Many others saw them and benefited from them. The records served as visible evidence that FDR was one of us.

A year or two later, in the late 1950s, I returned to Warm Springs for a checkup. I was pleased to note that the charts of FDR's muscle tests had been mounted in an exhibit case for all to see. By that time the President's Warm Springs cottage, "the Little White House," had been turned into a national historic site; and the cottage attracted thousands of tourists, many of them handicapped. The tourists were able to see the President's wheelchair, his hand-controlled car, the treatment tables and pool, and, of course, the muscle charts. These exhibits encouraged the disabled to identify with the late President, and helped the general population to improve their understanding of disability.

I began the research for this book in 1981, the International Year of Disabled Persons. I was, that year, a Fellow at the Woodrow Wilson International Center for Scholars. During the course of my work at the Presidential Library in Hyde Park, New York, I was astonished to learn that, so far as the archivists were aware, there were no medical records of Franklin D. Roosevelt's presidential years in existence anywhere. I was told the President's medical files had been in the care of his personal physician, the late Admiral Ross McIntire. They had been kept in a safe at the Bethesda Naval Hospital. The combination to this safe had been known to but two people: the hospital's commander and Admiral McIntire. Shortly after the President's death, the records were found to have "disappeared." What happened to them no one knows to this day.

This is a great loss to history. The President's health was failing during the last year of his life. This was the climactic year of World War II. During this period FDR made decisions of incomparable importance. In interpreting his behavior it would be helpful to have a detailed assessment of his health.

Learning of the disappearance of the records reminded me that I had seen some health records of the presidential years at Warm Springs—the muscle charts. Upon inquiry, I learned that the charts were, indeed, still in existence. They were in the possession of the Roosevelt Warm Springs Institute for Rehabilitation, the successor organization of the Georgia Warm Springs Foundation. I was told, however, that the FDR records were not available for public inspection. I could not see them nor could I copy them.

After several efforts to obtain access, I wrote for help to Congressman James Roosevelt, the President's eldest son and the surviving executor of his will. In response to my request, Roosevelt kindly wrote to the Institute asking that I be allowed to see the documents. I did see them—they were just as I had remembered them. Fortunately, I was able to make a transcription of these records for my own use.

In preparing my manuscript for the publisher, it seemed to me that paraplegics reading the book would find it interesting and, perhaps, encouraging to compare their own muscle patterns with those of the late President. I decided, therefore, that it would be of value to print a portion of the President's muscle test charts in the Appendix. I wrote to the Institute Executive Director, Mr. J. Ellics Moran, asking permission to do so.

Mr. Moran denied my request. He replied, "There are two problems: 1) the Department of Human Resources has a regulation that prohibits the release of medical information on a deceased patient without a court order or subpoena signed by a judge; and 2) there is a new State of Georgia law which prohibits the release of medical information which will be rereleased. The information is considered privileged and confidential. Under these conditions I am afraid that we cannot release to you the information that you have requested."

I reject the relevance of the two points raised by Mr. Moran: 1) Franklin Roosevelt was never a patient of the Georgia Department of Human Resources; the fact that his records are now in the department's file is an historical accident and nothing more; 2) The records have already been released and rereleased to the public many, many times. They are no longer privileged nor are they confidential.

It is my firm belief that the President's charts should be at the Presidential Library at Hyde Park where they will be available to scholars and to the public. Roosevelt willed his papers and associated documents to the nation. The Library has prepresidential health records in its collection, and the muscle charts should be with them—per the directions of FDR's will.

Roosevelt did all he could throughout his life to help his fellow paralytics. I cannot conceive of his objecting to the publication of the charts for the information and encouragement of today's paraplegics. Accordingly, in this appendix I am publishing my transcription of one of the charts.

Birthday January 1882

No.   Name: Roosevelt, Franklin D. Age:51   Diagnosis: Polio   Date of Onset 1921

Waist 39	Cannot Walk	Walks Unaided	With Braces	Left	Right	Crutches	Canes	Corset
Date:12/3/33	----	-------	XXXXX	XX	XX	------	XX 1	---

Characteristic gait

Date:12/3/33   Walks with cane and person's arm

Left 12/3/33		Trunk and Legs		Right 12/3/33
		Facial		
		Neck		
N		Back		N
N	Upper	Anterior abdominals	Upper	N
G	Lower	Anterior abdominals	Lower	N
G-		Lateral abdominals		G+
(over edge cannot lift)	F upper P lower	Gluteus maximus	upper P lower	P+ lifts ½ over edge
P+		Ilio psoas		P
P+ ½		Sartorius		P
P+ ½		Tensor fasciae latae		P+ starts
P+ distance F strength		Hip abductors		P starts
P+ grad		Hip adductors		P
P+		Inward rotators		P+
P+ starts		Outward rotators		F+
P+ ½		Quadriceps		P+ starts
F-	Inner	Hamstrings Inner		P+
P	Outer	Hamstrings Outer		P+ better
P+ good		Gastrocnemius		F
P+		Anterior tibial		P
F-		Posterior tibial		P+
P+		Peroneals		G+
G-		Extensor longus digitorum		G-
G		Extensor brevis digitorum		G-
F		Extensor proprius hallucis		F+
N	1	Flexor longus digitorum 1		F
N	2	" " " 2		G-
N	3	" " " 3		G
G	4	" " " 4		G
G	1	Flexor brevis digitorum 1		N
G	2	" " " 2		G+
G-	3	" " " 3		G
G-	4	" " " 4		G
F		Flexor lumbricales		G
G+		Flexor longus hallucis		F
G		Flexor brevis hallucis		F

MEASUREMENTS

Left		Right	
11½ (6)	Calf	11½	
16 5/8 - 13 1/4	Thigh	13 1/8 - 16 3/4	(10)
37 3/4	Length	37 3/4	

CONTRACTURES AND DEFORMITIES

Left		Right
	Hip lies in out rot	cont
flex. cont.	Knee	
	Ankle	
Ft. drop	Toes	Ft. drop

(Author's note: Physical therapist grades each muscle group according to the scale:
N, normal; G, good; F, fair; P, poor; T, trace.)

Reference Notes

This book began as a research project at the Woodrow Wilson International Center for Scholars while I was there as a visiting fellow. Additional research was done at the Franklin D. Roosevelt Presidential Library at Hyde Park, New York and the Roosevelt Warm Springs Institute for Rehabilitation at Warm Springs, Georgia. All three institutions were most helpful, and I thank them.

All Roosevelt family letters listed in the reference notes are available at the Presidential Library at Hyde Park.

Full details on the books and articles listed in the reference notes may be found in the bibliography.

The epigraph on the title page is from Earle Looker, "Is Franklin Roosevelt Fit to Be President," *Liberty Magazine*, July 25, 1931, pp. 6–10.

Introduction

[1] Hoover, Herbert, unpublished manuscript, 1962.

Chapter I Onset

[1] Graff, Robert, and Ginna, Robert, *F.D.R.*, p. 59.
[2] Looker, Earle, *This Man Roosevelt*, p. 111.
[3] *Ibid.*
[4] Roosevelt, James, and Shalett, Sidney, *Affectionately, F.D.R.*, p. 141.
[5] Looker, p. 111.
[6] Graff and Ginna, p. 46.
[7] Davis, Kenneth, *F.D.R., The Beckoning of Destiny 1882–1928*, p. 616.
[8] F.D.R. pieces quoted in Davis, p. 75.
[9] Roosevelt, Sara, *My Boy Franklin*, p. 15.
[10] Davis, p. 84.

[11] Roosevelt, Sara, p. 18.
[12] For polio details see Paul, John R., *A History of Poliomyelitis*, and Huckstep, R. L., *Poliomyelitis*.
[13] Roosevelt, James, *My Parents*, p. 101.
[14] For scandal details and quotations see Freidel, Frank, *Franklin D. Roosevelt*, vol. 2, pp. 95–7; Davis, pp. 642–5; U.S. 67th Congress 1st Session, Senate Committee on Naval Affairs, *Alleged Immoral Conditions at Newport (R.I.) Naval Training Station*, Report (Washington, 1921).
[15] Lash, Joseph P., *Eleanor and Franklin*, p. 266.
[16] Freidel, vol. 2, p. 97.
[17] Davis, p. 490.

Chapter II Crisis

[1] F.D.R. to Dr. William Egleston, October 11, 1924.
[2] Looker, Earle, *This Man Roosevelt*, p. 112.
[3] F.D.R. to Dr. William Egleston, *op. cit.*
[4] Eleanor Roosevelt to James Roosevelt Roosevelt, August 14, 1921.
[5] Davis, Kenneth, *F.D.R., The Beckoning of Destiny*, p. 656.
[6] Gould, Jean, *A Good Fight*, p. 26.
[7] Roosevelt, Eleanor, *Autobiography*, p. 114.
[8] Lash, Joseph P., *Eleanor and Franklin*, p. 268.
[9] Davis, p. 651.
[10] Graff, Robert, and Ginna, Robert, *F.D.R.*, p. 59.
[11] Asbell, Bernard, *The F.D.R. Memoirs*, p. 259.
[12] Eleanor Roosevelt to James Roosevelt Roosevelt, op. cit.
[13] Gould, p. 69.
[14] Asbell, p. 234.
[15] Freidel, Frank, *Franklin D. Roosevelt*, vol. 2, p. 100.
[16] Roosevelt, Eleanor, p. 117.
[17] Roosevelt, James, and Shalett, Sidney, *Affectionately, F.D.R.*, p. 143.
[18] Graff and Ginna, p. 192.
[19] *Ibid.*
[20] Davis, p. 661.
[21] Roosevelt, Elliott, and Brough, James, *An Untold Story: The Roosevelts of Hyde Park*, p. 149.
[22] Roosevelt, Eleanor, p. 116.

Chapter III Convalescence

[1] Graff, Robert, and Ginna, Robert, *F.D.R.*, p. 69.
[2] "F. D. Roosevelt Ill," *The New York Times*, September 16, 1921, p. 1; letter from F.D.R. to Adolph S. Ochs, September 16, 1921.
[3] Gunther, John, *Roosevelt in Retrospect*, pp. 227-28.
[4] Lindley, Ernest K., *Franklin D. Roosevelt*, p. 221.
[5] Roosevelt, Eleanor, *Autobiography*, p. 120.

[6] Harrity, Richard, and Martin, Ralph, *The Human Side of F.D.R.*, unpaged.
[7] Lindley, p. 206.
[8] Freidel, Frank, *Franklin D. Roosevelt*, vol. 2, p. 191.
[9] McIntire, Ross T., and Creel, George, *White House Physician*, p. 8.
[10] Graff and Ginna, p. 69.
[11] Sara Roosevelt to F.D.R., August 23, 1925.
[12] Lippman, Theo, Jr., *The Squire of Warm Springs*, p. 81.

Chapter IV Attitudes

[1] Lily Norton to Helen Whidden, November 14, 1921.
[2] *Ibid.*
[3] Davis, Gwilym G., "The Education of Crippled Children," in Phillips, William F., and Rosenburg, Janet, *The Origins of Modern Treatment and Education of Physically Handicapped Children*, William F., Janet, variously paged.
[4] Le Roy, S. H., "Hospital For Ruptured and Crippled," in Phillips and Rosenburg, variously paged.
[5] Elmslie, R. C. *The Care of Invalid and Crippled Children in School*, p. 9.
[6] Elmslie, p. 9.
[7] Elmslie, p. 40.
[8] Elmslie, p. 41.
[9] Davis, variously paged.

Chapter V Warm Springs

[1] F.D.R. to Eleanor Roosevelt, October 1924.
[2] For Warm Springs generally, see Walker, Turnley, *Roosevelt and the Warm Springs Story;* Gould, Jean, *A Good Fight;* Lippman, Theo, Jr. *The Squire of Warm Springs.* Additional material in uncatalogued archives of Georgia Warm Springs Foundation in care of Roosevelt Warm Springs Institute for Rehabilitation, Warm Springs, Georgia.
[3] F.D.R. to Eleanor Roosevelt, October 1924.
[4] Roosevelt, Eleanor, *This I Remember*, p. 27.
[5] Carmichael, Donald Scott, *F.D.R., Columnist*, p. 13.
[6] Gregory, Cleburne, "Franklin D. Roosevelt Will Swim To Health," *Atlanta Journal*, October 26, 1924.
[7] Roosevelt, F. D., *The Public Papers and Addresses of Franklin D. Roosevelt*, F.D.R. Remarks, Warm Springs, Georgia, November 29, 1934, vol. 3, p. 485.
[8] *Ibid.*
[9] Roosevelt, F.D., *Public Papers*, F.D.R. Remarks, Warm Springs, Georgia, November 25, 1983, vol. 7, p. 612.
[10] Botts, Fred, unpublished manuscript, undated, at F.D.R. Presidential Library.
[11] F.D.R. to Livingston Davis, April 25, 1925.
[12] Lash, Joseph, P., *Eleanor and Franklin*, p. 296.

[13] Freidel, Frank, *Franklin D. Roosevelt*, vol. 2, p. 197.
[14] *Ibid.*
[15] Walker, p. 82.

Chapter VI Rehabilitation

[1] F.D.R. to Mrs. W. S. Cowles, June 29, 1927.
[2] Roosevelt, Elliott, and Brough, James, *An Untold Story*, p. 250.
[3] Roosevelt, F. D., *Public Papers*, vol. 3, p. 488.
[4] Roosevelt, Elliott, *F.D.R. His Personal Letters*, p. 610.
[5] Lippman, Theo, Jr., *The Squire of Warm Springs*, p. 121.
[6] Boggs, D. M., to F.D.R., February 19, 1948.
[7] F.D.R. to Sara Roosevelt, February 1927.
[8] F.D.R. to Cowles, June 29, 1927.
[9] The Hydrotherapeutic Center, Pamphlet, Warm Springs, Georgia, undated.
[10] "Warm Springs Seeks to Expand," *The New York Times*, January 5, 1930.
[11] "Many Victims of Paralysis Aided at Warm Springs," *The Macon News*, Macon, Georgia, March 30, 1930.

Chapter VII Principles

[1] Author's interview with Anne Irwin Bray, July 16, 1981.

Chapter VIII Triumph

[1] Durant, Will, *The New York World*, June 28, 1928, quoted in Davis, p. 822.
[2] See accounts in Gould, Jean, *A Good Fight*; Walker, Turnley, *Roosevelt and the Warm Springs Story*; Davis, Kenneth, *F.D.R., The Beckoning of Destiny*; Freidel, Frank, *Franklin D. Roosevelt.*
[3] Roosevelt, James, and Shalett, Sidney, *Affectionately, F.D.R.*, p. 206.
[4] *Ibid.*, p. 207.
[5] Gould, p. 160.
[6] Roosevelt, Elliott, and Brough, James, *An Untold Story*, p. 242.
[7] Walker, Story.
[8] Lippman, Theo, Jr., *The Squire of Warm Springs*, p. 66.
[9] Durant, Will, *The New York World*, June 28, 1928.
[10] *The New York Times*, June 28, 1928.
[11] *Chicago Tribune*, July 1, 1928.

Chapter IX Governor

[1] Roosevelt, James, and Shalett, Sidney, *Affectionately, F.D.R.*, p. 208.
[2] Howe to F.D.R., September 25, 1928.
[3] F.D.R. to Smith, September 30, 1928.
[4] Howe to F.D.R., October 2, 1928.

[5] *New York Post,* October 2, 1928.
[6] Freidel, Frank, *Franklin D. Roosevelt,* vol. 2, p. 258.
[7] *New York Herald Tribune,* October 20, 1928.
[8] Roosevelt, Anna, "How Polio Helped Father," *Woman Magazine,* July 1949.
[9] Perkins, Frances, *The Roosevelt I Knew,* p. 44.
[10] *Ibid.,* p. 45.
[11] Roosevelt and Shalett, *Affectionately, F.D.R.,* p. 208.
[12] Perkins, p. 52.
[13] Roosevelt, F. D., *The Public Papers,* vol. 2, p. 84.
[14] Hamburger, Philip, in *The New Yorker,* November 17, 1962.
[15] Brownlow, Louis, *A Passion for Anonymity,* p. 270.
[16] As related to the author by Rex Tugwell and Col. Frank Mason. Incident referred to in Roosevelt, Eleanor, *This I Remember,* p. 61.
[17] Hoover, Herbert, unpublished manuscript, 1962.
[18] Freidel, vol. 3, p. 210.
[19] Looker, Earle, "Is Franklin D. Roosevelt Physically Fit to Be President?" *Liberty Magazine,* July 25, 1931.
[20] Moley, Raymond, *After Seven Years,* p. 52.
[21] Freidel, vol. 3, p. 370.
[22] Roosevelt, James, p. 232.

Chapter X President

[1] Moley, Raymond, *After Seven Years,* p. 139.
[2] *Ibid.*
[3] Lash, Joseph, P., *Eleanor and Franklin,* p. 510.
[4] Rosenman, Samuel, *Working with Roosevelts,* p. 2.
[5] Freidel, Frank, *Franklin D. Roosevelt,* vol. 3, p. 212.
[6] Rogers, Will, quoted in Morison, Samuel Eliot, *Oxford History of the American People,* p. 954.
[7] Gunther, John, *Roosevelt in Retrospect,* p. 239.
[8] Gould, Jean, *A Good Fight,* p. 197.
[9] Lippman, Theo, Jr., *The Squire of Warm Springs,* p. 189.
[10] Lash, p. 424.
[11] Gould, p. 191.
[12] Lippman, p. 178; Ickes, Harold, *The Secret Diaries,* vol. 1, p. 675.
[13] Lippman, p. 101.
[14] Asbell, Bernard, *The F.D.R. Memoirs,* p. 411.
[15] Dall, Curtis, *F.D.R.: My Exploited Father-in-Law,* p. 18.
[16] Daniel, Clifton, *Lords, Ladies and Gentlemen,* p. 73.
[17] Roosevelt, Nicholas, *A Front Row Seat,* p. 224.
[18] Roosevelt, F. D., *The Public Papers,* vol. 5, p. 230.
[19] Reilly, Michael, *Reilly of the White House,* pp. 98–100, and Roosevelt, James, and Shalett, Sidney, *Affectionately, F.D.R.,* p. 157.

Chapter XI Recreation

[1] Ickes, Harold, *The Secret Diaries*, vol. 1, p. 635.
[2] *Ibid.*
[3] Rigdon, William M., and Derieux, Jean, *White House Sailor*, p. 60.
[4] Ickes, vol. 1, pp. 449–50.
[5] Roosevelt, James, *My Parents: A Differing View*, p. 84.

Chapter XII Relations

[1] Pascal, Blaise, *Pensées*, p. 127.
[2] Shakespeare, William, *Hamlet*, Act III, Scene 5, line 145.
[3] Boettiger, John R., *A Love in Shadow*, p. 32.
[4] *Ibid.*
[5] Roosevelt, James, *My Parents: A Differing View*, p. 81.
[6] Harrity, Richard, and Martin, Ralph, *The Human Side of F.D.R.*, unpaged.
[7] Reilly, Michael F., *Reilly of the White House*, p. 85.
[8] Boettiger, p. 56.
[9] Reilly, p. 83.
[10] Roosevelt, Sara, to Frederick A. Delano, September 4, 1921.
[11] Boettiger, p. 90.
[12] Roosevelt, Eleanor, Foreword, *F.D.R. His Personal Letters*, 1905–1928, p. xviii.
[13] Davis, Kenneth, *Invincible Summer*, p. 65.
[14] Lorant, Stefan, *Eleanor Roosevelt*, p. 85.
[15] Boettiger, p. 73.
[16] Rollins, Alfred B., Jr., *Roosevelt and Howe*, p. 186.
[17] Lorant, p. 85.
[18] Oursler, Fulton, *Behold, This Dreamer!*, p. 429.
[19] Acheson, Dean, *Morning and Noon*, p. 164.

Chapter XIII Sex

[1] Oursler, Fulton, *Behold, This Dreamer!*, p. 423.
[2] Roosevelt, James, *My Parents: A Differing View*, p. 104.
[3] "Wife Says Doctors Cleared Roosevelt," *The New York Times*, August 9, 1956, p. 1.
[4] Asbell, Bernard, *The F.D.R. Memoirs*, p. 236.
[5] Acheson, Dean, *Morning and Noon*, pp. 211-12.
[6] Oursler, pp. 423-5.
[7] Asbell, p. 255.
[8] Asbell, p. 244.
[9] Freidel, Frank, *Franklin D. Roosevelt*, vol. 2, p. 191.
[10] Tully, Grace, *F.D.R. Was My Boss*, p. 36.
[11] Asbell, p. 405.
[12] Asbell, p. 413.

[13] Rutherfurd, Lucy M., to Anna R. Halsted, May 9, 1945, as printed in Boettiger, John R., *A Love in Shadow*, p. 262.
[14] Asbell, p. 413.
[15] Boettiger, p. 256.
[16] Cotten, Lyman A., "FDR and Lucy Mercer," Letter to the Editor, *Times Literary Supplement*, August 1, 1980, p. 874.

Chapter XIV The March Of Dimes

[1] Cohn, Victor, *Four Billion Dimes*, p. 52.
[2] Roosevelt, F. D., *The Public Papers*, vol. 3, pp. 485–90.
[4] Cohn, p. 39.
[5] Cohn, p. 43.
[6] Cohn, p. 46.
[7] Cohn, p. 51.
[8] Roosevelt, F. D., *The Public Papers*, vol. 6, pp. 374–76.
[9] Gould, Jean, *A Good Fight*, p. 174.
[10] Roosevelt, F. D., *The Public Papers*, vol. 6, pp. 374–76.
[11] Cohn, p. 52.
[12] *Ibid.*
[13] *Ibid.*

Chapter XV "Hi, Ho, Silver!"

[1] Smith, Merriman, *Merriman Smith's Book of Presidents: A White House Memoir*, edited by Smith, Tim, p. 202.
[2] *Ibid.*
[3] Roosevelt, F. D., memorandum to Secret Service, May 29, 1933.
[4] Hamlin, Mrs. Charles, "Some Memories of Franklin D. Roosevelt," manuscript in FDR Presidential Library, Hyde Park, New York.

Chapter XVI War

[1] Stimson, Henry, and Bundy, McGeorge, *On Active Service in Peace and War*, p. 667.
[2] Churchill, Winston S., *The Second World War Triumph and Tragedy*, vol. 6, p. 474.
[3] Roosevelt, F. D., *The Public Papers*, vol. 10, pp. 514–5.
[4] Holmes, Oliver Wendell, as quoted in Bingham, Colin, ed., *Men and Affairs*, p. 367.
[5] Freidel, Frank, *Franklin D. Roosevelt*, vol. 4, p. 245.
[6] Rosenman, Samuel, *Working with Roosevelts*, p. 325.
[7] Stimson and Bundy, p. 664.
[8] Churchill, vol. 6, p. 474.
[9] Rigdon, William M., and Creel, George, *White House Sailor*, p. 11.

[10] McIntire, Ross, *White House Physician*, p. 201.
[11] *Ibid.*, p. 12.
[12] Roosevelt, Elliott, *As He Saw It*, p. 106.
[13] Roosevelt, F. D. *The Public Papers*, vol. 10, p. 321.
[14] Gunther, John, *Roosevelt in Retrospect*, p. 149.
[15] Pogue, Forrest C., *George C. Marshall*, vol. 2, p. 22.

Chapter XVII Depression

[1] Sherwood, Robert E., *Roosevelt and Hopkins*, p. 880.
[2] McIntire, Ross, and Creel, George, *White House Physician*, p. 57.
[3] Bruenn, H. G., "Clinical Notes on the Illness and Death of President Franklin D. Roosevelt," *Annals of Internal Medicine*, 72, number 4 (April 1970), p. 579.
[4] Roosevelt, James, and Shalett, Sidney, *Affectionately, F.D.R.*, p. 319.
[5] Davis, Kenneth, *F.D.R., The Beckoning of Destiny 1882–1928*, p. 655.
[6] McIntire and Creel, p. 8.
[7] Roosevelt, James, p. 35.
[8] Bishop, Jim, *FDR's Last Year*, p. 293.
[9] *Encyclopaedia Britannica*, XV Edition, vol. 10, p. 170.
[10] *Harvard Guide to Psychiatric Illness*, pp. 191-3; *The Merck Manual of Diagnosis and Therapy*, Robert Berkow, M.D., ed. pp. 1494– 5.
[11] Tully, Grace, *F.D.R. Was My Boss*, p. 66.
[12] *Harvard Guide*, p. 191.
[13] Bishop, p. 8.

Chapter XVIII Farewell

[1] Archilochus, 7th century B.C.
[2] "Wife Says Doctors Cleared Roosevelt," *The New York Times*, August 9, 1956, p. 1.
[3] Lorant, Stefan, *FDR: A Pictorial Biography*, unpaged.
[4] Rosenman, Samuel, *Working With Roosevelts*, p. 478.
[5] Rosenman, p. 474.
[6] Burns, James MacGregor, *Roosevelt, The Soldier of Freedom*, p. 530.
[7] Rosenman, p. 516.
[8] Roosevelt, James, and Shalett, Sidney, *Affectionately, F.D.R.*, p. 354.
[9] Roosevelt, Franklin, *The Public Papers*, vol. 13, p. 523.
[10] *Congressional Record*, p. 1622, March 1, 1945.
[11] *Congressional Record*, p. 1620, March 1, 1945.
[12] *Congressional Record*, p. 1622, March 1, 1945.
[13] Churchill, Winston, *The Second World War*, vol. 6, p. 477.
[14] Moran, Charles, *Winston Churchill: The Struggle for Survival*, p. 242.
[15] Charlton, Michael, "The Eagle and the Small Birds," *Encounter*, June 1983, p. 27.
[16] *Ibid.*
[17] Burns, p. 580.

Chapter XIX Apotheosis

[1] Belsley, Dorothy, wife of Roosevelt Administration employee, to the author, 1983.

[2] *Congressional Record*, pp 1620-24, March 1, 1945.

[3] As told to author by the son.

[4] Bishop, Jim, FDR's Last Year, p. 482.

[5] Confidential communication to author.

[6] Tully, Grace, *F.D.R. Was My Boss*, p.357.

[7] As told to author by Hyde Park official.

[8] Tugwell, Rex, to author.

[9] Tully, Grace, to author.

[10] Belsley, Dorothy, to author.

[11] Graff, Robert, and Ginna, Robert, *F.D.R.*, p.14.

BIBLIOGRAPHY

Books

Acheson, Dean. *Morning and Noon*. Cambridge: Houghton Mifflin Company, 1965.

Adamic, Louis. *Dinner at the White House*. New York: Harper and Brothers Publishers, 1946.

Asbell, Bernard. *The F.D.R. Memoirs*. New York: Doubleday and Company, Inc., 1973.

Barber, James David. *The Presidential Character, Predicting Performance in the White House*. New Jersey: Prentice Hall, Inc., 1972.

Bellush, Bernard. *Franklin D. Roosevelt as Governor of New York*. New York: A.M.S. Press, 1968.

Bingham, Colin, ed. *Men and Affairs: A Modern Miscellany*. Sydney: Currawong Publishing Company, Inc., 1967.

Bishop, Jim, *FDR's Last Year, April 1944–April 1945*. New York: William Morrow and Company, Inc., 1974.

Boettiger, John R. *A Love in Shadow*. New York: W. W. Norton and Company, Inc., 1978.

Brownlow, Louis. *A Passion for Anonymity, the Autobiography of Louis Brownlow*. Chicago: The University of Chicago Press, 1958.

Brynes, James. *All in One Lifetime*. New York: Harper, 1958.

Brynes, James Francis. *Speaking Frankly*. New York: Harper, 1947.

Carmichael, Donald Scott. *F.D.R., Columnist*. Chicago: University of Chicago Press, 1947.

Cecil, Russell LaFayette. *Cecil-Loeb Textbook of Medicine*. Philadelphia: Saunders, 1967.

Dall, Curtis B. *F.D.R.: My Exploited Father-in-law*. Washington, D.C.: Action Associates, 1968.

Daniel, Clifton. *Lords, Ladies and Gentlemen: A Memoir.* New York: Arbor House, 1984.

Daniels, Jonathan. *White House Witness 1942–1945.* New York: Doubleday and Company, Inc. 1975.

Davis, Kenneth S. *F.D.R., The Beckoning of Destiny 1882–1928.* New York: G. P. Putnam's Sons, 1972.

Davis, Olin. *Franklin Roosevelt at Hyde Park.* New York: American Artists Group, Inc., 1949.

Elmslie, R. C. *The Care of Invalid and Crippled Children in School.* London: The School Hygiene Publishing Company, 1911.

Farley, James A. *Jim Farley's Story, The Roosevelt Years.* New York: McGraw-Hill Book Company, Inc., 1948.

Fisher, P. J. *Polio Story.* London: Heinemann Company, Ltd., 1967.

Flynn, John T. *Country Squire in the White House.* New York: Doubleday, Doron and Company, 1940.

Flynn, John T. *The Roosevelt Myth.* New York: The Devin-Adair Publishing Company, 1948.

Freidel, Frank. *Franklin D. Roosevelt.* 4 volumes. Boston: Little, Brown and Company, 1954.

Gies, Joseph. *Franklin D. Roosevelt, Portrait of a President.* New York: Doubleday and Company, Inc., 1971.

Gosnell, Harold F. *Champion Campaigner, Franklin D. Roosevelt.* New York: The Macmillan Company, 1952.

Gould, Jean. *A Good Fight, The Story of F.D.R.'s Conquest of Polio.* New York: Dodd, Mead and Company, 1960.

Graff, Robert D., and Ginna, Robert Emmett. *F.D.R.* New York: Harper and Row, 1962.

Gunther, John. *Roosevelt in Retrospect, A Profile in History.* New York: Harper and Brothers, 1950.

Haj, Fareed. *Disability in Antiquity.* New York: Philosophical Library Press, Inc., 1970.

Harrity, Richard, and Martin, Ralph G. *The Human Side of F.D.R.* New York: Duell, Sloan and Pearce, 1960.

Hassett, William D. *Off the Record with F.D.R. 1942–1945.* New Jersey: Rutgers University Press, 1958.

Hatch, Alden P. *Citizen of the World, Franklin D. Roosevelt.* Essex: Skeffington and Son Ltd., 1948.

Hickock, Lorena A. *The Road to the White House, FDR: The Pre-Presidential Years.* New York: Chilton Company Publishers, 1962.

Huckstep, R. L. *Poliomyelitis.* Edinburgh: Churchill Livingstone, 1975.

FDR'S SPLENDID DECEPTION

Hurd, Charles, *When the New Deal Was Young and Gay.* New York: Hawthorn Books, Inc., 1965.

Ickes, Harold L. *The Secret Diaries of Harold L. Ickes.* 3 volumes. New York: Simon and Schuster, 1953, 1953, 1954.

Jarzab, Leonard. *Secrets of Roosevelt's Last Election Campaign.* Chicago: Drawgas, 1977.

Kessler, Henry Howard. *Knife Is Not Enough.* New York: Norton Press, 1968.

Knutson, Jeanne N. *Handbook of Political Psychology.* San Francisco: Jossey-Bass Publishers, 1973.

Krusen, Frank Hammon. *Handbook of Physical Medicine.* Philadelphia: Saunders Press, 1965.

Lash, Joseph P. *Eleanor and Franklin.* New York: W. W. Norton and Company, Inc., 1971.

Licht, Sidney Herman, ed. *Rehabilitation and Medicine.* New Haven: E. Licht, 1968.

Lindley, Ernest K. *Franklin D. Roosevelt, A Career in Progressive Democracy.* Indianapolis: The Bobbs-Merrill Company, 1931.

Lippman, Theo, Jr. *The Squire of Warm Springs, F.D.R. in Georgia 1924–1945.* Chicago: Playboy Press, 1977.

Lloyd, Wyndham E. B. *A Hundred Years Of Medicine.* New York: Gerald Duckworth and Company, Ltd., 1971.

Looker, Earle. *This Man Roosevelt.* New York: Brewer, Warren and Putman, 1932.

McDaniel, James W. , Ph. D. *Physical Disability and Human Behavior.* New York: Pergamon Press, Inc., 1969.

McIntire, Ross T., and Creel, George. *White House Physician.* New York: G. P. Putnam's Sons, 1946.

McLellan, David S. *Dean Acheson: The State Department Years.* New York: Dodd, Mead and Company, 1976.

Moran, Charles McMoran Wilson. *Winston Churchill: The Struggle for Survival, 1940–1965, taken from the diaries of Lord Moran.* London: Constable, 1966.

Oursler, Fulton. *Behold, This Dreamer!* Boston: Little, Brown, 1964.

Parks, Lillian Rogers. *My Thirty Years Backstairs at the White House.* New York: Fleet Publishing Corporation, 1961.

Pascal, Blaise, *Pensées, Great Books of the Western World.* Volume 33. Chicago: Encyclopaedia Britannica, Inc., 1952.

Paul, John Rodman. *A History of Poliomyelitis.* New Haven: Yale University Press, 1971.

232

Perkins, Frances. *The Roosevelt I Knew.* New York: The Viking Press, 1946.

Phillips, William R. F., and Rosenburg, Janet. *The Origins of Modern Treatment and Education of Physically Handicapped Children.* New York: Arno Press, 1980.

Reilly, Michael F. *Reilly of the White House.* New York: Simon and Schuster, 1947.

Rigdon, William McKinley, and Derieux, James. *White House Sailor.* New York: Doubleday and Company, Inc., 1962.

Rollins, Alfred B., Jr. *Roosevelt and Howe.* New York: Alfred A. Knopf, 1962.

Roosevelt Eleanor. *This I Remember.* New York: Harper and Brothers, 1961.

Roosevelt, Eleanor. *The Autobiography of Eleanor Roosevelt.* New York: Harper and Brothers, 1949.

Roosevelt, Elliott. *As He Saw It.* New York: Duell, Sloan and Pierce, 1946.

Roosevelt, Elliott, and Brough, James. *An Untold Story, The Roosevelts of Hyde Park.* New York: G. P. Putnam's Sons, 1973.

Roosevelt, Elliott. *F.D.R. His Personal Letters 1905–1928.* New York: Duell, Sloan and Pierce, 1948.

Roosevelt, F. D. *The Public Papers and Addresses of Franklin D. Roosevelt.* 13 volumes. New York: Random House, Macmillan, Harper, 1938–1950.

Roosevelt, James. *My Parents, A Differing View.* Chicago: Playboy Press, 1976.

Roosevelt, James, and Shalett, Sidney. *Affectionately, F.D.R.* New York: Harcourt, Brace and Company, 1959.

Roosevelt, Nicholas. *A Front Row Seat.* Oklahoma: University of Oklahoma.

Rosenman, Samuel I. *Working with Roosevelt.* New York: Da Capo Press, 1972.

Sherwood, Robert E. *Roosevelt and Hopkins, An Intimate History.* New York: Harper and Brothers, 1948.

Rusk, Howard A. *Rehabilitation Medicine.* St. Louis: Mosby Press Ltd., 1977.

Smith, A. Merriman. *Merriman Smith's Book of Presidents: A White House Memoir.* New York: W. W. Norton and Company, Inc., 1972.

Smith, A. Merriman. *Thank You, Mr. President: A White House Notebook.* New York: Da Capo Press, 1976.

Starling, Edmund William. *Starling of the White House.* New York: Simon and Schuster, 1946.

Steel, Ronald. *Walter Lippmann and the American Century.* Boston: Little, Brown and Company, 1980.

Stimson, Henry L., and Bundy, McGeorge. *On Active Service in Peace and War.* New York: Harper and Brothers, 1947.

Sugrue, Thomas. *Starling of the White House.* New York: Simon and Schuster, 1946.

Truman, Margaret. *Harry Truman.* New York: William Morrow and Company, Inc., 1973.

Walker, Turnley. *Roosevelt and the Warm Springs Story.* New York: Story Press—A. A. Wyn, Inc., 1953.

White, Graham J. *FDR and the Press.* Chicago: University of Chicago Press, 1979.

Periodicals and Others

Asbell, Bernard. "FDR's Extra Burden." Adapted from book by author (1973).

Bray, Anne Irwin. "Roosevelt in Warm Springs: Once Upon a Thanksgiving." *Meriwether Progress,* Manchester, Georgia (undated).

Brown, Betty, and O'Connor (Dillmeier), Hazel Stephen, Letter from Warm Springs, Georgia. (April 15, 1945).

Bruenn, Howard G., M.D. "Clinical Notes on the Illness and Death of President Franklin D. Roosevelt," *Annals of Internal Medicine* 72, number 4 (April 1970): 579-91.

Burns, James MacGregor. "FDR: The Untold Story of His Last Year." *Saturday Review* (April 11, 1970): 12–15. 39.

Charlton, Michael. "The Eagle and the Small Birds." *Encounter* (June 1983): 7–27.

Cohn, Victor. *Four Billion Dimes.* Pamphlet by *Minneapolis Star and Tribune* (undated).

Cotten, Lyman A. "FDR and Lucy Mercer." Letter to the Editor, *Times Literary Supplement* (August 1, 1980).

Davis, Kenneth S. "FDR as a Biographer's Problem." *The American Scholar* (Winter 1983/84): 100–108.

Gallagher, Hugh G. "FDR: An Unusual Look at a Hero." *Disabled USA* (Spring 1982): 23–26.

Gallagher, Hugh G. "FDR's Cover Up: The Extent of His Handicap." *The Washington Post*, Washington D.C. (January 24, 1982).

Goldsmith, Harry S. "Unanswered Mysteries in the Death of Franklin D. Roosevelt." *Surgery, Gynecology and Obstetrics* 149 (December 1979): 899–907.

Hamlin, Mrs. Charles. "An Old River Friend." *The New Republic* (April 15, 1946).

High, Stanley. "Is President Roosevelt a Well Man Today?" *Liberty Magazine* (June 27, 1936): 22–23.

Hoover, Herbert. "My Personal Relations with Mr. Roosevelt." Unpublished manuscript, 1962. Herbert Hoover Presidential Library.

Irwin, C. E. "A Resume of the Treatment of Poliomyelitis as Practised at the Georgia Warm Springs Foundation" (undated).

Looker, Earle. "Is Franklin D. Roosevelt Physically Fit to Be President?" *Liberty Magazine* (July 25, 1931): 6–10.

Noel, John Vavasour. "Rambling Through the Mid-South." *The Spur of Warm Springs, Georgia* (February 1, 1927).

Rice, Diana. "Warm Springs Seeks to Expand. " *The New York Times* (January 5, 1930).

Roosevelt, Anna. "How Polio Helped Father." *Woman Magazine* (July 1949): 46–54, 112–15.

Roosevelt, F. D. "A Pioneering Opportunity." (photographs) from undated brochure from Georgia Warm Springs Foundation, Hydrotherapeutic Center, Warm Springs, Georgia.

Talley, Robert. "Many Victims of Paralysis Aided at Warm Springs." Macon, Georgia *News*. (March 30, 1930).

"Franklin D. Roosevelt's Little White House and Museum." Souvenir Tour Guide. Franklin D. Roosevelt Warm Springs Memorial Commission.

Undated brochure from the Hydrotherapeutic Center at Warm Springs, Georgia.

"Great Work Done for Sufferers from Infantile Paralysis by Gov. Roosevelt." Nashville *Banner* (October 20, 1929).

"Gov. Roosevelt Sponsors Plan for Treating 300,000 Infantile Paralysis Patients." *St. Louis Post-Dispatch* (November 6, 1929).

"Roosevelt's Health May Be Bar to 1932 Candidacy." Allentown, Pennsylvania *Leader* (May 12, 1930).

Twentieth Anniversary Report of the National Foundation for Infantile Paralysis, Warm Springs, Georgia (January 2–3, 1958).

Georgia Warm Springs Foundation Annual Report for the fiscal year ended September 30, 1941.

Congressional Record, House of Representatives (March 1, 1945): 1618–23.

Index